RUSSIAN FOR SCIENTISTS

THE MACMILLAN COMPANY
NEW YORK • CHICAGO
DALLAS • ATLANTA • SAN FRANCISCO
LONDON • MANILA
IN CANADA
BRETT-MACMILLAN LTD.
GALT, ONTARIO

RUSSIAN
FOR SCIENTISTS

DENNIS WARD

Head of the Russian Department and Senior Lecturer in Russian, University of Edinburgh

The Macmillan Company New York

Printed in the United States of America

First Printing 1961

Library of Congress Catalog Card Number 61-6891

CONTENTS

ACKNOWLEDGMENTS

Much of the English of this book was typed by Miss S. Millar, Secretary-Typist to the Departments of Modern Languages in the University of Edinburgh. Most of the Russian of the final version was typed in by the Reverend John Sotnikov, of Edinburgh. Dr. Militsa Greene, Lecturer in Russian in the University of Edinburgh, examined the Russian from the grammatical point of view and made some valuable suggestions for improvements. Miss Emmie Vosnesensky, Assistant Lecturer in Russian in the University of Edinburgh, gave extensive help in typing the first version and in preparing and typing the General Vocabulary. My wife, Mrs. D. Mary Ward, helped considerably in preparing the General Vocabulary and undertook the tedious business of inserting stress-marks in the body of the book and the General Vocabulary. It is a very pleasant duty to express my sincere gratitude to all these people. Any faults that remain are entirely my own responsibility. I should be happy to have any errors called to my attention and to receive suggestions for improvements.

Edinburgh, 1960 D.W.

ABBREVIATIONS

acc.	accusative.	*m.*	masculine.
adj.	adjective.	*n.*	neuter; noun.
dat.	dative.	*nom.*	nominative
f.	feminine.	*pfv.*	perfective.
fut.	future.	*pl.*	plural.
gen.	genitive.	*prep.*	prepositional.
impfv.	imperfective.	*pres.*	present.
inst.	instrumental.	*sing.*	singular.
loc.	locative.		

INTRODUCTION

The achievements of the Soviet Union in various fields of science have made it increasingly obvious in recent years that Russian is an essential foreign language for the non-Russian scientist. A vast bulk of scientific material is published in Russian and no more than a small proportion of this material is translated into other languages. More and more scientists, therefore, are taking up the study of Russian.

In many respects, Russian is a strange and difficult language for the English-speaking student : it has a complicated grammar and much of its word-stock is not as readily comprehensible as, say, that of French or German. It is particularly difficult for the English-speaking student to learn to write and speak Russian in a reasonably short space of time. Most scientists, however, are not primarily interested in learning how to ask the way to the nearest rocket-station, or comfort-station, in flawless colloquial Russian. Nor do they wish to read *Anna Karenina* or *Crime and Punishment* in the original : they are interested in learning Russian simply so that they can read technical material within the limited field of their own special study and perhaps one or two adjacent fields of study.

This book has been designed especially for this purpose : it provides a *recognition* course, the object of which is to help students to master as quickly as possible enough Russian to enable them to understand technical and scientific literature in Russian. For this reason, much of the hard and time-consuming labour associated with the learning of Russian for 'normal' purposes can be removed, though this is not to say that all the effort can be removed, nor that any essential grammar should be omitted. Thus, the grammatical elements to be committed to memory can often be reduced in size, as it were, though they are not reduced in number. For this reason, I shall not use the expression 'grammatical ending' in this book (the expression is, in any case, inappropriate when the indicator of the grammatical form of a word does not come at the end of the word) : I shall use instead the word 'marker' and shall mean by that word 'absolutely minimal grammatical marker'—that is to say the very smallest element of a word necessary for the recognition of its grammatical form. A 'marker' in this sense may be coterminous with, for example, a full grammatical ending, but in many cases it may be shorter than a full grammatical ending. In this respect, one should bear in mind that the context helps the reader to recognise a particular marker for what it is. Thus, although **–ть** is a marker of the infinitive, not all words ending in **–ть** are infinitives—some of them may be nouns. In such a sentence, however, as **Он начал нагревать металл** *He began to heat up the metal*, it is clear from the context that **нагревать** must be an infinitive and not a noun.

Another consequence of the limited purpose of this book is that the exercises may be all 'one-way' exercises. In fact the student is called upon to translate from Russian into English and not from English into Russian, which is a much harder undertaking.

Although the grammar can be simplified for recognition purposes, it is not possible to simplify the learning of vocabulary. For some time the student will find that his greatest handicap is the lack of vocabulary. He should therefore make every effort to learn as many words as possible, discriminating between those words which will be useful for his own particular field of study and those which will not, and always bearing in mind that even in the most highly technical matter the 'ordinary' words will probably outnumber the 'technical' words. In the individual vocabularies to the exercises the student will not find *all* the new words used in the exercises. If it is reasonably clear from the context what the meaning of a new word is, that word may not be given in the vocabulary. Words which have been used previously in exercises or which occur in the grammatical explanations (with English translation, of course) are also often omitted from the individual vocabularies. The object of this is to persuade the student to learn words as he comes across them.

Words which have been borrowed from English, as well as a few which have been borrowed from other languages, are usually omitted from the individual vocabularies. On meeting a new word in an exercise and discovering that it is not in the individual vocabulary, the student should try transliterating the word (i.e. should substitute Latin letters for the Russian ones), at the same time discounting or interpreting any Russian grammatical elements which the word may have.[1] Thus, **электрон** is immediately seen to be the English *electron*, **микробиология** is clearly *microbiology*, and once one appreciates that **-ция** is the equivalent of English *-tion* then **полимеризация** is clearly

[1] See the 'Hints on Transliteration' on page 25.

polymerisation. A student who continually makes intelligent guesses at the meaning of new words is more likely to feel that he is making good progress in understanding the language than one who is continually referring to the vocabulary.

To improve his word-stock, the student should read and re-read the vocabularies and exercises, make lists of words, particularly those which he has found difficult to remember, and he should also learn 'morphemes' as well as whole words. 'Morphemes' may be described as 'minimal units of meaning expressed linguistically' and they include roots, prefixes and suffixes (which last include many grammatical markers in Russian). Thus, when a student knows that the prefix **не-** means *non-*, *in-*, *a-*, that the word **раствор** (itself consisting of two morphemes) means *solution*, that the element **-им-** means *-able*, *-ble*, etc., and that the element **-ость** means 'abstract noun', he is likely to guess on first meeting the word **нерастворимость** that it means *insolubility*—especially with the help of the context.

A student should not expect to understand all the scientific words used in this book, since some of them may refer to highly specialised matters outside his own particular field of study. If a sentence does not concern his own particular field of study and the meaning of the entire sentence is not readily comprehensible, the student should translate the sentence literally, concentrating on understanding the grammatical structure. *All* the words used in the exercises, as well as some used in the grammatical explanations, are included in the general vocabulary at the end of the book.

Beginning with Exercise 17, Chapter 9, the exercises contain more difficult material, since nearly all the sentences in that exercise and thereafter are taken from the Transactions of the Academy of Sciences of the U.S.S.R. (**Доклады Академии наук СССР**) and were not specially designed for students, though some of them have been adapted for the purposes of this book. I have made extensive use of such admittedly difficult material, because I felt that most students would think the additional effort involved worth while since they would be translating actual material from recent scientific articles, the kind of material they are aiming to read. The student should not despair if, beginning with Exercise 17, the rate at which he translates the exercises becomes considerably slower and he should be prepared to find himself occasionally unable, without the help of a teacher,[1] to

[1] The course is intended to be used either with or without the help of a teacher. Naturally, better results will be obtained through working with a teacher or someone who knows Russian.

translate parts of sentences. Such sentences may be left partly translated and returned to later, since it is intended that, having worked through the book once, the student should return to Exercise 17 (or even to an earlier exercise) and work through the exercises once more, before going on to read technical articles in Russian.

Above all, the student should not try to rush through the exercises: it is better to come to an understanding of Russian slowly and *thoroughly*, rather than rapidly and *superficially*. Nevertheless, a few months' thorough study with the aid of this course (the length of study required depends, of course, not only on the individual aptitude of the student but also on the number of hours per day or week that he is able to devote to the task) should enable the average student to go on to reading technical literature in Russian, in his own field of study, with the aid of a dictionary at first and then with only occasional reference to a dictionary.

After the main body of the book there are four appendices. Appendix I gives complete paradigms (declension patterns) of nouns and adjectives, Appendices II and III are designed to help the student recognise one and the same morphemes in spite of their changing shapes, and Appendix IV is a ready reference-table of the commoner 'anomalous' verbs.

Though this book is designed primarily for scientists, the layman who wishes to obtain a reading knowledge of Russian will find that the method used here is equally valid for him. Much of the vocabulary will, of course, be strange to him and will be useless for general reading purposes but he will be able to obtain a basic knowledge of the grammar for recognition purposes. In its original form, this course was in fact used both with scientists and ordinary students of Russian.

1

THE ALPHABET AND PRONUNCIATION

The Russian alphabet has thirty-two symbols, most of which are derived ultimately from the capital forms of the ninth-century Greek alphabet. The easiest way of learning the letters of the Russian alphabet is to take them in groups, arranged progressively according to their unfamiliarity or dissimilarity to the alphabets of western European languages. In the following sections on the Russian alphabet only the briefest description of the phonetic value of the letters is given. This description is by no means sufficient to enable students to pronounce Russian correctly (for this a very lengthy description would be necessary) but it is sufficient to allow students to read words to themselves or to read them aloud in class-work with some rough approximation to Russian pronunciation.[1] Russian, like English, has a mobile accent or stress, so that for purposes of speaking the language correctly it is necessary to learn where the accent occurs in each word. For purposes of reading Russian it is not necessary, except in a very few instances, to know where the accent falls, but for the convenience of students the words in this book are provided with an accent mark (an 'acute' accent). The cursive forms of the letters are illustrated, so that the student may learn to write down Russian words without the inconvenience of printing every letter.

EXAMPLES FOR PRACTICE

(*a*) **А, а К, к М, м О, о Т, т Е, е**

All the letters in this section look like letters of the English alphabet and represent for the most part sounds fairly similar to the sounds which the corresponding English letters represent.

Russian letter	*Approximate pronunciation*[2]	*Written*
А, а	*a* in *cat* (not *a* in *father*)	As in English.

[1] Students who wish to learn more about the pronunciation of Russian should refer to the author's *Russian Pronunciation: a practical course* (Oliver & Boyd, Edinburgh, 1958).

[2] The phonetic values given in this column are the 'basic' values. Modifications of these basic values are given in broad outline on page 24.

Russian letter	*Approximate pronunciation*	*Written*
К, к	*k* in *king*, *c* in *cat*	Capital as in English, small usually written without a riser, thus *к*
М, м	*m* in *mat*	*М м* The initial loop is an integral part of the cursive form of this letter and must be written, no matter what letter precedes (see below).
О, о	*aw* in *thaw* (not *o* in *home* or *hot*)	As in English.
Т, т	*t* in *take*	Capital: *Т Т* Small: *т т* The first of the two variants is commoner and has the advantage of being easy to connect with other letters. A bar may be placed over it to avoid confusion with other letters, thus *т̄*
Е, е	*ye* in *yet*, except after **ц, ш, ж, ч, щ** (see below), when it simply represents *e* in *get*. Sometimes **Е, е** represent *yaw*, as in *yawn*, and they are then provided with a diaeresis in elementary books, thus **ё**, though not in normal Russian printed matter, except to avoid ambiguity[1]	As in English.

[1] Since the letter **е** with the value *yaw* occurs only in stressed position the diaeresis can, in elementary books of this kind, serve as a stress or accent mark.

EXAMPLES FOR PRACTICE

Printed form	*Cursive form*	*Meaning*
как	*как*	how
так	*так так*	thus
тот	*тот тот*	this
мак	*мак*	poppy
там	*там там*	there
том	*том том*	volume
áтом	*атом атом*	atom
ток	*ток ток*	current
те	*те те*	those
тема	*тема тема*	theme
тётка	*тётка тётка*	auntie

(*b*) **Р, р   С, с   Н, н   У, у   В, в   Х, х**

These letters, while looking, at least in their capital forms, like letters of the English alphabet, have values very different from those of their English likenesses.

Russian letter	*Approximate pronunciation*	*Written*
Р, р	*r* in *rod*—but a slightly trilled or rolled *r*	Like English P p.
С, с	*s* in *sun*	Like English C c.
Н, н	*n* in *not*	
У, у	*oo* in *soon*	Like English Y y.
В, в	*v* in *van*	Like English B b, the small one always having two loops, thus *в* not *в*
Х, х	*ch* in Scots *loch*, German *ach*, though with less friction. A good substitute for it is English *h*	Like English X x.

EXAMPLES FOR PRACTICE

Printed form	*Cursive form*	*Meaning*
рак	рак	crayfish ; cancer
сок	сок	juice
он	он	he
но	но	but
у́тка	утка	duck
ко́нус	конус	cone
ва́та	вата	wadding
ватт	ватт	watt
ваттме́тр	ваттметр	watt-meter
автома́т	автомат	automaton, sub-machine-gun
ве́ко	веко	eyelid
хао́с	хаос	chaos
хара́ктер	характер	character
хром	хром	chromium, chrome
хрен	хрен	horse-radish
хромосо́ма	хромосома	chromosome

(*c*) **Б, б И, и Й, й Э, э Я, я**

The letters in this group are not unlike some English letters in that they look like slight distortions or mirror-images of some English letters.

Russian letter	*Approximate pronunciation*	*Written*
Б, б	*b* in *but*	Capital : Б Small : б
И, и	*ea* in *yeast*, except after **ж**, **ш** and **ц** (see below) when it has the same value as the letter **ы** (see below)	Like English U u : И и
Й, й	*y* in *boy*, i.e. it is used after other vowel letters to represent the second part of a diphthong	

Э, э	*e* in *let*	*Э э*
Я, я	*ya* in *yap*	*Я я* (*Я*) The initial hook is an integral part of the cursive form of this letter and must not be omitted, no matter what precedes it.

EXAMPLES FOR PRACTICE

Printed form	*Cursive form*	*Meaning*
бор	*бор*	boron
бóмба	*бомба*	bomb
и́ва	*ива*	willow
рой	*рой*	swarm
экстра́кт	*экстракт*	extract
мя́со	*мясо*	meat, flesh
мя́та	*мята*	mint
хи́мия	*химия*	chemistry
а́томная бóмба	*атомная бомба*	atom bomb
макробиóтика	*макробиотика*	macrobiotics
энтеретóмия	*энтеретомия*	enterotomy

(*d*) **П, п Г, г Д, д Ф, ф З, з Л, л**

All these letters are similar to letters found in the Greek alphabet but quite unlike any letters found in the English alphabet.

Russian letter	*Approximate pronunciation*	*Written*
П, п	*p* in *put*	Small letter like English *n*. A bar may be placed over this to avoid confusion with other letters *n̄*. The capital letter is written *П* or *П*.
Г, г	*g* in *good*	*Г* ; small (N.B.) *г*

Д, д	*d* in *done*	Capital: *Д* Small: *д* or *∂*. To be strictly correct the upper loop of *∂* must not be carried round so as to run into the next letter. The form *д* does not have the disadvantage of this hiatus and may be run into the next letter (see below).
Ф, ф	*f* in *food*	*Ф*, *ф* the movement of the pen in forming this letter may be illustrated thus: *ф* or thus: *ф ф ф ф*
З, з	*z* in *zeta*	*З*, *з* (i.e. like the figure '3' with a run-in to the next letter; or *З з*
Л, л	*l* in *luck*	*Л*, *л* The initial hook is an integral part of the cursive form of this letter and must not be omitted, no matter what precedes it.

EXAMPLES FOR PRACTICE

Printed form	*Cursive form*	*Meaning*
пот	*пот*	sweat
пар	*пар*	steam
горн	*горн*	furnace
грани́т	*гранит*	granite
до́мна	*домна домна*	blast-furnace

Printed form	*Cursive form*	*Meaning*
диск	*диск диск*	disc
факт	*факт*	fact
фо́рма	*форма*	form, shape
зоб	*зоб зоб*	crop, goitre
зуб	*зуб зуб*	tooth, cog
ла́кмус	*лакмус*	litmus
ла́мпа	*лампа*	lamp, valve
лес	*лес*	wood, forest
газ	*газ газ*	gas
рези́на	*резина*	rubber
геликопте́р	*геликоптер*	helicopter
гекса́эдр	*гексаэдр*	hexahedron
дендри́т	*дендрит*	dendrite
диабе́т	*диабет*	diabetes
фа́за	*фаза*	phase
кислота́	*кислота*	acid
кислоро́д	*кислород*	oxygen
азо́т	*азот*	nitrogen
водоро́д	*водород*	hydrogen
зонд	*зонд*	probe
лесово́дство	*лесоводство*	forestry

(*e*) i. **Ш, ш   Ж, ж   Ц, ц   Ч, ч   Щ, щ**
ii. **Ю, ю   Ы, ы   Ь, ь   Ъ, ъ**

The letters in these two groups are quite unlike any letters found in western alphabets.

i. *Russian letter*	*Approximate pronunciation*	*Written*
Ш, ш	*sh* in *shoot*	*Ш, ш*. The third upright stroke must be completed; the letter must not look like English w (*w*). May be underlined: *ш*

Ж, ж	*z* in *azure* or *s* in *leisure*	*Ж*, *ж* or *ж*. The movement of the pen in forming this letter may be illustrated thus: *Э|С* or thus: *э ж ж ж*
Ц, ц	*ts* in *bits*	*Ц*, *ц*, i.e. like *u* in English, with a final hook or loop under the line.
Ч, ч	*ch* in *cheese*	*Ч*, *ч* (rather like one variety of cursive *r* in English).
Щ, щ	*shch* in *fresh cheese* (or *shsh* in *wash sheep*)	*Щ*, *щ*, i.e. like *ш* with a final hook or loop under the line.

EXAMPLES FOR PRACTICE

Printed form	*Cursive form*	*Meaning*
шар	*шар*	sphere
шок	*шок*	shock
жар	*жар*	heat
жир	*жир*	fat
живóтное	*животное*	animal
цинк	*цинк*	zinc
ци́фра	*цифра*	figure, numeral
цемéнт	*цемент*	cement
час	*час*	hour
чи́бис	*чибис*	lapwing
член	*член*	limb, member
чýвство	*чувство*	feeling
щекá	*щека*	cheek
щýка	*щука*	pike
óвощи	*овощи*	vegetables

ii. *Russian letter*	*Approximate pronunciation*	*Written*
Ю, ю	*you* in *youth*	Ю ю
Ы, ы	(very approximately) the *i* in *bib*. It has a ' cloudy ' quality, as if the *u* in p*ut* were fused with it	Small: ы (never occurs initially).
Ь, ь	Has no sound of its own, being used to indicate that the preceding consonant is pronounced ' soft.'[1] Its name is ' the soft sign.'	Small: ь (never occurs initially).
Ъ, ъ	Has no sound of its own, being used to indicate that the preceding consonant is not pronounced ' soft.' The name of this letter is ' the hard sign.'	Small: ъ (never occurs initially).

(The above descriptions of the functions of the hard and the soft signs are very rough but are sufficient for the purposes of this book.)

EXAMPLES FOR PRACTICE

Printed form	*Cursive form*	*Meaning*
юг	юг	south
Юпи́тер	Юпитер	Jupiter
лю́тик	лютик	buttercup
ты́сяча	тысяча	thousand
сыро́й	сырой	damp, raw
ры́ба	рыба	fish
чита́ть	читать	to read
ходи́ть	ходить	to go
кость	кость	bone
съесть	съесть	to eat up
объе́кт	объект	object, objective

[1] The soft sign has no effect on the letters **ш** and **ж**, which are pronounced in their normal way even when **ь** follows them. **ь** then has no phonetic function at all.

The thirty-two letters of the Russian alphabet, in the order of that alphabet, are:

А Б В Г Д Е Ж З И Й К Л М Н О П
а б в г д е ж з и й к л м н о п

Р С Т У Ф Х Ц Ч Ш Щ Ъ Ы Ь Э Ю Я
р с т у ф х ц ч ш щ ъ ы ь э ю я

There are nine vowel letters:

(i) **а ы у э о** (ii) **я и ю е**

The second group constitutes the so-called 'softening' vowel letters (see below).

There are twenty consonant letters:

б в г д ж з к л м н п р с т ф х ц ч ш щ

one diphthong letter: **й**
two auxiliary letters: **ъ** ('hard sign')
ь ('soft sign').

Further Remarks on Pronunciation

Vowels. When they are not in stressed position, the vowel letters **а о е** and **я** have phonetic values other than those given above.

The letter **е** then represents a sound rather like English *i*, as in *sit*, and so does the letter **а** when preceded in unstressed position by either **ч** or **щ**. Otherwise, in unstressed position, both **а** and **о** represent a sound approximately like English *u* in *sun*.

The letter **я** in positions in front of the stressed position has a phonetic value rather like English *yi* in *yip*, whereas after the stressed position it has a phonetic value rather like *you* in *young*.

After **ж ш** and **ц** the letter **и** has the same value as **ы**.

Consonants. Apart from the four consonant letters **л, м, н** and **р**, which always represent voiced consonants, and the four consonant letters **х, ц, ч** and **щ** which always represent voiceless consonants, there are six pairs of voiced and voiceless consonants:

voiced	**б**	**в**	**г**	**д**	**ж**	**з**
	|	|	|	|	|	|
voiceless	**п**	**ф**	**к**	**т**	**ш**	**с**

When one of the voiced consonant letters of the six pairs occurs at the end of a word or before any voiceless consonant letter, it represents its corresponding voiceless consonant. When one of the voiceless consonants of the six pairs occurs before a voiced consonant letter of the six pairs (other than **в**) it represents its corresponding voiced consonant. Thus:

нерв	*nerve*	is pronounced	as if spelt	**нерф**
рог	*horn*	,,	,,	**рок**
год	*year*	,,	,,	**гот**
рожь	*rye*	,,	,,	**рошь**
газ	*gas*	,,	,,	**гас**
автома́т	*automaton*	,,	,,	**афтама́т**
ло́дка	*boat*	,,	,,	**ло́тка**
сдвиг	*displacement*	,,	,,	**здвик**
сбо́рка	*assemblage*	,,	,,	**збо́рка**
о́тжиг[1]	*annealing*	,,	,,	**о́джик**[1]

When a consonant letter (other than **ш, ж** or **ц**) is followed by one of the 'softening' vowel letters (**я, и, ю, е**), the consonant represented is a 'soft' consonant. Very broadly speaking this means that it is pronounced with a very slight suggestion after it of a sound like that represented by the letter *y* in English *yield*.

The soft sign (**ь**) following a consonant letter also indicates that the consonant is to be pronounced 'soft'. When the soft sign *and* a softening vowel letter follow a consonant letter, there is a full *y* sound (as in *yield*) between the soft consonant and the following vowel. The letters **ш** and **ж** do not represent soft consonants when they are followed by the soft sign or one of the softening vowel letters.

The hard sign (**ъ**) occurs between a consonant letter and softening vowel letter. Its function is to indicate that the consonant is not pronounced soft but that there is a full *y* sound before the vowel. Thus **сесть** *to sit down* is pronounced approximately $s^{y}est^{y}$, while **съесть** is pronounced approximately $syest^{y}$.

There are other modifications of consonants which occur but the student who is learning Russian simply for reading purposes need not trouble himself with them and they are therefore not described in this book.

[1]Also **отжи́г**, pronounced as if spelt **аджи́к**.

Hints on Transliteration

Russian has borrowed many words from west European languages, particularly technical words, during the last few decades. In transferring these words into Russian certain conventions are usually observed and the following notes include those conventions which may not be immediately obvious, as well as some of the more obvious ones. The sign = means 'may represent . . . in loan-words'.

ав and **ау** = *au*, as in **автомоби́ль, автомати́ческий** (*automatic*, note that **-ический** = *-ic*), **тра́вма, аудито́рия,ауто́псия.**

в = *w*, as in **ватт, ваго́н** (*waggon*). Occasionally **у** = *w*, as in **уэ́льский** (*Welsh*).

г = *h*, as in **гормо́н, га́битус.**

е = *ö* or *oe* in words of German origin, as in **рентгеногра́мма** (*roentgenogram*, *x-ray plate*).

ев and **эв** = *eu*, as in **евге́ника** (*eugenics*), **эвте́ктика** (*eutectics*).

-ий = *-ium* in the names of chemical elements particularly, as in **алюми́ний** (*aluminium*), **ге́лий** (*helium*). (It does not follow that *-ium* always appears as **-ий** in Russian: cp. **ура́н** with *uranium*).

кв = *qu*, as in **эквивале́нт, квант** (*quantum*).

кз and **кс** = *x*, as in **э́кзосмос** (*exosmosis*), **экстра́кт.**

т = *th*, as in **те́зис, тео́рия.** Occasionally *th* appears as **ф,** as in **эфи́р** (*ether*).

ф = *ph*, as in **физиоло́гия, фи́зика.**

х = *ch* (when this does not have the sound of *ch* in e.g. *chip*), as in **хромосо́ма, евста́хиева труба́** (*Fustachian tube*).

ц = *c* before **е** and **и,** as in **центр, цеме́нт, це́зий** (*caesium*), **цитоло́гия** but **цинк** = *zinc*. The elements **-ция** (with modifications due to case-changes) and **-цион** correspond to *-tion*, as in **эволю́ция, эволю́ционный** (*evolutionary*).

2

THE NOMINATIVE SINGULAR AND SIMPLE SENTENCES

A

There are three grammatical genders in Russian: masculine, feminine, neuter. The grammatical gender does not necessarily depend on the nature of the object; thus the word for *table*, **стол,** is masculine, the word for *sea*, **мо́ре,** is neuter, the word for *moon*, **луна́,** is feminine. It is in most instances, however, easy to tell the grammatical gender of a word in Russian by the markers of its various cases.

The marker of the nominative singular case for masculine nouns is a final consonant letter, final **й,** or final **ь.** The following are masculine nouns:

азо́т	*nitrogen*	**нитра́т**	*nitrate*
объём	*volume*	**сантиме́тр**	*centimetre*
строй	*structure*	**слу́чай**	*incident*
дели́тель	*divisor*	**путь**	*path, way*

The marker of the nominative singular case for feminine nouns is final **а, я** or **ь.** The following are feminine nouns:

фо́рма	*form*	**ли́ния**	*line*
кишка́	*gut*	**до́ля**	*lot, portion*
мазь	*grease*	**боле́знь**	*disease*

The marker of the nominative singular case for neuter nouns is final **о** or **е** (and **ё**). The following are neuter nouns:

о́лово	*tin*	**сырьё**	*raw material*
то́пливо	*fuel*	**умноже́ние**	*multiplication*
по́ле	*field*		

It will be seen later that the above formulations apply also to the nominative singular of the adjective and to certain verb and pronoun forms. The formulations may therefore be extended thus:

1. The marker of masculine subject forms in the singular is a consonant, **й** or **ь**.[1]
2. The marker of feminine subject forms in the singular is **а**, **я** or **ь**.
3. The marker of neuter subject forms in the singular is **о** or **е**.

To this must be added the rider that a few masculine nouns end in **а** and a very few neuter nouns end in **-мя**. (These will be treated later.) Thus:

Masc.	*Fem.*	*Neuter*
consonant	**а**	**о**
й	**я**	**е** (and **ё**)
ь	**ь**	. . . .
. . . .		**-мя**
а		

B

Read the following sentences and observe the structure of the Russian:

1.	**Газ — вещество́.**	*Gas is matter.*
2.	**Желе́зо — вещество́.**	*Iron is matter.*
3.	**Квадра́т — фигура.**	*A square is a figure.*
4.	**Два — число́.**	*Two is a number.*
5.	**Ци́фра 3 — число́ три.**	*The figure 3 is the number three.*
6.	**Энзи́м — катализа́тор.**	*An enzyme is a catalyst.*
7.	**Вода́ — вещество́.**	*Water is a substance.*
8.	**Алма́з — углеро́д.**	*A diamond is a carbon.*
9.	**Каучу́к — углеводоро́д.**	*Rubber is a hydrocarbon.*
10.	**Мета́лл — цинк.**	*The metal is zinc.*
11.	**Цинк — мета́лл.**	*Zinc is a metal.*
12.	**Я мужчи́на.**	*I am a man.*
13.	**Вы же́нщина.**	*You are a woman.*
14.	**Они́ тут.**	*They are here.*

From these examples it will be seen that (1) there is no word for *the* or *a* in Russian; (2) the present tense of the verb *to be* is not expressed. The word **есть,** having the meaning *there is, there are,* can also be used, usually for emphatic purposes only, in the meaning *is, are, am.* There are also some substitutes for the verb *to be* and these *can* be used in the present tense. In most cases, however, the present tense of the verb *to be* is not expressed other than by a dash in writing, and *even this is optional,* as the last examples show.

[1] Hereinafter, unless otherwise stated, a marker is understood to consist of a *final* letter or group of letters.

C

Read the following sentences:

1.	**Желéзо твёрдый метáлл.**	*Iron is a hard metal.*
2.	**Бакели́т — хру́пкий материáл.**	*Bakelite is a brittle material.*
3.	**Э́то большóй квадрáт.**	*This is a big square.*
4.	**Э́то дли́нная ли́ния.**	*This is a long line.*
5.	**Кровь — густáя крáсная жи́дкость.**	*Blood is a thick, red liquid.*
6.	**Желéзо твердое веществó.**	*Iron is a hard substance.*
7.	**Э́то магни́тное пóле.**	*It is a magnetic field.*
8.	**Инди́го — си́нее веществó.**	*Indigo is a blue substance.*

From these examples it will be seen that the nominative singular of the adjective has the following markers : masculine, **-й** (preceded by **ы, и** or **o**) ; feminine, **я** (preceded by **а** or **я**), neuter, **-е** (preceded by **о** or **е**). It will also be seen that these markers correspond to the formulations given at the end of the first section of this chapter.

Exercise 1

Vocabulary[1]

сто, *hundred*
сталь (*f.*), *steel*
вели́кий, *great*
слепóй, *blind*
кишкá, *gut*
зарáзный, *infectious*
чугу́н, *cast-iron*
мя́гкий, *soft*
прóчный, *durable*
серьёзный, *serious*
снег, *snow*
а, *and, but*
кость (*f.*), *bone*
и, *and*
простóй, *simple*
не, *not*
части́ца, *particle*
мáленький, *small*

1. Водá — жи́дкость.
2. Сто — большóе числó.
3. Э́та[2] фигу́ра — гексаэ́др.
4. Сталь твёрдый метáлл.
5. Там большóй кóнус.
6. Вы вели́кий зоóлог.

[1] As a general rule, words used earlier in the book and those whose meaning is obvious either because of the context or their similarity to English words are not given in the vocabularies for the exercises. All words used in the exercises are in the general vocabulary at the end of the book. Adjectives are given in the nom. sing. masc. form.

[2] Fem. form of **э́то** *this, that,* which is neuter and is often used as an 'introductory' demonstrative : *this (thing) is . . ., it is . . .,* cf. sentence No. 7.

7. Э́то слепа́я кишка́.
8. Туберкулёз зара́зная боле́знь.
9. Чугу́н хру́пкий мета́лл.
10. Цинк — мя́гкий мета́лл, но про́чный.
11. Рак — серьёзная боле́знь.
12. Мо́ре си́нее, а снег бе́лый.
13. Кость — бе́лая и твёрдая.
14. Э́то дли́нная хромосо́ма.
15. Электри́ческая ла́мпа тут.
16. Умноже́ние — просто́й проце́сс.
17. Юпи́тер плане́та, а Си́риус звезда́.
18. Э́то твёрдое веществó не желе́зо, а эбони́т.
19. Э́та сталь твёрдая и про́чная.
20. Больша́я части́ца — прото́н, а ма́ленькая части́ца — электро́н.

3

THE PREPOSITIONAL CASE OF THE NOUN

There are six cases in Russian: nominative, genitive, dative, accusative, instrumental, prepositional. All these cases, except the nominative, can be used with a preposition. All of them can be used without a preposition, except the prepositional case, which always has a preposition with it. Though some of the other cases can express location, it is the prepositional case which above all others expresses location. Hence its alternative name: the locative case.

The preposition **при** *at, near, by, during,*[1] cannot take any case other than the prepositional, while the prepositions **в** (sometimes **во**) *in,* **по** *after,* **о** (sometimes **об, обо**) *about,* **на** *on,* while taking other cases with other meanings, take the prepositional case with the meanings given here.

The markers of the prepositional case of nouns are as follows:

1. In the plural, for all genders, **-х** (preceded by **а** or **я**):

моле́кула	**в моле́кулах**	*in the molecules*
а́том	**в а́томах**	*in the atoms*
ли́ния	**на ли́ниях**	*on the lines*
сосу́д	**в сосу́дах**	*in the vessels*
влия́ние	**о влия́ниях**	*about the influences*

2. In the singular, for most types of masculine nouns, **-е**:

сосу́д	**в сосу́де**	*in the vessel*
а́том	**об а́томе**	*about the atom*
луч	**о луче́**	*about the ray*
зно́й	**при зно́е**	*in the heat*
учи́тель	**об учи́теле**	*about the teacher*

Masculine nouns ending in **-ий** in the nominative singular (there are only a few of these) have **-и** as marker for the prepositional case, e.g. **ра́дий — в ра́дии** *in radium.*

[1] The meaning of the preposition **при** cannot be given by a few simple correspondents in English. Its meaning, or variety of meanings, will become evident from the sentences and lessons that follow.

The anomalous masculine noun **путь** *way, path,* also has its prepositional in **-и,** e.g. **на пути́** *on the way.*

3. In the singular, for most types of feminine nouns, **-е** :

нау́ка	**в нау́ке**	*in science*
моле́кула	**при моле́куле**	*near, by the molecule*
луна́	**на луне́**	*on the moon*

Feminine nouns ending in the nominative singular in **-ь** or **-ия** have as marker for the prepositional case **-и**. Thus :

анато́мия	**об анато́мии**	*about anatomy*
тео́рия	**в тео́рии**	*in the theory*
смесь	**в сме́си**	*in the mixture*
кость	**на кости́**	*on the bone*

4. In the singular, for most types of neuter nouns, **-е** :

вещество́	**о веществе́**	*about the substance*
по́ле	**в по́ле**	*in the field*
мо́ре	**на мо́ре**	*on the sea*

Neuter nouns ending in **-ие** have as marker for the prepositional case **-и**. Thus :

явле́ние	**о явле́нии**	*about the phenomenon*
расте́ние	**на расте́нии**	*on the plant*
зна́ние	**при зна́нии**	*with the knowledge*

Notice that, except in the instance of masculine nouns with the nominative singular ending in a consonant, the marker of the nominative singular is replaced by the prepositional case ending : **нау́к-а — в нау́к-е, тео́ри-я — в тео́ри-и, смес-ь — в сме́с-и,** etc. It happens that with such nouns as **по́ле, мо́ре,** etc. the marker of the prepositional singular is identical with that of the nominative singular : **по́ле — в по́л-е, мо́р-е — на мо́р-е.** If one takes the nominative singular marker of masculine nouns ending in a consonant to be zero, then one can say that, in general, the nominative singular marker is replaced by the prepositional case ending. This general rule applies to all the other cases too : i.e. the nominative singular marker is replaced in other cases by the appropriate ending. For reading purposes, however, it is necessary to learn only the markers (minimal markers) which in some instances are shorter than the case endings.

The neuter nouns which end in the nominative singular in **-мя** (of which there are ten only) have the peculiar feature that the **-я** of the nominative singular is replaced by **-ен** before the endings of the other cases are added. The prepositional marker for these nouns is **-и**. Thus:

Nom. sing.		*Prep. sing.*	*Prep. pl.*
вре́м-я	*time*	**о вре́м-ен-и**	**о врем-ен-а́х**
се́м-я	*seed*	**в се́м-ен-и**	**в сем-ен-а́х**

Bearing the above points in mind, we may state that:

1. The marker of the prep. sing. of nouns is **-е** or **-и**;
2. The marker of the prep. pl. of nouns is **-х**.

For immediate recognition purposes, this is all that it is necessary to learn. The distribution of the two alternatives of the prep. sing. (though this is not essential information) is as follows:

The prep. sing. marker **и** is shared by

1. All nouns with penultimate **и** in the nom. sing.: **радий — в ра́дии, тео́рия — в тео́рии, явле́ние — о явле́нии.**
2. Feminine nouns having the marker **ь** in the nom. sing.: **смесь — в сме́си, кость — на кости́.**
3. The masculine noun **путь — на пути́.**
4. The ten neuter nouns having nom. sing. in **-мя — вре́мя — о вре́мени**;

while all other nouns, masculine, feminine or neuter, have the prep. sing. marker **-е**.

There are some masculine nouns which have a normal prep. sing. in **-е** and also a special marker, **-у** or **-ю,** with purely locative meaning (i.e. when used with either of the prepositions **в** or **на**). Thus:

лес	**о ле́се**	*about the wood*	**в лесу́**	*in the wood*
край	**о кра́е**	*about the edge*	**на краю**	*on the edge*
снег	**о сне́ге**	*about the snow*	**в снегу́**	*in the snow*

The adjective, while having different markers for the prep. sing. (these will be described later), has the same marker for the prep. pl. as the noun, i.e. **-х.** In the adjective this marker is preceded by **ы** or **и,** whereas in the noun it is preceded by **а** or **я**. Thus:

твёрдый — твёрдых	**кра́сный — кра́сных**
хру́пкий — хру́пких	**си́ний — си́них**

See Chapter 11

Exercise 2

Vocabulary

то́чка, *point*
соль (*f.*), *salt*
пла́мя (*n.*), *flame*
он, *he, it*
она́, *she, it*
оно́, *it*
недоста́ток, *fault, flaw*
где, *where*
де́рево, *tree*
пле́сень (*f.*), *mould*
ядро́, *nucleus, kernel*
тёмный, *dark*
пятно́, *stain, patch*
тяжёлый, *heavy*
что (*pronounced* **што**), *what*
иску́сственный, *artificial*
радиопереда́тчик, *radio-transmitter*
бензи́н, *petrol*
бензо́л, *benzol, benzene*
круг, *circle*
уже́, *already*
тако́й, *such*

Translate into English:

1. На ли́нии то́чка.
2. В мо́ре соль.
3. Мета́лл в пла́мени. Он в пла́мени.
4. Есть серьёзный недоста́ток в тео́рии.
5. Кость бе́лая. Она́ бе́лая.
6. Где де́рево? Де́рево в лесу́. Оно́ в лесу́.
7. В сме́си — соль и вода́.
8. На расте́ниях си́няя пле́сень.
9. В э́тих[1] расте́ниях кра́сный сок.
10. Бе́лое ядро́ в семена́х — твёрдое.
11. На луне́ тёмное пятно́. Э́то ма́ленький кра́тер.
12. В океа́не тяжёлый водоро́д.
13. Что э́то? Э́то иску́сственный спу́тник.
14. В спу́тнике электри́ческая аппарату́ра и радиопереда́тчик.
15. В сосу́де густа́я си́няя жи́дкость.
16. В ма́леньких сосу́дах — кероси́н, а в больши́х — бензи́н.
17. Э́то не бензи́н в сосу́дах, а бензо́л.
18. Ма́ленькая геометри́ческая фигу́ра в квадра́те — круг.
19. Где профе́ссор? Он в Росси́и на конфере́нции.
20. В Росси́и уже́ есть тако́й аппара́т.

[1] Prep. pl. of the word meaning *this, that*.

4

THE INFINITIVE AND THE PAST TENSE

Infinitive

There are two markers of the infinitive in Russian: final **ь** or final **и.** Of these the commoner is **ь** and in most verbs it is preceded by the letter **т,** thus **-ть.** Some examples of infinitives of this type are:

чита́ть	*to read*	**ходи́ть**	*to go*
писа́ть	*to write*	**увели́чить**	*to increase*
сплавля́ть[1]	*to fuse*	**прони́кнуть**[2]	*to penetrate*
лить	*to pour*	**пасть**	*to fall*
стере́ть[1]	*to wipe off*	**дуть**	*to blow*
греть	*to warm*		

In a few infinitives the **ь**-marker is preceded by **ч,** while the **и**-marker is always preceded by **т.** Verbs of these two types are:

нести́	*to be carrying, bearing*	**произвести́**	*to produce*
вести́	*to be leading, to bring*	**жечь**	*to burn* (*transitive*)
перевести́	*to translate*	**мочь**	*to be able*

Some students may find it easier to think of the infinitive markers as **-ть, -ти** and **-чь.**[3]

[1] The prefix **с-** (sometimes **со-**) has two meanings: (1) *together* (con-, com-, etc.); (2) *off, from* (a-, ab-, etc.).
[2] The prefix **про-** means *through* (trans-, pro-).
[3] This is not to say that *all* words ending in **-ть, -ти** or **-чь** are infinitives. Some of them may be nouns and several such nouns have been used in previous lessons, e.g. **кость, жи́дкость, на кости́,** etc.

Past Tense

In Russian the endings of the past tense change according to gender and number, not according to person and number, as they do, for example, in Latin. This is to say that there are no forms which of themselves express, for example, *I went, you went, he went, we went*, etc., but instead there are four forms only—masculine singular, feminine singular, neuter singular and a plural which is common to all genders. Thus a past tense masculine indicates that an action took place or has taken place in the past and that the subject which performed the action was grammatically masculine. The past tense masculine **ходи́л,** for example, means *went* and the subject may be *he* or *I*, *you* (sing.) or *it*, provided that *I*, *you* or *it* are masculine in grammatical gender. Similarly the past tense feminine **ходи́ла** means *went* and the subject may be *she* or *I*, *you* (sing.) or *it*, provided that *I*, *you* or *it* are feminine in grammatical gender. Thus:

Masc.		*Fem.*	
я ходи́л	*I went*	**я ходи́ла**	*I went*
ты ходи́л	*you* (sing.) *went*	**ты ходи́ла**	*you* (sing.) *went*
он ходи́л	*he, it went*	**она́ ходи́ла**	*she, it went*

The marker for nearly all past tense forms is **л,** to which is added the gender marker 'zero' for masculine forms, **-а** for feminine forms, **-о** for neuter forms,[1] and **-и** for plural forms of any gender.

With most verbs in which the infinitive ends in **ть** preceded by a vowel the past tense is formed by removing the **ть** of the infinitive and adding to the resultant stem the marker **л** plus one of the gender-number markers. Thus:

	Past Tense			
Infin.	*Masc.*	*Fem.*	*Neuter*	*Pl.*
ходи́-ть	**ходи́-л**	**ходи́-л-а**	**ходи́-л-о**	**ходи́-л-и**
чита́-ть	**чита́-л**	**чита́-л-а**	**чита́-л-о**	**чита́-л-и**
ли-ть	**ли-л**	**ли-л-а́**	**ли́-л-о**	**ли́-л-и**
гре-ть	**гре-л**	**гре́-л-а**	**гре́-л-о**	**гре́-л-и**
увели́чи-ть	**увели́чи-л**	**увели́чи-л-а**	**увели́чи-л-о**	**увели́чи-л-и**

The expression of the idea of 'pastness' is not particularised into a variety of past tenses, as it is in English. There is only one past tense in Russian, though the past tense *and* the future tense are modified by the system of 'aspects' (which will be treated in Chapter 10 and may be ignored until then). The past tense masculine **писа́л** means, therefore (masculine subject) *wrote, was writing, used to write*, etc., according to the context.

[1] Compare the markers of the nominative singular (Ch. 2).

Exercise 3

Vocabulary

мы, *we*
хоте́ть, *to want*
быть, *to be*
ры́ба, *fish*
со́лнце,[1] *sun*
сиде́ть, *to sit*
сад,[2] *garden*
нагре́ть, *to heat up*
те́ло, *body*
лете́ть, *to be flying, to fly*
пустота́, *vacuum*
самолёт, *aircraft*
реакти́вный самолёт, *jet aircraft*
бы́стро, *swiftly*
гу́бка, *sponge*
отчёт, *report*
о́пыт, *experiment*
учёный, *scientist, scholar*
ви́деть, *to see*
чёрный, *black*
хи́мик, *chemist*
узна́ть, *to find out, get to know*
показа́ть, *to show*
потому́ что, *because*
хиру́рг, *surgeon*
пе́рвый, *first*
примени́ть, *to apply*
о́лово, *tin*
зелёный, *green*
но́вый, *new*
преврати́ть, *to convert*
обсужда́ть, *to discuss*
когда́-то, *at some time*
о́пухоль (*f.*), *tumour*

[1] The **л** is not pronounced in this word.
[2] Has a special locative in **-у**: **в саду́.**

Translate into English:

1. Профе́ссор писа́л.
2. Студе́нт чита́л.
3. Мы ходи́ли.
4. Я хоте́л чита́ть.
5. В воде́ была́ больша́я ры́ба.
6. Со́лнце гре́ло по́ле и мо́ре.[1]
7. Она́ хоте́ла писа́ть.
8. Где вы хоте́ли сиде́ть?
9. Мы хоте́ли сиде́ть в саду́.
10. Студе́нт нагре́л жи́дкость.[2]
11. Те́ло абсорби́ровало газ.[2]
12. Баллисти́ческая раке́та лете́ла в пустоте́.
13. Реакти́вный самолёт лете́л бы́стро.
14. Гу́бка абсорби́ровала жи́дкость.
15. В тео́рии был серьёзный недоста́ток.
16. Профе́ссор писа́л отчёт об о́пыте.
17. Учёный хоте́л чита́ть дли́нный отчёт об о́пыте.
18. На рентгеногра́мме до́ктор ви́дел ма́ленькое чёрное пятно́.

19. Хи́мик анализи́ровал жи́дкость; он хоте́л узна́ть, что э́то за жи́дкость.[3]
20. Ана́лиз показа́л, что э́то вода́.
21. Я уже́ знал, что э́то вода́, потому́ что э́то я влил[4] жи́дкость в сосу́д.
22. Англи́йский хиру́рг Джо́зеф Ли́стер пе́рвый примени́л[5] анти-септи́ческий ме́тод в хирурги́и.
23. В то вре́мя[6] профе́ссор был в Росси́и на конфере́нции.
24. Металлу́рг сплавля́л желе́зо и о́лово в сосу́де.
25. В зелёных семена́х бы́ло твёрдое, бе́лое ядро́.
26. Они́ изоли́ровали но́вый витами́н.
27. Хи́мик влил бензи́н в ма́ленький сосу́д, а в большо́й сосу́д он влил бензо́л.
28. Они́ преврати́ли U^{238} в но́вый элеме́нт, плуто́ний.
29. На конфере́нции обсужда́ли вопро́с о но́вых радиоакти́вных элеме́нтах.
30. Опера́ция показа́ла, что на кости́ когда́-то была́ о́пухоль.

NOTES:

(1) **по́ле** and **мо́ре** are objects of the action expressed by **гре́ло.** They are in the accusative case, which for neuter nouns, many masculine nouns and some feminine nouns is identical with the nominative case. Accusatives which are different from the nominative are not used until Chapter 9.

(2) cf. note 1.

(3) **э́то** *this* (neuter sing.) is used when English often has *it.* **что за** means *what sort of* (cf. German *was für*) and the entire expression **что . . . . жи́дкость** means *what sort of liquid it was.* There is no verb in this clause because the ' sequence of tenses ' used in English does not apply to Russian. In such sentences as this, that tense is used in Russian which would be applicable at the time of the occurrence. Thus, at the time of the occurrence, *he wanted to find out*: *what sort of liquid is it.* The use of the past tense in this clause would mean *he wanted to find out: what sort of liquid was it*, i.e. *he wanted to find out what sort of liquid it had been.*

(4) **влил**: prefixed form of **лил,** which is past tense masculine of **лить.** The prefix **в** = *in.* **э́то я влил**: *it was I who had poured . . . . in.*

(5) **пе́рвый примени́л**: *first applied*, i.e. *was the first to apply.*

(6) *At that time.*

5

THE GENITIVE SINGULAR

Nouns. For masculine and neuter nouns the marker of the genitive singular is **а** or **я.** This marker replaces the nominative singular marker (see Chapter 3). Thus:

температу́ра га́за	*the temperature of the gas*
строе́ние а́тома	*the structure of the atom*
проце́сс умноже́ния	*the process of multiplication*
кни́га учи́теля	*the teacher's book*
вес те́ла	*the weight of the body*

Exceptions to this general rule for masculine and neuter nouns are **путь,** which has genitive singular **пути́,** and neuter nouns ending in the nominative singular **-мя,** which have genitive singular in **-ени,** e.g. **вре́мя — вре́мени.** (Cf. prepositional case of such nouns, Chapter 3.)

A number of masculine nouns have two genitives, one formed as described above and another with the marker **у** or **ю** instead of **а** or **я.** This second form is used principally in 'partitive' phrases, i.e. phrases expressing 'part of,' 'some of,' 'a certain quantity of,' etc. Thus:

са́хар	*sugar*	**за́пах са́хара**	*the smell of sugar*
		BUT	
		кусо́к са́хару	*a piece of sugar*
чай	*tea*	**цена́ ча́я**	*the price of tea*
		BUT	
		фунт ча́ю	*a pound of tea*
лес	*wood*	**цена́ ле́са**	*the price of wood*
		BUT	
		то́нна ле́су	*a ton of wood*

For feminine nouns the marker of the genitive singular is **ы** or **и.** This replaces the last letter of the nominative singular. Thus:

строе́ние моле́кулы	*the structure of the molecule*
длина́ ли́нии	*the length of the line*
серьёзность боле́зни	*the seriousness of the disease*

кни́га студе́нтки	*the student's book*
амплиту́да фа́зы	*the amplitude of the phase*

EXERCISE 4[1]

Give the nominative singular and meaning of the following nouns:

1. га́за, а́тома, зу́ба, самолёта, азо́та.
2. по́ля, мо́ря, умноже́ния, сосу́да, вре́мени.
3. ли́нии, фа́зы, амплиту́ды, боле́зни, фо́рмы.
4. ле́су, пла́мени, стро́я, учи́теля, желе́за, воды́.
5. со́лнца, пустоты́, гу́бки, раке́ты, влия́ния, со́ли, пути́, расте́ния.

[1] Students who find it difficult to operate with isolated words may, at their discretion, omit exercises of this type.

Adjectives. The declension of the adjectives differs largely from that of nouns in Russian, and it is only at certain points that the two types of declension are similar. The genitive singular of the adjective, for instance, is quite unlike that of the noun.

For the masculine and neuter adjective the marker of the genitive singular is **го,** preceded by **о** or **е.** The entire ending **ого** or **его,** *pronounced as if spelt* **ово, ево,** replaces the nominative singular endings **ый, ий, ой, ое** or **ее.** Thus:

	Nom. sing.	*Gen. sing.*	
Masc.	**твёрдый**	**твёрдого**	*hard*
Neuter	**твёрдое**		
Masc.	**хру́пкий**	**хру́пкого**	*brittle*
Neuter	**хру́пкое**		
Masc.	**большо́й**	**большо́го**	*big*
Neuter	**большо́е**		
Masc.	**си́ний**	**си́него**	*blue*
Neuter	**си́нее**		

For the feminine adjective the marker of the genitive singular is **й,** preceded by **о** or **е.** The entire ending **ой** or **ей** replaces the nominative singular endings **ая** and **яя.** Thus:

Nom. sing.	*Gen. sing.*	
твёрдая	**твёрдой**	*hard*
больша́я	**большо́й**	*big*
си́няя	**си́ней**	*blue*

EXERCISE 5[1]

Give the case, gender and meaning of the following:

1. твёрдого, хру́пкий, си́него, большо́го, магни́тное.
2. густо́е, серьёзной, дли́нного, си́ней, чёрной.
3. зара́зный, бе́лого, вели́кой, мя́гкого, просто́й.
4. твёрдого материа́ла, большо́й моле́кулы, ма́ленького квадра́та, просто́го а́тома.
5. густо́й жи́дкости, си́него вещества́, кра́сной воды́, хру́пкой ко́сти.

[1] See note 1, page 40.

USE OF THE GENITIVE CASE

The genitive case in Russian is used in much the same way as *of* and apostrophe *s* are used in English. It is also used in ways which are strange to the English-speaking student. Particular attention should be paid to these latter usages of the genitive case.

The following are some of the functions of the genitive case:

(*a*) In expressions of possession and 'of-expressions,' including adjectival expressions.

(*b*) In expressions of quantity.

(*c*) With many prepositions.

(*d*) In numerical expressions: with the numbers 2, 3 and 4, and larger numbers (other than the 'teens) of which the last unit is 2, 3 or 4, the genitive *singular* of nouns is used. With these same numbers the nominative or genitive *plural* of adjectives is used. With the numbers 5 to 20 and upwards (excluding larger numbers of which the last unit is 1, 2, 3 or 4) the genitive plural of nouns *and* adjectives is used.[1] For the present we are concerned only with the use of the genitive singular of nouns with the numbers 2, 3 and 4.[2]

[1] With compound numbers of which the last unit is 1 (other than 11) the nominative *singular* is used. Numbers ending in 'teens, including ... 11, ... 12, ... 13, ... 14, have the genitive plural of noun and adjective. (See Chapter 19.)

[2] This usage occurs only when the *entire* numerical expression is to be construed as nominative (subject) or accusative (object). Otherwise the entire expression is in the genitive, dative or whatever the appropriate case may be. (See Chapter 19.)

(*e*) In negative expressions with **нет** *there is not/no, there are not/no,* **нé было** *there was not/no, there were not/no,* and with negated verbs (i.e. verbs used in conjunction with the negative particle **не**). In this latter usage the accusative case is also used. Note that **не** without a verb, when it has the meaning *is not, are not,* does not govern the genitive. Since the use of the genitive with **нет** and **нé было** is an extension of the use of the genitive in expressions of quantity, being, so to speak, an expression of ' negative quantity,' the special partitive genitive of certain masculine nouns may be found in expressions of this type.

(*f*) With certain verbs.

Examples of these usages of the genitive are :

(*a*) Possession, etc. : see examples at the beginning of this lesson. With some adjectives : this is similar to the English usage of *of* after adjectives—*full of, worthy of,* etc.

пóлный	*full* (*of*)	**достóйный**	*worthy* (*of*)

(*b*) Expressions of quantity :

мнóго[1] **материáла**	*much material*
мáло материáла	*little material*
немнóго[1] **материáла**	*a little material*
скóлько мáзи	*how much ointment*
он вы́пил воды́[2]	*he drank some water*[2]

(*c*) With prepositions :

от ли́нии	*from the line*
для профéссора	*for the professor*
из дéрева	*out of wood, i.e. made of wood* (**дéрево,** *tree, wood*)
без азóта	*without nitrogen*
и́з лесу[3]	*out of the wood*

(*d*) In numerical expressions :

два кýба	*two cubes* (**оди́н куб,** *one cube*)
два пóля	*two fields* (**однó пóле,** *one field*)

[1] This is not the genitive ending **ого** and therefore the **г** is pronounced as **г,** not as **в.**

[2] The genitive is sufficient here to express *some water.*

[3] After the prepositions **из, от** and one or two others the genitive in **у** or **ю** of those masculine nouns which have such a genitive (see above) may be found instead of the genitive in **а** or **я.** In such instances the stress is on the preposition and the noun has no stress. (Cf. stress of **нé было** above.)

две фóрмы[1]	*two shapes* (**однá**[2] **фóрма,** *one shape*)
три кýба	*three cubes*
три фóрмы	*three shapes*
три пóля	*three fields*
четы́ре изотóпа	*four isotopes*
четы́ре фáзы	*four phases*
четы́ре дéрева	*four trees*

(*e*) In negative expressions:

Нет[3] **воды́**	*There is no water.*
Нé было воды́	*There was no water.*
Сáхару нé было	*There was no sugar.*
Мы не ви́дели óпыта	*We did not see the experiment.*
Он не читáл кни́ги	*He did not* (*has not, etc.*) *read the book.*

(*f*) With many verbs. Many verbs which govern the genitive express either the idea of aiming at or achieving a goal, or avoidance of or aversion from something.

искáть	*to seek*	**избегáть**	*to avoid*
дости́гнуть	*to reach, achieve*	**лишáть**	*to deprive*

[1] The number 2 has the form **два** with masculine and neuter nouns and the form **две** with feminine nouns.

[2] The number 1 has a masculine form **оди́н,** a neuter form **однó** and a feminine form **однá.** There is also a plural form **одни́** which means *some.* Note the **и** in the masculine nominative singular. Cardinal numbers other than 1 and 2 and compounds thereof do not have gender distinctions.

[3] **нет**: *there is not, there are not.* An alternative form, found occasionally, is **нéту,** which may have a slightly emphatic value.

Exercise 6

Vocabulary

край, *edge*
далекó, *far, a long way*
полéзный, *useful*
свáрка, *welding*
внéшний, *external*
пыль (*f.*), *dust*
вóздух, *air*
вес, *weight*
нáтрий, *sodium*
произвóдство, *production*
внутри́ (+ gen.), *within*
óчень, *very*
высóкий, *high*
упрýгость (*f.*), *elasticity*
явлéние, *phenomenon*
гéлий, *helium*
когдá, *when*
пи́ща, *food*
вкус, *taste*
лýчше, *better*
основнóй, *basic*
довóльно, *enough, fairly*

Translate into English:

1. В воде́ океа́на мно́го со́ли.
2. На ли́нии я ви́дел три то́чки.
3. У квадра́та[1] четы́ре кра́я.
4. У ди́ска оди́н край.
5. От Эдинбу́рга до Ло́ндона — далеко́.
6. Проду́кт мета́на CHCl3 — хлорофо́рм.
7. У водоро́да три изото́па.
8. Ацетиле́н — вещество́ поле́зное для сва́рки мета́лла.
9. У сфе́ры одна́ вне́шняя пове́рхность.
10. Профе́ссор чита́л дли́нный отчёт учёного[2] об экспериме́нте.
11. В пыли́ и во́здухе есть микро́б туберкулёза.
12. Вес одного́[3] куби́ческого сантиме́тра э́того вещества́ — два гра́мма.
13. Хлори́д на́трия вещество́ поле́зное в произво́дстве со́ды.
14. Внутри́ со́лнца о́чень высо́кая температу́ра.
15. Упру́гость га́за явле́ние о́чень поле́зное в те́хнике.
16. В а́томе просто́го водоро́да — ядро́ (оди́н прото́н) и электро́н.
17. Ма́сса ге́лия — четы́ре; в ядре́ два прото́на и два нейтро́на.
18. Когда́ в пи́ще бы́ло немно́го со́ли, вкус был лу́чше.
19. Основно́й при́нцип радиолокацио́нной те́хники дово́льно просто́й.
20. Ру́сский учёный И. И. Ме́чников рабо́тал в сфе́ре микробиоло́гии.

NOTES:

(1) The preposition **у,** meaning *at,* requires the genitive case. This construction is the common way of expressing in Russian *has, have* or, with the past tense of the verb **быть,** *had.* **У квадра́та** means *a square has.*

(2) Some adjectives are used as nouns and, naturally, have adjectival endings.

(3) **одного́** is the genitive of **оди́н** and **одно́.**

EXERCISE 7a

VOCABULARY

никто́, *nobody*
удиви́тельный, *surprising*
причи́на, *cause*
возвра́тный тиф, *typhoid*
нить (*f.*), *thread*
изуча́ть, *to study*
гла́вным о́бразом, *for the most part, principally*
откры́ть, *to discover*
впервы́е, *first* (used with a verb in the sense ‘ was the first to,’ etc.)

расщепи́ть, *to split*
определи́ть, *to determine*
заря́д, *charge*
ва́жный, *important*
значе́ние, *significance*
име́ть, *to have*
примене́ние, *application*
всеми́рный, *universal*
тяготе́ние, *gravitation*
нача́ла (*pl.*), *principles*
труд, *work*
оказа́ть, *to exert*
разви́тие, *development*
сомне́ние, *doubt*
проведе́ние, *conduct*
сам, *self*
оши́бка, *mistake, error*
хотя́, *although*
ещё, *yet*
дать, *to give*
положи́тельный, *positive*
одна́ко, *however*
мне́ние, *opinion*
и, *and* ; **и . . . и** — *both . . and* ; **и** alone is sometimes used for purposes of emphasis (see sentence 10—*even, too*)
избежа́ть, *to avoid*
по́этому, *therefore*
повтори́ть, *to repeat*
коренно́й, *fundamental*
измене́ние, *change, alteration*
отноше́ние, *attitude, relation* ; **в отноше́нии** (+gen.), *as regards*

Translate into English:

1. Никто́ не[1] предви́дел[2] тако́го удиви́тельного результа́та от тако́го просто́го экспериме́нта.
2. Студе́нт чита́л в кни́ге, что причи́на возвра́тного ти́фа — спирохе́та, т.е.[3] бакте́рия в фо́рме дли́нной спира́льной ни́ти.
3. Вели́кий англи́йский фи́зик Э́рнест Ре́зерфорд[4] изуча́л гла́вным о́бразом строе́ние а́тома.
4. В 1900 г.[5] Ре́зерфорд откры́л но́вый радиоакти́вный элеме́нт а в 1919 г. он впервы́е расщепи́л ядро́ а́тома.
5. Уже́ в 1910 Ми́лликен эксперимента́льно[6] определи́л заря́д электро́на.
6. Ва́жное значе́ние в исто́рии астроно́мии име́ло примене́ние телеско́па[7] и откры́тие[8] всеми́рного тяготе́ния.
7. „Нача́ла" Эвкли́да[9] о́чень ва́жный труд в исто́рии матема́тики; он оказа́л большо́е влия́ние на разви́тие э́той нау́ки.
8. Нет сомне́ния, что в тео́рии серьёзный недоста́ток, потому́ что в проведе́нии самого́ о́пыта не́ было оши́бки.
9. В при́нципе э́то тео́рия досто́йная вели́кого учёного, хотя́ на пра́ктике она́ ещё не дала́ положи́тельного результа́та.
10. Профе́ссор, одна́ко, был того́[10] мне́ния, что и в проведе́нии о́пыта мы не избежа́ли оши́бки, и по́этому не хоте́л повтори́ть о́пыт без коренно́го измене́ния и в отноше́нии тео́рии и в отноше́нии ме́тода.

NOTES:

(1) The accumulation of negatives is common in Russian: one negative word does not negate another in Russian and thus the entire phrase or sentence remains negative.

(2) **пред-** is a prefix equivalent to English *pre-, fore-*.

(3) **т.е. — то есть,** *that is, i.e.*

(4) The Russian spelling of *Rutherford*.

(5) **г.**—abbreviation of the word for *year* (**год**), which is sometimes omitted (see next sentence for example).

(6) **-о** is a common adverbial marker, English *-ly*.

(7) This sentence shows an inversion common in Russian. The subject of the verb is **примене́ние телеско́па.**

(8) A noun connected with the verb **откры́ть.**

(9) The Russian spelling of *Euclid*.

(10) Genitive of **тот** (*masc.*) and **то** (*neuter*), *that*.

EXERCISE 7b

VOCABULARY

давно́, *long ago*
свине́ц, *lead*
проводи́ть, *to conduct*
ток, *current*
заключи́ть, *to conclude*
чи́стый, *pure*
удо́бный слу́чай, *convenient occasion, opportunity*
иссле́дование, *research, investigation*
размноже́ние, *reproduction*
нагре́ть, *to heat up*
печь (*f.*), *stove*
пото́м, *then*
охлажде́ние, *cooling*
пря́мо, *straight*
предложи́ть, *to propose*
щелочно́й, *alkaline*
о́бласть (*f.*), *region, sphere, province*
та́кже, *also*
основополо́жник, *founder*
неме́цкий, *German*
нача́ть, *to begin*
тече́ние, *course*
Акаде́мия нау́к СССР, *Academy of Sciences of the U.S.S.R.*
ядови́тый, *poisonous*
грибо́к, *fungus*
осо́бый, *special*
нали́чие, *presence*
позволя́ть, *to allow*
избега́ть, *to avoid* (cf. **избежа́ть** above)
перемеще́ние, *transference, shifting*
нау́чный сотру́дник, *scientific collaborator, scientific worker, scientist*
лече́бный, *medicinal, therapeutic*
лече́ние, *treatment*

Translate into English:

1. Уже давно́ узна́ли,[1] что желе́зо магни́тное вещество́, а свине́ц не магни́тное.
2. Жи́дкость в сосу́де не проводи́ла электри́ческого то́ка, поэ́тому заключи́ли, что э́то не чи́стая вода́.
3. Она́ иска́ла удо́бного слу́чая для иссле́дования ци́кла размноже́ния э́того живо́тного.
4. Сосу́д, по́лный густо́й си́ней жи́дкости, нагре́ли в печи́ до 600° и пото́м без охлажде́ния вы́лили[2] жи́дкость пря́мо в резерву́ар.
5. В 1900 Эдисо́н впервы́е предложи́л электри́ческий аккумуля́тор щелочно́го ти́па.
6. Эдисо́н рабо́тал гла́вным о́бразом в о́бласти электроте́хники, но та́кже рабо́тал и в о́бласти телефони́и, киноте́хники и хи́мии.
7. Основополо́жник ква́нтовой фи́зики — неме́цкий фи́зик-теоре́тик Макс Планк.
8. В тече́нии э́того иссле́дования откры́ли в лаборато́рии Институ́та Микробиоло́гии Акаде́мии нау́к СССР но́вый ядови́тый микроскопи́ческий грибо́к.
9. Осо́бая констру́кция электро́да и нали́чие коммута́тора позволя́ли избега́ть ча́стого перемеще́ния электро́да.
10. Нау́чный сотру́дник Институ́та Микробиоло́гии Ве́ра Иосифовна Била́й откры́ла но́вый лече́бный препара́т — микроци́д, вещество́ о́чень поле́зное в хирурги́и, в стоматоло́гии, в гинеколо́гии, а та́кже при[3] лече́нии анги́ны.

NOTES:

(1) The use of the past tense plural (and the third person plural of the present tense) without a subject is roughly equivalent to English *one* (*learnt*), or the passive *it was* (*learnt*), or an unspecified *they* as in *they* (*learnt*).

(2) The prefix **вы-** corresponds to English *out*, *ex-*, *e-*, etc.

(3) Here **при** = *in*.

6

THE PAST TENSE (continued) AND REFLEXIVE VERBS

Past Tense

Most verbs with an infinitive in **-ти** (e.g. **нести́**) form the past tense masculine by means of the verb ' stem ' alone, without the marker **л.** This stem is to be obtained in some cases simply by removing the last syllable **-ти**, thus: **нести́**, stem **нес-**, past tense masculine **нёс.** In other cases, however, the stem is not, so to speak, visible in the infinitive, but is to be found in the present tense. An example of this is **грести́** *to row, paddle*, stem **греб-** (present tense 1st person singular **гребу́**), past tense masculine **грёб.**

The stem is similarly ' hidden ' in infinitives ending in **-чь.** Such verbs have a stem ending in **к** or **г** and also form the past tense masculine without the marker **л.** Thus: **мочь** *to be able*, stem **мог-** (present tense 1st person singular **могу́**), past tense masculine **мог**; **печь** *to bake*, stem **пек-** (present tense 1st person singular **пеку́**), past tense masculine **пёк**; **бере́чь** *to take care of*, stem **берег-** (present tense 1st person singular **берегу́**), past tense masculine **берёг.**

There are two fairly large groups of verbs with the infinitive ending in **-нуть.** The verbs of one of these groups form the past tense in the ' normal ' way by replacing **-ть** by **-л.** Thus: **дви́нуть** *to move*, past tense masculine **дви́нул.** The verbs of the other group form the past tense masculine without **-л,** by removing the last syllable **-нуть.** Thus: **пога́снуть** *to go out, be extinguished*, past tense masculine **пога́с**; **исче́знуть** *to disappear*, past tense masculine **исче́з.**

There are a few verbs which have as the last five letters of the infinitive **-ереть.** They form the past tense masculine by removing **-еть.** Thus: **умере́ть** *to die*, past tense masculine **у́мер; тереть** *to rub*, past tense masculine **тёр.**

One or two verbs are formed from a root **-шиб-.** Verbs formed from this root and having an infinitive in **-ить** have a past tense masculine without **-л,** thus: **ушиби́ть** *to bruise, contuse*, past tense masculine **уши́б.**

All the verbs of the types described above have the past tense marker **л** in the feminine, neuter and plural forms of the past tense.

Thus:

Infin.	*Past masc.*	*Fem.*	*Neuter*	*Pl.*
нести́	**нёс**	**несло́**	**несло**	**несли́**
грести́	**грёб**	**гребла́**	**гребло́**	**гребли́**
мочь	**мог**	**могла́**	**могло́**	**могли́**
печь	**пёк**	**пекла́**	**пекло́**	**пекли́**
бере́чь	**берёг**	**берегла́**	**берегло́**	**берегли́**
пога́снуть	**пога́с**	**пога́сла**	**пога́сло**	**пога́сли**
исче́знуть	**исче́з**	**исче́зла**	**исче́зло**	**исче́зли**
умере́ть	**у́мер**	**умерла́**	**у́мерло**	**у́мерли**
тере́ть	**тёр**	**тёрла**	**тёрло**	**тёрли**
ушиби́ть	**ушиб**	**ушибла**	**ушибло**	**ушибли**

Some verbs with an infinitive in **-ти** or **ть** preceded by **с** form the past tense masculine with **л**, after removing the last three letters of the infinitive. Thus:

вести́	*to be leading*, past tense masculine			**вёл**
сесть	*to sit down*,	,,	,,	**сел**
плести́	*to weave*,	,,	,,	**плёл**
упа́сть	*to fall*,	,,	,,	**упа́л**

The verb **итти́** or **идти́** *to be going* forms its past tense from a different root, thus: masculine **шёл**, feminine **шла**, neuter **шло**, plural **шли**.[1]

Some of the verbs in this and the preceding section are of frequent occurrence in compound forms (i.e. prefixed forms). These compound verbs form their past tenses in the same way as the simple verbs. Among such compounds are:

перенести́	*to carry across*; *to undergo, suffer*
перевести́	*to translate*
перейти́[2]	*to go across*
внести́	*to bring in*
ввести́	*to lead/bring in*
войти́	*to go/come in*

[1] Note the presence of the vowel letter **е** in the masculine form and its absence in the other forms. This phenomenon of the 'fugitive vowel' is found in nouns and adjectives too, and attention will be called to it whenever it arises. The entire phenomenon is described in Appendix III.

[2] The compounding form of **идти́/итти́** is **-йти** in most cases; an exception is **придти́/притти́** *to come*. The past tense of these compounds is formed by the replacement of **-йти, -дти** or **-тти** by **-шёл, -шла, -шло, -шли.** (See Appendix IV.)

вы́нести	*to take/bring out*
вы́вести	*to lead, bring out, to draw (a conclusion)*
вы́йти	*to come/go out*
произвести́	*to produce*
придти́, притти́[1]	*to come*
произойти́	*to issue, arise (from); to occur*
найти́	*to find* (cf. English *to come upon*)

[1] Also **прийти́.**

The material contained in this and the preceding section may seem somewhat complicated, but the student should bear in mind that all he is required to do is to learn to recognise these forms. Moreover, a little practice in reading Russian will soon establish these apparently anomalous forms in the memory, especially as knowledge of the present tense often helps in recognition of the past tense and *vice versa*. Verbs of the types described here are in any case included in the reference table in Appendix IV.

Reflexive Verbs

Another verbal compound of the root **-шиб-** (cf. **ушиби́ть** above) is **ошиби́ться** *to make a mistake*. The past tense of this verb is **оши́бся, оши́блась, оши́блось, оши́блись.**

The elements **ся** and **сь** are 'reflexive particles' and one or the other of them may be added to a verb form to make it 'reflexive.' The infinitive, the past tense, the present tense, the future tense and several of the participles may occur with the reflexive particle, which always comes in the final position.

Reflexive verbs in Russian may express a 'passive' idea:

кни́га	**чита́лась**	**везде́**
the book	*read-self* (i.e. *was read*)	*everywhere*

or an action performed (voluntarily or involuntarily) by the agent or actor upon himself:

до́ктор	**ушибся**	**о**	**стол**
the doctor	*bruised-self*	*against*	*the table*

or they may simply be 'formally reflexive,' i.e. they may have no apparent reflexive or passive idea:

ошиби́ться	*to make a mistake*	**смея́ться**	*to laugh*
боя́ться	*to be afraid, to fear*		

Exercise 8

Give the infinitive (with meaning) to which the following past tenses correspond (refer to Appendix IV, if necessary):

1. грёб, нёс, вёл, пёк, сел.
2. мог, плёл, берёг, пал, уга́с.
3. исче́з, у́мер, шёл, ушиб, вела́.
4. тёрла, ошибся, перенесла́, вы́вело, нашли́.
5. ушиблась, произошло́, смея́лась, могло́, пога́сла, перешли́.

Exercise 9

Vocabulary

про́бный, *test* (*adj.*)
раз, *once*
бы́стро, *swiftly*
дать, *to give*
соверше́нно, *completely*
пластма́сса, *plastic*
врач, (*medical*) *doctor*
сказа́ть, *to say*
помо́чь (*compound of* **мочь**), *to help*
второ́й, *second*
чахо́тка, *consumption*
рак, *cancer*
лёгкое (*adjectival n.*), *lung*
со́лнечный, *solar*
вспы́шка, *flare*
с (+ *gen.*), *from, off*
сторона́, *side*
криво́й, *curved, bent*
друго́й, *other*
прямо́й, *straight*
восто́рг, *rapture, delight*
тума́нность (*f.*), *nebula*
созве́здие, *constellation*
тща́тельный, *thorough*
осмо́тр, *inspection, examination*
пласти́нка, *plate*
боль (*f.*), *pain*
печь, *to bake, to roast*
по́сле (+ *gen.*), *after*
вы́глядеть, *to look, seem*
ре́зко, *sharply*
всё-таки, *nevertheless*
рециди́в, *relapse*
спустя́, *later*
моча́, *urine*
бело́к, *albumen*
вы́вод, *conclusion*; **сде́лать вы́вод,** *to come to the conclusion*

Translate into English:

1. Реакти́вный самолёт не мог лете́ть в пустоте́.
2. Про́бная баллисти́ческая раке́та не могла́ взлете́ть.[1]
3. Раз она́ взлете́ла, она бы́стро дости́гла большо́й ско́рости.
4. Они́ хоте́ли произвести́ но́вый си́нтез, но не могли́.
5. Э́та рабо́та дала́ оди́н о́чень интере́сный результа́т.
6. Из сме́си мы произвели́ соверше́нно но́вый тип пластма́ссы.

7. Врач оши́бся, когда́ он сказа́л, что боле́знь полиомиели́т.
8. Профе́ссор физиоло́гии перевёл две кни́ги ру́сского учёного Па́влова о рефле́ксах.
9. Э́то вещество́ помогло́ абсорби́ровать жи́дкость.
10. Пе́рвый метеори́т упа́л на по́ле, а второ́й упа́л в мо́ре.
11. Больно́й у́мер от чахо́тки, а не от ра́ка лёгкого.
12. Больша́я со́лнечная вспы́шка уже́ пога́сла.
13. С одно́й стороны́ шла крива́я ли́ния, а с друго́й шла пряма́я ли́ния.
14. Астроно́м вы́шел из обсервато́рии в восто́рге, потому́ что он нашёл тума́нность в созве́здии Орио́на.
15. Откры́тие но́вой тума́нности произошло́ в результа́те тща́тельного осмо́тра фотографи́ческой пласти́нки.
16. Больна́я перенесла́ мно́го бо́ли от ра́ка лёгкого.
17. Мы пекли́[2] препара́т в тече́ние ча́са и по́сле э́того кра́сное пятно́ у́же соверше́нно исче́зло.
18. Хотя́ больно́й у́же вы́глядел лу́чше и температу́ра ре́зко упа́ла, мы всё-таки боя́лись рециди́ва.[3]
19. Четы́ре часа́ спустя́ мы нашли́ в моче́ 21% белка́.[4]
20. Из э́того мы сде́лали вы́вод, что у больно́го начался́ рециди́в.

NOTES:

(1) **вз-, воз-,** a prefix signifying *up*.
(2) Past tense plural of **печь.**
(3) **боя́ться** governs the genitive case.
(4) **бело́к** is a noun with a fugitive vowel (in this instance **о**). Masculine nouns which have a fugitive vowel have the vowel only in the nominative case.

7

THE INSTRUMENTAL CASE

Nouns

For masculine and neuter nouns the marker of the instrumental singular is **м,** preceded by **о** or **е.** Thus:

по́ле	*field*	**по́лем**	**cocу́д**	*vessel*	**сосу́дом**
то́пливо	*fuel*	**то́пливом**	**а́том**	*atom*	**а́томом**
строй	*order*	**стро́ем**	**путь**	*way*	**путём**

Neuter nouns with the nominative singular in **-мя** have the additional syllable **ен** before the instrumental ending:

вре́мя	*time*	**вре́менем**	**пла́мя**	*flame*	**пла́менем**

(cf. genitive and prepositional singular of such nouns: **вре́мени**).

For feminine nouns with the nominative singular in **а** or **я** the marker of the instrumental singular is **й,** preceded by **о** or **е.** Thus:

вода́	*water*	**водо́й**	**ли́ния**	*line*	**ли́нией**
сестра́	*sister*	**сестро́й**	**до́ля**	*portion*	**до́лей**
моле́кула	*molecule*	**моле́кулой**	**тео́рия**	*theory*	**тео́рией**

An alternative marker for feminine nouns of this type is **ю,** preceded by **о** or **е.** Thus: **водо́ю, сестро́ю, до́лею,** etc. This marker is now much less common than **й** and is given here simply because it may be found occasionally in technical literature.

For feminine nouns with the nominative singular ending in a soft sign the marker of the instrumental singular is **ю,** added to the nominative singular (i.e. the **ю** is preceded by **ь**). Thus:

кость	*bone*	**ко́стью**	**жи́дкость**	*liquid*	**жи́дкостью**
ско́рость	*velocity*	**ско́ростью**			

For all nouns the marker of the instrumental plural, irrespective of gender, is **-ми,** preceded by **а** or **я.** Thus:

сосу́д	—	**сосу́дами**	**по́ле**	—	**поля́ми**
путь	—	**путя́ми**	**а́том**	—	**а́томами**
ли́ния	—	**ли́ниями**	**сестра́**	—	**сёстрами**
моле́кула	—	**моле́кулами**	**тео́рия**	—	**тео́риями**
кость	—	**костя́ми**	**жи́дкость**	—	**жи́дкостями**

Neuter nouns with the nominative singular in **-мя** again have the additional syllable **ен** before the instrumental plural ending.

вре́мя *time* **времена́ми** **се́мя** *seed* **семена́ми**

In one or two nouns, the instrumental plural marker **ми** is preceded by **ь** instead of **а** or **я.** Examples of this are **детьми́,** instrumental plural of **де́ти** *children*; **людьми́,** instrumental plural of **лю́ди** *people*.

Exercise 10

State (i) the case,[1] (ii) the meaning of the following nouns:

1. проце́ссом, строе́нием, вре́мени, фа́зами, са́харом.
2. ко́сти, пути́, те́лом, водо́й, врачо́м.
3. жи́дкостью, са́хару, амплиту́дой, боле́знью, фо́рмой.
4. ско́ростью, времена́ми, со́лнцем, пустото́й, осмо́тра.
5. раке́той, ли́цами, тума́нностью, созве́здиями, ли́нией.
6. пласти́нкой, во́здухе, на́трием, ни́тями, упру́гостью.

[1] By no means all of the nouns are in the instrumental case.

Adjectives

For the masculine and neuter adjective the marker of the instrumental singular is **-м,** preceded, however, not by **о** or **е,** but by **ы** or **и.** Thus:

Nom. sing.			*Inst. sing.*
Masc.	*Neuter*		*Masc. and Neuter*
кра́сный	**кра́сное**	*red*	**кра́сным**
густо́й	**густо́е**	*thick*	**густы́м**
си́ний	**си́нее**	*blue*	**си́ним**
большо́й	**большо́е**	*big*	**больши́м**

For the feminine adjective the marker of the instrumental singular is identical with that for feminine nouns having the nominative singular in **а** or **я,** i.e. **й** (preceded by **о** or **е**). Thus:

кра́сная — кра́сной **густа́я — густо́й**
си́няя — си́ней **больша́я — большо́й**

It will be seen that this ending is identical with that of the genitive singular of feminine adjectives. There is the alternative marker **ю** (preceded by **о** or **е**) for the instrumental singular of the feminine adjectives : **кра́сною, густо́ю, си́нею, большо́ю,** but these forms are less common than the ones given above.

For adjectives of any gender the marker of the instrumental plural is **-ми,** as for nouns, but it is preceded by **ы** or **и,** not by **а** or **я.** Thus : **кра́сными, густы́ми, си́ними, больши́ми.**

Exercise 11

State (i) the case,[1] (ii) the meaning of the following adjectives :

1. твёрдым, хру́пкой, дли́нными, одноро́дного, магни́тной.
2. бе́лой, си́ней, мя́гкими, просто́й, тяжёлым.
3. коро́ткого, серьёзной, учёным, чёрными, основно́й.
4. поле́зными, вторы́м, больно́й, про́бной, пе́рвого.
5. но́вым, ру́сской, высо́кими, вне́шней, ма́леньким.

[1] Note that not all these adjectives are in the instrumental case and that there may be more than one answer to some parts of these questions.

Use of the Instrumental Case

The instrumental case is used in a variety of ways :

(*a*) To denote the means or instrument whereby an action is performed (hence the name of the case) or the agent by whom an action is performed.

(*b*) With certain prepositions.

(*c*) With the verb **быть** and substitutes for this verb.

(*d*) With certain other verbs.

(*e*) In a number of other idiomatic expressions.

The following are examples of these usages :

(*a*)	**Студе́нт писа́л си́ним карандашо́м.**	*The student wrote with a blue pencil.*
	бомбардирова́ть нейтро́нами	*to bombard with neutrons*
	разбавля́ть водо́й	*to dilute with water*
	Кни́га чита́лась учёными везде́.	*The book was read by scholars everywhere.*

(*b*)	**Он вы́шел с сестро́й.**	*He went out with his sister.*
	Принима́ть лека́рство с водо́й.	*Take the medicine with water.*
	над атмосфе́рой	*above the atmosphere*
	пе́ред до́мом	*in front of the house*
	за со́лнцем	*behind the sun*
	ме́жду зуба́ми	*between the teeth*
(*c*)	**Он был профе́ссором.**	*He was a professor.*
	Он был до́ктором.	*He was a doctor.*
	Лу́чшим студе́нтом явля́лся Черно́в.	*Chernov was the best student.*
	(But **Он профе́ссор.**	*He is a professor.*
	Он до́ктор.	*He is a doctor.*)
(*d*)	**Отве́т оказа́лся непра́вильным.**	*The answer turned out (to be) wrong.*
	Мы занима́лись ра́зными пробле́мами.	*We were occupied with various problems.*
	Студе́нт владе́л ру́сским языко́м.	*The student had a command of the Russian language.*
	Вы интересова́лись ра́зными вопро́сами.	*You were interested in various questions.*

(*e*)	**но́чью**	*at night*	(**ночь,** *night*)
	у́тром	*in the morning*	(**у́тро,** *morning*)
	ле́том	*in the summer*	(**ле́то,** *summer*)
	весно́й	*in spring*	(**весна́,** *spring*)
	по́лем	*through the field*	
	други́ми слова́ми	*in other words*	(**сло́во,** *word*)
	длино́й в три ми́ли	*three miles long*	
	бо́льшей ча́стью	*for the most part, for the greater part* (**бо́льший,** *greater*; **часть** (*f.*), *part*)	
	таки́м о́бразом	*in this manner* (**о́браз,** *way, shape, form*)	

Exercise 12

Vocabulary

под (+ *inst.*), *under*
ко́жа, *skin*
обнару́жить, *to discover*
кусо́к, *piece*
удовлетвори́тельный, *satisfactory*

па́лочка, *a little stick, rod*
наблюда́ть, *to observe*
размножа́ться,[1] *to reproduce, multiply*
быстрота́, *rapidity*
цвет, *colour*
зима́, *winter*
борьба́, *struggle*
про́тив (+ *gen.*), *against*
части́ца,[2] *particle*
слой, *layer*
толщина́, *thickness*
райо́н, *region*
вы́сший, *higher, upper*
по́льзоваться, *to make use of*
спать, *to sleep*
есть, *to eat*
тем вре́менем, *meanwhile*
саме́ц, *male*
са́мка, *female*
са́мый, *most, very*
прожо́рливый, *gluttonous*
отрывно́й, *escape* (*adj.*)
цель (*f.*), *object*
хорошо́, *well*
согласова́ться, *to agree*
ста́дия, *stage*
перегруппиро́вка, *regrouping*
получи́ть, *to obtain*
ре́зкий, *sharp, pronounced*
преоблада́ние, *preponderance*

[1] Compare **умноже́ние** *multiplication,* and **мно́го** *many.* (Alternation of **г** and **ж**: see Appendix II.)
[2] cf. **часть** *part.*

Translate into English:

1. Вода́ в сосу́де абсорби́ровалась ма́ленькой гу́бкой.
2. Под ко́жей до́ктор обнару́жил кусо́к желе́за длино́й в два сантиме́тра.
3. Результа́т экспериме́нта явля́лся удовлетвори́тельным.
4. Под микроско́пом профе́ссор ви́дел микро́б в фо́рме па́лочки.
5. Други́ми слова́ми, то, что он наблюда́л, была́ баци́лла.
6. Микро́б мог размножа́ться с большо́й быстрото́й.
7. Ме́жду по́люсом и эква́тором астроно́мами наблюда́лась зо́на си́него цве́та.
8. Зимо́й до́ктор занима́лся борьбо́й про́тив туберкулёза.
9. Фи́зик бомбардирова́л а́льфа-части́цами слой мета́лла толщино́й в три миллиме́тра.
10. Над сло́ем Хе́висейда[1] Э́ппельтон[2] обнару́жил друго́й райо́н иониза́ции.[3]
11. Иску́сственный спу́тник оказа́лся идеа́льным инструме́нтом иссле́дования вы́сшей атмосфе́ры.
12. В рабо́те над[4] дифтери́том мы по́льзовались контро́льным экспериме́нтом.[5]
13. Но́чью саме́ц не спал и не хоте́л есть.
14. Тем вре́менем са́мка е́ла са́мым прожо́рливым о́бразом.

15. О́чень ва́жной пробле́мой межплане́тной[6] навига́ции явля́лся вопро́с; как дости́гнуть отрывно́й ско́рости?
16. Парамагни́тный резона́нс впервы́е наблюда́лся сове́тским учёным Е. К. Заво́йским в 1944.
17. С э́той це́лью мы по́льзовались ме́тодом дегенера́ции.
18. Э́тот факт хорошо́ согласова́лся с ио́нным механи́змом реа́кции дие́нового си́нтеза.
19. Второ́й ста́дией проце́сса явля́лась перегруппиро́вка ио́нного ко́мплекса.
20. При реа́кции пентадие́на-1,3[7] с акролеи́ном мы получи́ли смесь с ре́зким преоблада́нием о-изоме́ра.

NOTES:

(1) **Хе́висейд** *Heaviside.*

(2) **Э́ппельтон** *Appleton.*

(3) The ending **-ция** corresponds to *-tion* in words borrowed from Western European languages.

(4) Here **над** = *on.*

(5) **по́льзоваться** governs the instrumental case.

(6) The prefix **меж-** = *inter-.*

(7) In Russian a comma is used instead of a point in the decimal notation.

8

THE PRESENT TENSE AND THE NOMINATIVE PLURAL

Present Tense

The present tense in Russian, as is usual in inflected languages, changes according to person and number (not according to gender and number, as the past tense does in Russian), and the markers for the present tense are as follows:

1st	person	singular	**-у** or **-ю**
2nd	,,	,,	**-шь**
3rd	,,	,,	**-ет** or **-ит**
1st	,,	plural	**-м**
2nd	,,	,,	**-те**
2rd	,,	,,	**-ут, -ют, -ат** or **-ят**

The markers for the 3rd person singular and plural may be broken down even further, thus: the 3rd person marker is **-т,** the preceding vowel indicating number (**е** or **и** — singular, other vowels — plural).

The second person singular will not be met with in technical literature except possibly in an idiomatic usage corresponding to the English *one does so-and-so* or *you do so-and-so* (see below).

Here are some examples of typical conjugations:

ЧИТА́ТЬ	**ГРЕТЬ**	**НЕСТИ́**	**ИДТИ́**
чита́ю	**гре́ю**	**несу́**	**иду́**
чита́ешь	**гре́ешь**	**несёшь**	**идёшь**
чита́ет	**гре́ет**	**несёт**	**идёт**
чита́ем	**гре́ем**	**несём**	**идём**
чита́ете	**гре́ете**	**несёте**	**идёте**
чита́ют	**гре́ют**	**несу́т**	**иду́т**

ХОДИ́ТЬ	**ГОРЕ́ТЬ**	**БОЯ́ТЬСЯ**
хожу́	**горю́**	**бою́сь**
хо́дишь	**гори́шь**	**бои́шься**
хо́дит	**гори́т**	**бои́тся**
хо́дим	**гори́м**	**бои́мся**
хо́дите	**гори́те**	**бои́тесь**
хо́дят	**горя́т**	**боя́тся**

The only exception to these conjugation patterns for the present tense is the verb **есть** *to eat*, which is 'irregular' in the 1st and 3rd persons singular:

1st	person	singular	**ем**
2nd	,,	,,	**ешь**
3rd	,,	,,	**ест**
1st	,,	plural	**еди́м**
2nd	,,	,,	**еди́те**
3rd	,,	,,	**едя́т**

The infinitive **есть** *to eat* must be distinguished from the word **есть,** which has already been used and means *there is, there are* or, on occasions, simply *am, is* or *are*. **есть** in these senses is a vestige of the old present tense of the verb **быть.** Another vestige of this present tense is **суть,**[1] now extremely rare and meaning (*they*) *are.*

It is not necessary that a verb form (present tense, past or future) should have with it a noun or pronoun expressing the subject. If it is clear from the context who or what the subject of a verb is, the verb may be found without a word indicating the subject. Thus **гре́ет** means *he, she* or *it warms,* **чита́ю** *I read,* **идём** *we are going,* and so on.

Nearly all verbs with an infinitive ending in **-овать** or **-евать** have the curious feature that the syllable **ов** or **ев** is replaced in the present tense by **у** or **ю.** Thus: **анализи́ровать** *to analyse,* **анализи́рую, анализи́руешь, анализи́рует, анализи́руем,** etc., **клева́ть** *to peck,* **клюю́, клюёшь, клюёт,** etc. If therefore, a new present tense form is found ending in, say, **-ует,** the probability is that the infinitive ends in **-овать** or **-евать** and this should be borne in mind when looking up verbs in a dictionary. Thus, the infinitive of **сове́тует** is **сове́товать** *to advise,* that of **жуёт** is **жева́ть** *to chew.* Similarly, the probability is that a present tense form ending in **-юет, -юем,** etc., is derived from an infinitive ending in **-евать.** Thus the infinitive of **плюёт** is **плева́ть** *to spit.*

In a large number of verbs the final consonant of the root, visible in the infinitive and/or the past tense, is replaced by another consonant in the present tense. This replacement may occur in only one personal form of the present tense, in several forms or throughout the conjugation. Thus:

мочь (past tense **мог,** etc.) **могу́, мо́жешь, мо́жет, мо́жем, мо́жете, мо́гут**

[1] Not to be confused with the noun **суть** (*f.*), *essence, kernel.*

ходи́ть **хожу́, хо́дишь, хо́дит, хо́дим, хо́дите, хо́дят**
писа́ть **пишу́, пи́шешь, пи́шет, пи́шем, пи́шете, пи́шут**

All such interchanges of consonants are reducible to a limited number of patterns and are summarised in Appendix II ('Consonant Interchanges'), to which reference should be made as the occasion arises.

Vowel interchanges are not of such frequent occurrence in verbs as in other parts of speech. The following should be noted for the moment:

лить *to pour*	**бить** *to beat*	**пить** *to drink*
лью	**бью**	**пью**
льёшь	**бьёшь**	**пьёшь**
льёт	**бьёт**	**пьёт**
льём	**бьём**	**пьём**
льёте	**бьёте**	**пьёте**
льют	**бьют**	**пьют**

шить *to sew*	**вить** *to twine*
шью	**вью**
шьёшь	**вьёшь**
шьёт	**вьёт**
шьём	**вьём**
шьёте	**вьёте**
шьют	**вьют**

and

мыть *to wash*	**рыть** *to dig, delve*	**дава́ть** *to give*
мо́ю	**ро́ю**	**даю́**
мо́ешь	**ро́ешь**	**даёшь**
мо́ет	**ро́ет**	**даёт**
мо́ем	**ро́ем**	**даём**
мо́ете	**ро́ете**	**даёте**
мо́ют	**ро́ют**	**даю́т**

The commoner or more useful 'anomalous' verbs are contained in Appendix IV, which gives information about the present tense as well as about other verb forms. Having learnt the markers given at the beginning of this lesson, the student will be able, by referring when necessary to Appendices II and IV, to recognise any present tense forms and after some practice will find himself recognising present tense forms at sight and, often enough, without referring to the Appendices.

Exercise 13

Translate into English, referring where necessary to the Appendices, the following present tense forms:

1. чита́ем, несу́т, горя́т, ввóзим, пишу́.
2. идёте, анализи́руете, зна́ет, хóдят, гре́ю.
3. пьёт, ведём, ду́ет, хóчет, явля́ется.
4. сове́туете, льёт, кладу́, бои́тся, летя́т.
5. абсорби́руют, бережём, вьёт, несёшь, мóет.
6. мóжет, жую́т, жгу, ест, размножа́ются.
7. жжёт, клюю́т, печём, спит, едя́т.

Nominative Plural

For nouns, the markers of the nominative plural are **ы, и, а** or **я.** Thus:

самолёт	*aircraft*	**самолёты**
ла́мпа	*lamp*	**ла́мпы**
путь	*way*	**пути́**
кость	*bone*	**кóсти**
земля́	*earth*	**зе́мли**
кни́га	*book*	**кни́ги**
дóктор	*doctor*	**доктора́**
учи́тель	*teacher*	**учителя́**
ядрó	*nucleus*	**я́дра**
пóле	*field*	**поля́**
стул	*chair*	**сту́лья**
перó	*feather, pen*	**пе́рья**

The markers **ы** and **и** are restricted to feminine and masculine nouns, the markers **а** and **я** to neuter and masculine nouns.

Nouns of the type of **вре́мя** have the additional syllable **-ен-** before the nominative plural marker:

вре́мя	*time*	**времена́**
се́мя	*seed*	**семена́**

The noun **сын** *son* has the additional syllable **-ов-** in the plural, thus nominative plural, **сыновья́.**[1]

[1] Some other nouns have this feature too.

Nouns denoting the young of animals, ending in the nominative singular in **-ёнок,** have the nominative plural in **-áта,** or **-я́та,** thus:

мышёнок	*young mouse*	**мышáта**
жеребёнок	*foal*	**жеребя́та**
цыплёнок	*chicken*	**цыпля́та**

The noun **нéбо,** meaning *sky,* has the additional syllable **-ес-** in the plural, thus nominative plural, **небесá.**

Nouns ending in the nominative singular in **-анин** or **-янин,** all of which denote persons of various social categories or nationalities, lose the syllable **-ин** in the plural and have the anomalous nominative plural marker **е,** thus:

граждани́н	*citizen*	**грáждане**
крестья́нин	*peasant*	**крестья́не**
англичáнин	*Englishman*	**англичáне**

This marker **е,** which is anomalous for nouns, is the typical marker of the nominative plural for adjectives. It is preceded by **ы** or **и** and is constant, no matter what the gender of the noun accompanied by the adjective. Thus:

крáсные самолёты	*red aeroplanes*
си́ние лáмпы	*blue lamps*
крáсные семенá	*red seeds*
си́ние пéрья	*blue feathers*
пусты́е сосýды	*empty vessels*

It should be noted that, except where stated in the next chapter to be otherwise, the accusative is identical with the nominative, so that many of the nominatives plural quoted in this chapter also serve as accusatives plural.

Exercise 14

Vocabulary

напримéр, *for example*
таблица, *table*
значéние, *value*
недовóльный, *dissatisfied*
оснóва, *basis*
совремéнный, *contemporary* (cf. **врéмя**)
учéние, *teaching* (cf. **учи́тель**)
изучéние, *study*
я́дерный, *nuclear* (cf. **ядрó**)

осуша́ть, *to dry*
вычища́ть, *to clean out*
кузне́ц, *smith*
нагрева́ть, *to warm up, heat up*
доводи́ть, *to bring* (*to*)
его́,[1] *him, it*
состоя́ние, *state*
кова́ть (кую́, куёт), *to forge*
мо́лот, *hammer*
вытека́ть, *to flow out, exude*
называ́ть, *to name, call*
содержа́ть, *to contain*
каучу́к, *rubber, caoutchouc*
соста́в, *composition*
рези́на, (*hard*) *rubber*
се́ра, *sulphur*
е́сли, *if*
прибавля́ть, *to add*
коли́чество, *quantity*
получа́ть, *to obtain*
рогово́й, *horny*
земля́, *earth*
снижа́ть, *to lower*
распа́д, *decay*
существова́ть, *to exist*
испуска́ть, *to emit*
и́ли, *or*
захва́тывать, *to capture*
оболо́чка, *envelope, shell*
образо́вывать, *to form*
огро́мный, *huge*
успе́шно, *successfully*
защи́та, *defence*
кро́ме (+ gen.), *apart from*
рабо́чий, *worker*
сре́дство, *means, instrument*

[1] Pronounced as if spelt **ево́.**

Translate into English:

1. Наприме́р, в табли́це 1 даётся значе́ние фу́нкции z.
2. Осно́вой совреме́нной сове́тской физиоло́гии явля́ется материалисти́ческое уче́ние И. П. Па́влова.
3. Чита́ешь отчёт об экспериме́нтах и всё-таки ока́зываешься недово́льным.
4. А́томная фи́зика занима́ется изуче́нием строе́ния а́тома, я́дерная фи́зика занима́ется изуче́нием ядра́ а́тома.
5. Мо́ем сосу́д водо́й, осуша́ем и вычища́ем спи́ртом.
6. Мы зна́ем, наприме́р, что кузне́ц нагрева́ет желе́зо.
7. Он дово́дит его́ до тако́го состоя́ния, что он мо́жет кова́ть его́; мо́лотом он и[1] куёт его́.
8. Из де́рева вытека́ет бе́лый сок; э́тот сок соде́ржит каучу́к.
9. Э́то де́рево называ́ется каучу́ковым де́ревом.
10. В соста́в рези́ны и́ли вулканизи́рованного каучу́ка вхо́дит[2] и се́ра.
11. Е́сли мы прибавля́ем большо́е коли́чество се́ры, мы получа́ем рогово́й каучу́к, — одни́м[3] сло́вом — эбони́т.
12. Со́лнце гре́ет пове́рхность земли́, а но́чью температу́ра пове́рхности снижа́ется.
13. В ра́дии и́ли в ура́не происхо́дит я́дерный распа́д.

14. Существу́ет два ти́па а́томного распа́да — а́льфа-распа́д и бе́та-распа́д.
15. При а́льфа-распа́де испуска́ется а́льфа-части́ца — ядро́ изото́па ге́лия $_2He^4$.
16. При бе́та-распа́де испуска́ется бе́та-части́ца (электро́н) и́ли ядро́ а́тома захва́тывает электро́н из а́томной оболо́чки.
17. В результа́те распа́да ра́дия образо́вывается радиоакти́вный газ — радо́н.
18. Огро́мные пла́ны разви́тия а́томной энерге́тики успе́шно реализу́ются.
19. Вопро́сы защи́ты персона́ла а́томной электроста́нции явля́ются о́чень ва́жными.
20. Кро́ме того́,[4] у персона́ла на электроста́нции есть индивидуа́льные дозиметри́ческие сре́дства.
21. В табли́це 2 даю́тся значе́ния фу́нкции z.
22. Доктора́ чита́ют дли́нные отчёты об экспериме́нтах.
23. Они́ вычища́ли пусты́е сосу́ды спи́ртом.
24. Со́лнце гре́ет кра́сные семена́ в земле́.
25. Испуска́ются а́льфа-части́цы — я́дра изото́па ге́лия $_2He^4$.
26. Я́дра захва́тывают электро́ны из а́томной оболо́чки.

NOTES:

(1) The word **и** means *and, also, as well* and is also used as an 'emphatic participle,' so that the second part of sentence 7 could be translated *and then he does forge it, with a hammer.*
(2) **в** is a prefix signifying *in.*
(3) **одни́м** is instrumental of **оди́н** and **одно́.**
(4) Genitive of **тот** and **то,** the **г** being pronounced as **в.**

9

THE GENITIVE PLURAL AND THE ACCUSATIVE CASE

Genitive Plural

The markers of the genitive plural for nouns are **в** (preceded by **о** or **е**), **й** (preceded by **и** or **е**), zero, and **ь** (preceded, of course, by a consonant). A ' zero ' marker means simply that any final vowel of the nominative singular is removed and nothing replaces it.

The following are examples of the genitive plural:

	Nom. sing.		*Gen. pl.*
Marker **в**	**самолёт**	*aircraft*	**самолётов**
	край	*edge*	**краёв**
	профе́ссор	*professor*	**профессоро́в**
	перо́	*feather, pen*	**пе́рьев**
Marker **й**	**ли́ния**	*line*	**ли́ний**
	кость	*bone*	**косте́й**
	путь	*way*	**путе́й**
	по́ле	*field*	**поле́й**
Marker zero	**ла́мпа**	*lamp*	**ламп**
	фа́за	*phase*	**фаз**
	вещество́	*matter*	**веще́ств**
	сло́во	*word*	**слов**
	глаз[1]	*eye*	**глаз**
Marker **ь**	**ми́ля**	*mile*	**ми́ль**
	земля́	*earth*	**земе́ль**[2]

The distribution of these markers is as follows:

The marker **в** occurs largely with masculine nouns and also with a few neuter nouns; the marker **й** occurs with masculine, feminine and neuter nouns; the zero marker occurs with feminine and neuter nouns and also a few masculine nouns; and the marker **ь** occurs with feminine nouns.

Neuter nouns of the **вре́мя** type form their genitive plural with

[1] One of the very few masculine nouns which have zero marker in the genitive plural.

[2] The genitive plural of **земля́** has a fugitive vowel, which does not appear in any of the other cases.

a zero marker but the syllable **-ен-** replaces the final **я** of the nominative singular, as it does in all other cases of nouns of this type. Thus: **вре́мя**, genitive plural **времён.** The noun **се́мя,** however, has the genitive plural **семя́н.**

The marker of the genitive plural for adjectives, irrespective of their gender, is **х** (preceded by **ы** or **и**). Thus:

кра́сных самолётов	*red aircraft*
си́них пе́рьев	*blue feathers*
дли́нных ли́ний	*long lines*
бе́лых косте́й	*white bones*
си́них ламп	*blue lamps*

ACCUSATIVE CASE

The only nouns which have a special form for the accusative case are feminine nouns with the nominative singular ending in **а** or **я.** This marker is replaced by **у** or **ю** to form the accusative singular. Thus:

Nom. sing.		*Acc. sing.*
фа́за	*phase*	**фа́зу**
раке́та	*rocket*	**раке́ту**
до́ля	*portion*	**до́лю**
земля́	*earth*	**зе́млю**

Otherwise the accusative case is identical either with the nominative or the genitive case. Thus, neuter nouns and masculine nouns denoting inanimate objects, as well as feminine nouns having the nominative singular in **ь,** have an accusative singular identical with the nominative singular.

Those masculine nouns which denote animate beings have an accusative singular identical with the genitive singular. In the plural, all nouns, of whatever gender, have an accusative identical with their nominative if they denote inanimate objects but identical with their genitive if they denote animate beings. Thus:

Nom. sing.		*Acc. sing.*	*Acc. pl.*
сло́во	*word*	**сло́во**	**слова́**
самолёт	*aircraft*	**самолёт**	**самолёты**
кость	*bone*	**кость**	**ко́сти**
до́ктор	*doctor*	**до́ктора**	**доктор́ов**[1]
ла́мпа	*lamp*	**ла́мпу**	**ла́мпы**
же́нщина	*woman*	**же́нщину**	**же́нщин**[1]

[1] i.e. identical with genitive plural.

There is a special marker for the accusative singular feminine of the adjective, namely **ю** (preceded by **у** or **ю**). Thus:

Nom. sing. fem.		*Acc. sing. fem.*
дли́нная ли́ния	*long line*	**дли́нную ли́нию**
бе́лая кость	*white bone*	**бе́лую кость**
си́няя ла́мпа	*blue lamp*	**си́нюю ла́мпу**

Otherwise the accusative case of the adjective is identical either with the nominative or with the genitive. If the accompanying or implied noun is neuter or masculine denoting an inanimate object then the accusative singular of the adjective is identical with the nominative singular. If, however, the noun is masculine and denotes an animate being then the accusative singular of the adjective is identical with the genitive singular. In the plural, irrespective of gender, the accusative is identical with the nominative if the noun denotes an inanimate object but identical with the genitive if the noun denotes an animate being. Thus:

Nom. sing.		*Acc. sing.*	*Acc. pl.*
дли́нная ли́ния	*long line*	**дли́нную ли́нию**	**дли́нные ли́нии**
бе́лая кость	*white bone*	**бе́лую кость**	**бе́лые ко́сти**
кра́сный самолёт	*red aircraft*	**кра́сный самолёт**	**кра́сные самолёты**
пусто́е сло́во	*empty word*	**пусто́е сло́во**	**пусты́е слова́**
ру́сский профе́ссор	*Russian professor*	**ру́сского профе́ссора**	**ру́сских профессоро́в**
англи́йский до́ктор	*English doctor*	**англи́йского до́ктора**	**англи́йских докторо́в**
ма́ленькая же́нщина	*small woman*	**ма́ленькую же́нщину**	**ма́леньких же́нщин**

Adjectives which are used as nouns follow the same rules:

Nom. sing.		*Acc. sing.*	*Acc. pl.*
больно́й	*patient* (*m.*)	**больно́го**	**больны́х**
больна́я	*patient* (*f.*)	**больну́ю**	**больны́х**
учёный	*scholar*	**учёного**	**учёных**
живо́тное	*animal*	**живо́тного**	**живо́тных**

The accusative case is used to express the direct object of an action, unless there is a partitive idea, when the genitive will be used, or a negative, when the genitive *may* be used. It is also used in expressions of time, distance, value; and with certain prepositions. The following are examples of these latter usages :

Она́ была́ там це́лый год.	*She was there a whole year.*
Он был там це́лую неде́лю.	*He was there a whole week.*
Мы прошли́ одну́ ми́лю.	*We have gone one mile.*
Э́та кни́га сто́ит фунт.	*This book costs a pound.*
в то вре́мя	*at that time*
во вре́мя	*at the time* (*of*), *during*
в стратосфе́ру	*into the stratosphere*
на кость	*on to the bone*
на до́ктора	*on to the doctor*
че́рез ли́нию	*across the line*
че́рез день	*in a day's time* (i.e. *after one day has elapsed*)
за ли́нию	*behind, beyond the line*
за день	*in a day* (i.e. *in the space of a day*)
за рубль	*for a rouble*

It will be noticed that some of the prepositions used above have been used previously with other cases. The prepositions **в, на, за** and **под** are used with the accusative in spatial expressions where movement is implied and with another case in spatial expressions where location is implied (**в** and **на** with the prepositional, **за** and **под** with the instrumental).

Exercise 15

Give the meaning of the following and state in what case are the nouns and adjectives :

1. сы́на, желе́зо, же́нщину, роди́теля, раке́т.
2. кра́сных дере́вьев, большу́ю фо́рму, иску́сственные спу́тники, вели́кого учёного, моле́кулы.
3. си́нюю жи́дкость, а́льфа-части́ц, кра́сные пе́рья, хромосо́м.
4. поле́зные проце́ссы, шесть фаз, серьёзных вопро́сов, твёрдое веществó, де́вять тел.
5. мно́го пе́рьев, пять слоёв, немно́го слов, спирохе́ты, ру́сские доктора́.
6. непра́вильных отве́тов, чёрные глаза́, магни́тных поле́й, интегра́льных фу́нкций, фотоэлектри́ческого эффе́кта.

EXERCISE 16

VOCABULARY

основополо́жник,[1] *founder*
сравни́тельный, *comparative*
совме́стно,[2] *jointly*
вме́сте,[2] *together*
установи́ть, *to establish*
закономе́рность, *regularity*
позвоно́чный, *vertebrate*
заложи́ть, *to lay*
созда́ть, *to create*
многокле́точный, *multicellular*
счита́ть, *to consider*
устро́енный, *organised, arranged*
о́бщий, *general, common*
пре́док (gen. **пре́дка**), *ancestor*
состоя́ть, *to consist*
нару́жный, *external, outer*
вну́тренний, *internal*
перева́ривать, *to digest*
разли́чный, *various*
подвижно́й, *mobile*
воспале́ние, *inflammation*
сво́йство, *property*

[1] cf. **осно́ва** *basis*; root **лож-** means *put* (*in a lying position*).
[2] cf. **ме́сто** *place*.

Translate into English:

МЕ́ЧНИКОВ

Илья́ Ильи́ч Ме́чников — ру́сский био́лог, оди́н из основополо́жников сравни́тельной патоло́гии, эволюцио́нной эмбриоло́гии, микробиоло́гии и иммуноло́гии. Он был чле́ном Петербу́ргской Акаде́мии нау́к.

Совме́стно с други́м учёным он организова́л в Оде́ссе пе́рвую в Росси́и бактериологи́ческую ста́нцию. Вме́сте с А. О. Ковале́вским, Ме́чников установи́л закономе́рности в разви́тии позвоно́чных и беспозвоно́чных[1] живо́тных. Таки́м о́бразом он заложи́л осно́вы эволюцио́нной эмбриоло́гии.

Ме́чников та́кже со́здал тео́рию многокле́точных живо́тных. Э́та тео́рия счита́ет, что все многокле́точные произошли́ от примити́вно[2] устро́енного о́бщего пре́дка.[3] Те́ло тако́го пре́дка состоя́ло из сло́я нару́жных кле́ток[4] и ма́ссы вну́тренних кле́ток. Э́ти кле́тки могли́ захва́тывать и перева́ривать пи́щу.

У[5] разли́чных многокле́точных Ме́чников обнару́жил подвижны́е кле́тки. Э́ти кле́тки перева́ривают части́цы пи́щи. Они́ называ́ются фагоци́тами. На осно́ве изуче́ния проце́ссов воспале́ния, патоге́нных свойств холе́рных и други́х микро́бов он со́здал фагоцита́рную тео́рию иммуните́та.

NOTES:

(1) **бес-, без-** — prefix signifying *without, in-, -less.*.
(2) **-о** is an adverb marker, = English *-ly*.
(3) **пре́док** has a fugitive **о** in the nom. sing. only.

(4) **клётка** has a fugitive **о** in the gen. pl. only.
(5) **у** here = *in*.

Exercise 17

Translate into English:

1. Материа́л показа́л, что электромагни́тные си́лы игра́ют суще́ственную роль в дина́мике планета́рных тума́нностей.

   си́ла = *force;* **игра́ть** = *to play;* **суще́ственный** = *essential, fundamental.*

2. Осо́бенности их структу́ры мо́жно объясни́ть предположе́нием, что в планета́рных тума́нностях существу́ют магни́тные поля́.

   осо́бенность (*f.*) = *peculiarity;* **их** is genitive and accusative plural of **они́** and therefore means *their* or *them;* **мо́жно** = *one can, one may, it is possible;* **объясни́ть** = *to explain;* **предположе́ние** = *supposition.*

3. У звёздных систе́м ти́па норма́льных спира́лей углова́я ско́рость не мо́жет значи́тельно отлича́ться от преде́ла Пуанкаре́.

   у here = *in;* **звёздный** = *stellar;* **углово́й** = *angular;* **значи́тельно** = *significantly, considerably;* **отлича́ть** = *to distinguish, to differentiate;* **преде́л** = *limit;* **Пуанкаре́** = *Poincaré.*

4. О неэлектромагни́тных взаимоде́йствиях μ-мезо́нов с нукло́нами в настоя́щее вре́мя име́ется о́чень ма́ло эксперимента́льных да́нных.

   взаимоде́йствие = *interaction;* **настоя́щий** = *present;* **име́ется** = '*has itself,*' i.e. *there is, there are;* **ма́ло, мно́го, немно́го** take the genitive plural when they mean, respectively, *few, many, a few;* **да́нное** = *datum, fact.*

5. Их э́тих да́нных сле́дует то́лько тот факт, что э́то взаимоде́йствие „сла́бое".

   э́тих is genitive plural of **э́тот, э́то** and **э́та**; **сле́довать** = *to follow;* **то́лько** = *only;* **сла́бый** = *weak.*

6. Спин — механи́ческий моме́нт коли́чества движе́ния электро́на и́ли други́х элемента́рных части́ц (позитро́нов, нейтро́нов, прото́нов и др.); от величины́ спи́на суще́ственно зави́сят сво́йства элемента́рных части́ц.

   коли́чество = *quantity;* **движе́ние** = *movement;* **др.** is an abbreviation of **други́х**; **величина́** = *magnitude, size;* **суще́ственно** is the adverb derived from **суще́ственный**; **зави́сеть** = *to depend;* **сво́йство** = *property.*

7. Решéние задáчи о движéнии снаря́да позволя́ет получи́ть систéму дифференциáльных уравнéний в вариáциях, на оснóве котóрой выбирáются парáметры систéмы автомати́ческого управлéния.

решéние = *solution;* **задáча** = *problem;* **снаря́д** = *missile;* between **позволя́ет** and **получи́ть** one must in translating insert ' one,' ' you ' or ' us '; **уравнéние** = *equation;* **котóрой** is genitive singular feminine of **котóрый,** which means *which* or *who;* **выбирáть** = *to select, choose;* **управлéние** = *guidance, guiding.*

8. Среди́ глáвных момéнтов инéрции тéла A, B, C нет рáвных: центр тя́жести тéла располагáется на однóй из глáвных осéй инéрции.

среди́ (+ gen.) = *among;* **глáвный** = *chief, main, principal;* A, B, C refer to **глáвных момéнтов**; **рáвный** = *equal;* **тя́жесть** (*f.*) = *gravity;* **располагáть** = *to distribute, dispose;* **ось** (*f.*) = *axis, axle.*

9. Впервы́е асимптоти́ческое решéние задáчи о затухáнии удáрных волн нашёл Л. Д. Ландáу: он получи́л пéрвый член решéния для сфери́ческого и цилиндри́ческого слу́чаев.

затухáние = *damping, fading;* **удáрный** = *shock;* **волнá** = *wave;* the first half of this sentence is ' inverted '; **член** = *member, limb;* **слу́чай** = *case;* the last word is in the genitive plural but the accompanying adjectives are in the genitive singular since each refers to a different ' case '—' for the spherical case and the cylindrical case.'

10. Во врéмя рабóты шесть насóсов заставля́ют дистилли́рованную вóду под давлéнием 100 атмосфéр циркули́ровать в пéрвом кóнтуре.

шесть = *six;* the numbers 5 to 20 and above, other than those ending in 1, 2, 3 or 4 (i.e. 21, 32, etc.) govern the genitive plural; **насóс** = *pump;* **заставля́ть** = *to compel, make;* **давлéние** = *pressure;* 100 is read here as **ста,** the genitive of **сто**; **кóнтур** = *circuit.*

10

VERBAL ASPECTS

Russian has only three tenses—past, present and future—while English has about a dozen, so that some of the fine distinctions in tense observed by English are ignored in Russian and a single Russian tense-form may be translated by several tense-forms in English. The choice of the appropriate English tense-form is then determined by the context.

In addition to the three tenses, however, Russian has two 'aspects' in its verbal system. These aspects modify the meaning of tenses, participles and infinitive so that in fact the range of expression available in the verb system is greater than the presence of three simple tenses would lead one to expect. The two aspects are known as 'imperfective' and 'perfective'[1] and combine with the tenses to form the past imperfective, the past perfective, the present imperfective (there is no present perfective), the future imperfective and the future perfective. The infinitive also appears in two aspects—imperfective and perfective—and so do some of the participles.

When a verb is in the perfective aspect the meaning additional to the basic meaning of the verb and the tense is that the action is thought of as *completed* in some sense: the perfective aspect refers to a *point* in time. When a verb is in the imperfective aspect there is no such additional meaning involved.

Naturally, an action or state expressed in the *past* tense must in some sense be completed but, whereas in the perfective aspect particular attention is drawn to this fact, in the imperfective aspect no particular attention is drawn to the fact of completion. Hence, what is important in terms of the imperfective aspect is the action or state as such—without special reference to a point in time except such as is inevitably implied by the tense used. The imperfective aspect, therefore, often expresses *duration* of an action or state, or even *repetition*. The perfective, on the other hand, often expresses *result, finishing* or even *beginning* (i.e. the completion, at a point in time, of an act of beginning).

The following are some examples of the contrasting usage of imperfective and perfective in the past:

[1] Not to be confused with 'imperfect' and 'perfect.'

	Imperfective	*Perfective*
1.	**Он анализи́ровал жи́дкость.** *He was analysing the liquid.* *He analysed the liquid* (but no special reference to completion).	**Он проанализи́ровал жи́дкость.** *He analysed the liquid* (action completed). *He has analysed the liquid.* *He had analysed the liquid.*
2.	**Она́ писа́ла письмо́.** *She was writing a letter.* *She wrote a letter* (but no special reference to completion).	**Она́ написа́ла письмо́.** *She wrote a letter* (action completed). *She has written a letter.* *She had written a letter.*
3.	**Я получа́л хоро́шие результа́ты.** *I was getting good results.* *I got good results* (but no special reference to completion).	**Я получи́л хоро́шие результа́ты.** *I got good results* (action completed). *I have got good results.* *I had got good results.*
4.	**Кузне́ц нагрева́л желе́зо.** *The smith was heating up the iron.* *The smith heated up the iron* (but no special reference to completion).	**Кузне́ц нагре́л желе́зо.** *The smith heated up the iron* (action completed). *The smith has heated up the iron.* *The smith had heated up the iron.*

It is not possible to establish a simple system of minimum markers of the aspects. The remarks contained in this section are for general guidance so that the student may be able to recognise, after a little practice, which is the aspect of a particular verb-form and even, by applying one or more of the techniques described here, to understand the meaning of what are at first sight completely new and incomprehensible verb-forms.

Any good dictionary, of course, will give both aspects of a verb (in the infinitive). Usually the imperfective is given as the principal item, the perfective following it or appearing in the dictionary as a separate item with a reference to the imperfective item. Thus :

сде́лать, see **де́лать**

or

сде́лать, pfv. (or 'perf.') of **де́лать**

or

сде́лать, см.[1] **де́лать**

or

сде́лать, сов. к[2] **де́лать**

[1] **см. = смотри́те** = *see.*
[2] **сов. к = соверше́нный вид к** = *perfective aspect to.*

The information which follows, however, will save the student the time-consuming effort of looking up every aspect-form in a dictionary.

(*a*) The commonest way of forming the perfective is by means of a prefix added to the imperfective. The prefixes used are various and one cannot, as is sometimes done, say that any one of them is commoner than the others, being a perfectivising prefix *par excellence*. In some instances the prefix merely makes a verb perfective, while in others it makes the verb perfective and also adds to it the meaning contained in the prefix. The prefixes used, together with any additional meaning they may carry, are as follows:

в-, во-, въ-	*in*
вы-	*out*
воз-, вз-, вос-, вс-, взо-, взъ-	*up*
до-	*up to*
за-	*begin; beyond; finish*
из-, ис-, изо-, изъ-	*out, from*
на-	*on*
о-, об-, обо-, объ-	*around*
обез-, обес-	*deprive, de-*
от-, ото-, отъ-	*from*
по-	*a little*
пере-	*across, trans-; again*
пре-	*across, trans-*
пред-, предо-, предъ-	*before, in front of*
при-	*up to; addition; ad-; a-*
про	*through, pro-*
раз-, разо-, рас-, разъ-	*asunder*
с-, со-, съ-	*together; off, from*
у-	*away*

One's first action on meeting a new verb, therefore, should be to ascertain whether it has a prefix. When the prefix is removed, the residue may be a familiar verb and will in most cases be an imperfective verb, since all but a few simple imperfective verbs become perfective when prefixed.

(*b*) Another way of forming perfective infinitives is by replacing an **а** preceding the infinitive marker **ть** by **и,** thus:

Imperfective		*Perfective*
броса́ть	*to throw*	**бро́сить**
получа́ть	*to obtain, receive*	**получи́ть**

One should therefore try, where appropriate, to replace **и** by **а,** or *vice versa,* and see whether the result is a familiar verb.

(*c*) Imperfective infinitives may be formed from perfective infinitives by means of the elements **-ва-, -ыва-** or **-ива-.** The element **-ва-** is inserted before the infinitive marker to form an imperfective infinitive in the manner shown by the following examples:

Perfective		*Imperfective*
дать	*to give*	**дава́ть**
узна́ть	*to find out*	**узнава́ть**
забы́ть	*to forget*	**забыва́ть**
нагре́ть	*to heat up*	**нагрева́ть**
наду́ть	*to inflate*	**надува́ть**

The elements **-ыва-** or **-ива-** replace the vowel before the infinitive marker to form imperfective infinitives, as the following examples show:

Perfective		*Imperfective*
приписа́ть	*to ascribe*	**припи́сывать**
отде́лать	*to finish off*	**отде́лывать**
отвинти́ть	*to unscrew*	**отви́нчивать**
уговори́ть	*to persuade*	**угова́ривать**
осмотре́ть	*to inspect*	**осма́тривать**
спроси́ть	*to ask*	**спра́шивать**

With all these verbs the forms in the left-hand column are historically the earlier forms, from which the ones in the right-hand column have been derived by means of the infix. An example of this process may help in coming to an understanding of the aspect system.

Писáть *to write* is imperfective. Its perfective is **написáть.** From **писáть,** however, several other perfectives have been derived —each with specialised meaning. Thus **приписáть** arises from the prefixing of a simple imperfective verb and is therefore perfective. It also has the additional meaning carried by the prefix (*to, addition, ad-, a-*). From **приписáть** by means of the element **-ыва-,** is derived **припи́сывать,** which is imperfective but retains the specialised meaning *to ascribe*.

Note that this type of ' back-formation ' sometimes involves a consonant interchange. Reference should be made, where necessary, to the table of consonant interchanges (Appendix II). Vowel interchange occurs only if the vowel involved is **o,** i.e. if in the basic simple verb the vowel **o** occurs in the penultimate syllable, then in this type of formation **o** may be replaced by **a** in the prefixed imperfective verb. Thus:

	Imperfective	*Perfective*	
to work	**рабóтать** →	**зарабóтать**	*to earn*
to earn	**зарабáтывать** ←		
to speak	**говори́ть** →	**уговори́ть**	*to persuade*
to persuade	**уговáривать** ←		

This change does not occur in the verbs with infinitive ending in **-овать**:

Perfective		*Imperfective*
опубликовáть	*to publish*	**опубликóвывать**

With verbs of this type, therefore, the procedure should be:

1. Remove the imperfectivising element, ascertaining at the same time whether consonant substitution and/or substitution of **a** by **o** is necessary.

2. If the resultant perfective verb is not familiar and there is a prefix, resolve the verb into prefix and simple verb and see if the separate meanings of prefix and verb combine into something meaningful in the context.

The foregoing instructions may seem somewhat complicated and it may be objected that a new verb can in any event be sought in a dictionary quite easily. This is undeniable, but the object of these procedures is to reduce to a minimum the constant and time-consuming references to the dictionary which students usually practise. Moreover, with a little practice the time required for these procedures will amount to no more than a fraction of a second, and a student who finds he is continually making correct estimations of the meanings of new words is more likely to persist in his study of the language than one whose rate of progress is retarded by continual reference to the dictionary.

A few verbs have two simple imperfectives, one with a 'generalised' meaning, the other with a 'specific' meaning. The commoner of these verbs are set out in the following table:

Generalised (on more than one occasion and/or in more than one direction)	*Specific* (on one occasion and in one direction)
'move on foot'	
ходи́ть, *to go, come*	**идти́** or **итти́,** *to be going, coming*
'carry on foot'	
носи́ть, *to carry, bring*	**нести́,** *to be carrying, bringing*
'lead'	
води́ть, *to lead, bring*	**вести́,** *to be leading, bringing*
'carry in a vehicle'	
вози́ть, *to carry, bring*	**везти́,** *to be carrying, bringing*
'move in a vehicle'	
е́здить, *to go, come*	**е́хать,** *to be going, coming*

These verbs have the additional peculiarity that, when prefixed, the generalised forms (the ones in the left-hand column) remain imperfective, the specific ones (the ones in the right-hand column) become perfective, the two resultant verbs then forming an imperfective-perfective pair, without the generalised-specific contrast of the simple verbs. In other words the resultant pairs are just like, say, **анализи́ровать** — **проанализи́ровать.** The following are examples of this:[1]

[1] The student should try to guess the meanings of the new verbs in this list from his knowledge of the basic verbs and the meaning of the prefixes given above.

Imperfective	*Perfective*
переходи́ть	**перейти́**[1]
уходи́ть	**уйти́**
переноси́ть	**перенести́**
вноси́ть	**внести́**
уводи́ть	**увести́**
приводи́ть	**привести́**
ввози́ть	**ввезти́**
перевози́ть	**перевезти́**
уезжа́ть[2]	**уйти́**
въезжа́ть	**войти́**
вводи́ть	**ввести́**
выноси́ть	**вы́нести**
выводи́ть	**вы́вести**
выходи́ть	**вы́йти**

[1] **-йти** is a 'compounding' form of **идти́.**
[2] **-езжа́ть** is a 'compounding' form of **е́здить.**

Several of these compounds, and others not given here, are of frequent occurrence. It is worth while, therefore, learning thoroughly the formation of these imperfective-perfective pairs, and also their past tenses and conjugations.

Exercise 18

Vocabulary

основополо́жник, *founder*
мир, *world*
пото́м, *then*
соверша́ть, -и́ть,[1] *to accomplish, perform*
кругосве́тный, *round the world*
путеше́ствие, *journey*
кора́бль (*m.*), *ship*
собира́ть, собра́ть, *to gather*
поря́док, *order*
гото́вить, при-,[1] *to prepare*
опублико́вывать, опублико-ва́ть, *to publish*
набро́сок, *sketch, draft*
де́лать, с-, *to do, make*
сообще́ние, *communication*
происхожде́ние, *origin*
вид, *species*
есте́ственный, *natural*
отбо́р, *selection*
свет, *world*

[1] Henceforth infinitives given in the vocabularies will be given in both aspects, the imperfective first. If the difference between the two aspects concerns only the vowel before the infinitive marker, the infinitives will be given thus: **соверша́ть, -и́ть** (= **соверши́ть**). If the perfective consists simply of the imperfective with a prefix, the infinitives will be given thus: **гото́вить, при-** (= **пригото́вить**).

Translate into English:

ДА́РВИН

Чарлз Да́рвин, основополо́жник тео́рии разви́тия органи́ческого ми́ра, учи́лся в Ке́мбриджском университе́те. Пото́м он соверши́л как натурали́ст кругосве́тное путеше́ствие на корабле́ „Бигль". Во вре́мя э́того путеше́ствия он всё[1] собира́л материа́л и таки́м о́бразом за шесть лет[2] путеше́ствия собра́л огро́мное коли́чество материа́ла. В тече́ние шести́[3] лет он приводи́л э́тот материа́л в поря́док и, когда́ он привёл его́ в поря́док, опубликова́л результа́ты рабо́ты и путеше́ствия на „Би́гле" в пяти́[3] тома́х.

Пе́рвый набро́сок тео́рии эволю́ции сде́лал он уже́ в 1842, второ́й же[4] набро́сок в 1844. Одна́ко, э́тих набро́сков[5] он не опублико́вывал. Пе́рвое сообще́ние о тео́рии эволю́ции он опубликова́л ле́том 1858. Основно́й труд Да́рвина — „Происхожде́ние ви́дов путём[6] есте́ственного отбо́ра" — вы́шел в свет в 1859.

Notes

(1) **всё** = *all* or, as an adverb, *always, continually*.
(2) To express *year* Russian uses the word **год** with the cardinal numbers 1, 2, 3 or 4 and higher numbers, other than 'teens,' ending in 1, 2, 3 or 4, otherwise the word **ле́то** (literally *summer*).
(3) When a number itself is in a case other than the nominative the accompanying noun or adjective is in the same case— **три то́ма** *three volumes*, **пять томо́в** *five volumes*, **в пяти́ тома́х** *in five volumes*, **в трёх тома́х** *in three volumes*, **с пятью́ тома́ми** *with five volumes*, etc. (see Chapter 19).
(4) **же** is an 'emphatic particle;' here it could be ignored in translation, or translated *while*.
(5) **набро́сок** has a fugitive **о** in the nominative singular.
(6) Instrumental of **путь** = *by means, by way* (*of*).

Exercise 19

Vocabulary

гениа́льный, *of genius*
ока́нчивать, око́нчить, *to complete*
избира́ть, избра́ть, *to elect*
короле́вский, *royal*
о́бщество, *society*
станови́ться, стать, *to become*
Моне́тный двор, *mint*
перечека́нка, *recoinage*
моне́та, *coin, coinage*
широ́кий, *broad, widespread*
изве́стность (*f.*), *fame*

стрóить, по-, *to build*
зеркáльный, *mirror*
свобóдный, *free*
большинствó, *majority*
пóмощь (*f.*), *help*
пытáться, по-, *to try*
соединя́ть, -и́ть, *to unite, combine*
начáло, *beginning*; *principle*
закóн, *law*
тяготéние, *gravitation*
течéние, *course, current*
столéтие, *century*

Translate into English:

НЬЮ́ТОН

Исáак Нью́тон — гениáльный англи́йский фи́зик, мехáник, астронóм и математик. Он окóнчил университéт в Кéмбридже и потóм читáл лéкции в том же[1] университéте. Егó избрáли члéном Лóндонского королéвского óбщества. В 1699 Нью́тон стал дирéктором Монéтного двора́, где он провёл перечекáнку англи́йской монéты.

Ширóкую извéстность получи́ли опти́ческие исслéдования Нью́тона. Э́то он пострóил пéрвые зеркáльные телескóпы-рефлéкторы, свобóдные от хромати́ческой аберрáции. Большинствó световы́х[2] явлéний Нью́тон объясня́л[3] с пóмощью корпускуля́рной теóрии свéта. Вмéсте с тем он пытáлся соедини́ть э́ту теóрию с волновóй[4] теóрией свéта.

В 1687 вы́шел глáвный труд Нью́тона — „Математи́ческие начáла натурáльной филосóфии", в котóром он сформули́ровал[5] три основны́х закóна класси́ческой мехáники. В том же[1] трудé он сформули́ровал закóн всеми́рного тяготéния. В течéние двух столéтий[6] труды́ Нью́тона окáзывали[7] большóе влия́ние на разви́тие мехáники, óптики и математики.

Notes

(1) The emphatic particle **же** in conjunction with the demonstrative **тот, та, то,** etc., renders the English *the same* (the word **сáмый** does not mean *same*, it means *most, very*).
(2) Adjective pertaining to **свет** *light*.
(3) Imperfective of **объясни́ть** *to explain*.
(4) Adjective pertaining to **волнá** *wave*.
(5) Perfective of **формули́ровать** *to formulate*.
(6) See note 3 to preceding exercise. **двух** is genitive of **два.**
(7) Imperfective to **оказáть** *to exert*.

EXERCISE 20

Translate into English:

1. Англи́йский учёный Ро́берт Бойль дал пе́рвое определе́ние хими́ческого элеме́нта и пыта́лся ввести́ в хи́мию иде́ю механи́ческой атоми́стики.

   Бойль = *Boyle;* **определе́ние** = *definition.*

2. Бойль откры́л оди́н из га́зовых зако́нов и разраба́тывал ка́чественный хими́ческий ана́лиз.

   га́зовый—adjective pertaining to **газ**; **разраба́тывать, разрабо́тать** = *to work out, elaborate;* **ка́чественный** = *qualitative.*

3. Сове́тский фи́зик Серге́й Ива́нович Вави́лов разрабо́тал тео́рию люминесце́нтного свече́ния раство́ра.

   свече́ние = *luminosity, shimmer,* **люминесце́нтное с—** = *chemi-luminescence;* **раство́р** = *solution;* in this sentence **разрабо́тал** is perfective because Vavilov completed the action, i.e. was successful, whereas in the previous sentence the statement is merely that Boyle 'was working out, etc.', i.e. 'tried to work out, etc.'

4. Вави́лов доказа́л, что мо́жно непосре́дственно обнару́жить ква́нтовый хара́ктер све́та при наблюде́нии светов́ых пучко́в сла́бой интенси́вности.

   дока́зывать, доказа́ть = *to prove, demonstrate;* **непосре́дственно** = *immediately, directly;* **наблюде́ние** = *observation* (**при** here may be translated as *by*); **пучо́к** = *cluster, bunch, beam* (this word has a fugitive vowel).

5. Зада́ча настоя́щего иссле́дования — проследи́ть распростране́ние Calanus tenuicornis в се́веро-за́падной ча́сти Ти́хого океа́на.

   просле́живать, проследи́ть = *to trace;* **распростране́ние** = *expansion, spreading, diffusion;* **се́веро-за́падный** = *north-western*—compound words in Russian are often formed by means of the 'compounding' vowels **о** and **е**; **ти́хий** = *quiet, pacific.*

6. Измере́ния с по́мощью конденса́торного дозиме́тра показа́ли, что ле́вый парабио́нт в э́тих усло́виях получа́л до 1 % излуче́ния.

   измере́ние = *measurement;* **усло́вие** = *condition, circumstance;* **излуче́ние** = *radiation.*

7. В пе́рвой се́рии о́пытов облуча́ли пра́вого партнёра до́зой 700*r*: во второ́й се́рии у пра́вого партнёра экрани́ровали го́лову свинцо́вой пласти́нкой толщино́й 3 мм и облуча́ли остальны́е уча́стки те́ла.

   облуча́ть, облучи́ть = *to irradiate;* **пра́вый** = *right-hand;* **экрани́ровать** = *to screen;* **голова́** = *head;* **у пра́вого партнёра** refers to **го́лову** and **у** means simply *of;* **свинцо́вый** = *lead* (*adj.*); **остально́й** = *remaining;* **уча́сток** (fugitive **о**) = *part, section.*

8. Таки́м о́бразом, да́нные пе́рвой се́рии о́пытов показа́ли, что при лучево́й боле́зни в крови́ име́ются вещества́, спосо́бные вызыва́ть вре́менное угнете́ние митоти́ческой акти́вности.

таки́м о́бразом = *thus, in this way;* **лучево́й**—adjective pertaining to **луч** *ray*, means *radial* or, as here, (*pertaining to*) *radiation;* **спосо́бный** = *capable;* **вызыва́ть, вы́звать** = *to call forth, provoke;* **вре́менный** = *temporary;* **угнете́ние** = *oppression, depression, suppression.*

9. Для э́той рабо́ты тре́бовались больши́е коли́чества стиро́ла с минима́льным коли́чеством вла́ги: в ка́честве осуши́теля мы вы́брали перхлора́т ма́гния.

тре́бовать, вос- = *to demand, require;* **вла́га** = *moisture;* **ка́чество** = *quality,* **в ка́честве** = *as;* **осуши́тель** = *drying agent;* **выбира́ть, вы́брать** = *to choose, select.*

10. Мы хоте́ли прове́рить э́тот факт и вы́яснить влия́ние не́которых други́х перхлора́тов (ба́рия, ка́лия и аммо́ния) на полимериза́цию стиро́ла.

проверя́ть, -ить = *to verify;* **выясня́ть, -ить** = *to ascertain;* **не́которые** = *several;* **ка́лий** = *potassium.*

11

THE PREPOSITIONAL CASE OF ADJECTIVES; ADVERBS; THE PAST PASSIVE PARTICIPLE

Prepositional Case of Adjectives

The marker for the prepositional plural of adjectives is **-х,** like that for nouns, preceded, however, by **ы** or **и,** not **а** or **я.** Thus:

в твёрдых мета́ллах	*in hard metals*
в пусты́х сосу́дах	*in empty vessels*
на си́них ла́мпах	*on the blue lamps*

The marker for the prepositional singular of masculine and neuter adjectives is **-м,** *preceded by* **о** *or* **е** *and not* **ы** *or* **и,** thus **-ом, -ем.** Care should be taken to avoid confusing this with the identical *instrumental* singular ending of masculine and neuter *nouns.* Examples of the prepositional singular of masculine and neuter adjectives are:

в твёрдом мета́лле	*in the hard metal*
в пусто́м сосу́де	*in the empty vessel*
на си́нем мо́ре	*on the blue sea*

The marker for the prepositional singular of feminine adjectives is **-й,** preceded by **о** or **е,** i.e. is identical with the genitive marker, thus:

на си́ней ла́мпе	*on the blue lamp*
в твёрдой кости́	*in a hard bone*
в техни́ческой литерату́ре	*in technical literature*

Exercise 21

Give the meaning of the following words and phrases, stating in what case are the adjectives and nouns:

1. пусты́х, твёрдой, си́нем, ва́жным, патоге́нном.
2. просто́й, мя́гкого мета́лла, тяжёлом, коро́тких, поле́зной.
3. пе́рвым, вторы́х, но́вой, высо́кую, дли́нным.
4. интере́сном, сло́жной, се́верные зи́мы, сравни́тельных, о́бщем.

5. **разли́чные эффе́кты, в непра́вильном отве́те, во́семь ли́ний, в си́ней жи́дкости, три фа́зы.**

Adverbs

The great majority of Russian adverbs have been derived at some time or other from other parts of speech, i.e. from adjectives, verbs, participles, nouns, numbers. The derivation of many of them is no longer immediately apparent, either because of phonetic (and hence orthographical) changes which have taken place or because the words from which they have been derived are no longer used. There are, however, a few types whose formation can easily be recognised and which, moreover, include a great number of adverbs. Some of these types are still 'productive,' i.e. new adverbs can be formed in the same manner.

1. The most productive type of adverb-formation is that with the marker **-o** from adjectives. Thus:

хо́лодно	cf. **холо́дный**	*cold*
глубоко́	cf. **глубо́кий**	*deep*
высоко́	cf. **высо́кий**	*high*
реши́тельно	cf. **реши́тельный**	*determined, decisive*

2. The marker **-e** is also used to form adverbs from adjectives:

кра́йне	cf. **кра́йний**	*extreme*
бо́льше (*more*)	cf. **бо́льший**	*bigger*

3. From adjectives in **-ский** adverbs in **-ски** are formed:

автомати́чески	cf. **автомати́ческий**	*automatic*
органи́чески	cf. **органи́ческий**	*organic*
ритми́чески	cf. **ритми́ческий**	*rhythmic*

4. Adverbs are formed from some present active participles (see Chapter 12) by replacing the adjective-ending with **-e**:

поража́юще	cf. **поража́ющий**	*striking*
вызыва́юще	cf. **вызыва́ющий**	*challenging*
волну́юще	cf. **волну́ющий**	*disturbing*

5. A common way of forming adverbs is with the prefix **по-**.

(*a*) **по-** has the meaning *by the, every,* e.g.:

помину́тно	*by the minute, every minute*
поме́сячно	*by the month* (cf. **ме́сяц** *month*)
поочерёдно	*by turns* (cf. **о́чередь** *turn*)

These adverbs have corresponding adjectives, from which in fact they may be considered to have been derived in the manner of Type 1. (Cf. **помину́тный, поме́сячный, поочерёдный,** etc.)

(*b*) **по-** has the meaning *in the manner of.*

(i) Together with the adverbial ending **-ски** (see 3 above):

по-де́тски	cf. **де́тский**	*childish, child's*
по-маркси́стски	cf. **маркси́стский**	*Marxist*
по-большеви́стски	cf. **большеви́стский**	*Bolshevik*

This type is used to express *in the .... language*: **по-ру́сски, по-англи́йски, по-францу́зски.**

These could equally mean *in the Russian, etc., manner.*

по-неме́цки *in German* or *in the German manner,* is formed without **-с-**.

(ii) Together with the dative singular masculine or neuter of adjectives:

по-но́вому	(**но́вый**	*new*)
по-ста́рому	(**ста́рый**	*old*)
по-пти́чьи	(**пти́чий**	*bird-like, bird's*)

The expressions **по-мо́ему, по-ва́шему, по-на́шему,** etc., besides the meaning *in my .... fashion,* also have —and more usually—the meaning *according to my .... wish, desire* or *in my .... opinion,* e.g.:

Он де́лает это по-на́шему.	*He does this in our way.*
По-мо́ему э́то не так.	*In my opinion this is not so.*
де́лать по-сво́ему	*to do it one's own way* (i.e. *as one wishes*)

6. Many adverbs are formed from prepositions (used as prefixes) with adjective or noun forms. Some of these are written as one word and are recorded as separate items in dictionaries, others are written as two words (and are, therefore, adverbial phrases) and, if recorded in a dictionary, will be found under the item referring to the second word. A few examples are:

до́красна e.g. **нагре́ть до́красна** *to heat till red-hot*
до́суха e.g. **вы́тереть до́суха** *to wipe dry*

издалёка	*from afar*
сле́ва	*on the left*
спра́ва	*on the right*
свысока́	*from on high*
сгоряча́	*rashly, in the heat of passion*
навы́ворот	*inside out*
наконе́ц	*at last*
нале́во	*to the left*
напра́во	*to the right*
вслед	*following*
вмиг	*in a flash, suddenly*

7. Note too the use of the instrumental of nouns to express time, place or manner of an action:

у́тром	*in the morning*
ве́чером	*in the evening*
днём (inst. sing. of **день**)	*in the daytime, in the afternoon*
но́чью	*at night*
ле́том	*in the summer*
зимо́й	*in the winter*
бего́м	*running, at a run*
по́лем	*through, across the field(s)*
ша́гом	*at walking pace*
шо́потом	*in a whisper*

Past Passive Participle

The past passive participle is one of the commoner participles in Russian. Its meaning is that the action expressed by the participle has been performed on the thing or person delimited by the participle. It expresses therefore the idea common to the italicised forms in the following English sentences:

It was *rubbed* with a damp cloth.
The resulting mixture, *collected* in a small vessel, was then *boiled*.
The experiment was *begun* under favourable conditions.
Everything will be *done* to save the life of the mother.
The results *given* by this method were most unsatisfactory.

There are two markers of the past passive participle in Russian. Most verbs which have a past passive participle form it with the marker **нн**, preceded by **а**, **я** or **е**, while some verbs form the past passive participle with the marker **т**, which may be preceded by a vowel or a consonant. In both instances the marker of the past passive participle is followed by the adjectival case-endings described in this and previous chapters, except in the so-called 'short forms' (see Chapter 12). With very few exceptions this participle is formed only from perfective verbs since it always implies a completed action. The following are examples of the past passive participle:

Infinitive	*Past Passive Participle*	*Meaning*
Type 1		
сде́лать	**сде́ланный**	*done*
проанализи́ровать	**проанализи́рованный**	*analysed*
дать	**да́нный**	*given*
унести́	**унесённый**	*carried off*
собра́ть	**со́бранный**	*collected*
Type 2		
нагре́ть	**нагре́тый**	*heated up*
нача́ть	**на́чатый**	*begun*
стере́ть	**стёртый**	*wiped off*
бить	**би́тый**	*struck*
откры́ть	**откры́тый**	*opened*

EXERCISE 22

Translate into English:

1. Структу́ра сохраня́ется да́же при о́чень ре́зком измене́нии физиологи́ческого состоя́ния органи́зма.

сохраня́ть, -и́ть = *to preserve;* **измене́ние** = *change.*

2. Числó микроорганúзмов в сéверо-зáпадном райóне Чёрного мóря колéблется от 14 тысяч до 495 тысяч в см³.

   сéверо-зáпадный = *north-western;* **колебáться, по-** = *to fluctuate.*

3. При огрóмной вáжности проблéмы нéкоторые вопрóсы и до настоящего врéмени остáлись далекó не пóлностью изýченными.

   The first three words might be translated *Despite the enormous importance;* **оставáться, остáться** = *to remain;* **пóлностью** = *completely, exhaustively;* **изучáть, -йть** = *to study.*

4. Такáя корреляция действúтельно обнарýживается в нáшем óпыте.

   действúтельный = *actual;* **нáшем** is prep. of **наш** *our.*

5. При óчень большóм содержáнии Ni_5Si_2 в сплáвах наблюдáется нóвый подъём жаропрóчности.

   содержáние = *contents, content;* **сплав** = *alloy;* **наблюдáть** = *to observe;* **подъём** = *rise;* **жаропрóчность** = *heat-resistance.*

6. Тщáтельно очúщенный с повéрхности в сúльном тóке сухóго углекúслого гáза образéц метáлла вéсом в 0,1-3 г. помещáлся в квáрцевую трýбку.

   тщáтельный = *careful;* **очищáть, очúстить** = *to clean;* **сухóй** = *dry;* **углекúслый газ** = *carbon dioxide;* **образéц** = *sample;* **поместúть** = *to place;* **квáрцевый**—adjective from **кварц.** The first ten words describe **образéц;** *A carefully cleaned from the surface in a strong current of dry carbon dioxide sample,* i.e. *A sample of metal,* etc., *which had been carefully cleaned* (='*shaved*') *from,* etc.

7. В закалённом состоянии у всех сплáвов в харáктере распределéния углерóда наблюдáется нéкоторая óбщая тендéнция.

   закáливать, закалúть = *to temper;* **всех** is genitive plural of **весь** *all* (see Chapter 18); **распределéние** = *distribution;* **нéкоторый** = *a certain;* **óбщий** = *common, general.*

8. Полýченную по окончáнии реáкции мáссу отсáсывают на ворóнке Бюхнера.

   по + prepositional = *after;* **окончáние** = *completion;* **отсáсывать, отсосáть** = *to suck off;* **ворóнка** = *funnel;* **Бюхнер** = *Büchner.*

9. Подрóбный анáлиз спирáлей осаждéния даёт возмóжность схематúчно, в пéрвом приближéнии, провестú зóну А для всегó сéверного полушáрия.

   подрóбный = *detailed;* **осаждéние** = *precipitation, deposit;* **возмóжность** = *possibility;* **приближéние** = *approximation;* **проводúть, провестú** here = *to draw, to put in;* **всегó** is genitive singular of **весь** *all;* **полушáрие** = *hemisphere.*

10. В э́той зóне приблизúтельно в 14 — 15 час. мéстного врéмени происхóдит повы́шенное вторжéние протóнов.

э́той is prepositional singular of **э́та** (see Chapter 17); **приблизи́тельный** = *approximate;* **происходи́ть, произойти́** = *to occur;* **повыша́ть, повы́сить** = *to raise, heighten;* **вторже́ние** = *intrusion.*

11. При прохожде́нии а́томного пучка́ че́рез ЛМ-2 он ионизи́руется электро́нами, эмитти́рованными като́дом и уско́ренными потенциа́лом се́тки.

прохожде́ние = *passage;* **ускоря́ть, уско́рить** = *to accelerate;* **се́тка** = *net, grid.*

12. О́бластью иониза́ции в да́нном слу́чае явля́ется простра́нство внутри́ се́тки.

слу́чай = *case;* **простра́нство** = *space;* **внутри́** (+ gen.) = *within.*

13. При периоди́ческой прове́рке станда́ртного соста́ва на ве́рхней криво́й наблюда́ются вспле́ски интенси́вности.

прове́рка = *checking, verification;* **соста́в** = *composition;* **ве́рхний** = *upper;* **криво́й** = *curved* (**крива́я** as noun = *curved line, curve*); **всплеск** = *splash, burst.*

14. В пе́рвых о́пытах мы испо́льзовали эксперимента́льную устано́вку, опи́санную в статье́ Виногра́дова.

испо́льзовать = *to use;* **устано́вка** = *apparatus;* **опи́сывать, описа́ть** = *to describe;* **статья́** = *article.*

15. На на́ших сни́мках во́зле ли́ний $L\alpha_{1,2}$ и $L\beta_1$ с коротково́лновой стороны́ обнару́жились я́ркие ли́нии.

сни́мок (fugitive **о**) = *photograph;* **во́зле** (+ gen.) = *beside, alongside;* **сторона́** = *side;* **я́ркий** = *vivid, bright.*

16. Полу́ченный алкила́т тру́дно растворя́ется в бензо́ле, хорошо́ растворя́ется в ацето́не, у́ксусной кислоте́, эфи́ре и хлорофо́рме.

тру́дный = *difficult;* **растворя́ть, -и́ть** = *to dissolve;* **хорошо́** = *well;* **у́ксусная кислота́** = *acetic acid.*

17. Основна́я ма́сса ферме́нта вхо́дит в соста́в коацерва́тных ка́пель: одна́ко ферме́нт прису́тствует та́кже и в равнове́сной жи́дкости.

ка́пля = *drop* (gen. pl. **ка́пель**); **одна́ко** = *however;* **прису́тствовать** = *to be present;* **равнове́сный** = *balanced, equilibrium (adj.)*

18. Практи́чески по́лное разложе́ние H_2O_2, при избы́точной концентра́ции ферме́нта, име́ет ме́сто в раство́ре, тогда́ как в коацерва́тных ка́плях, да́же и в э́том слу́чае, разложе́ние H_2O_2 дохо́дит то́лько до 60%.

разложе́ние = *resolution, decomposition;* **избы́точная** = *surplus, over-, super-;* **име́ть ме́сто** = *to take place;* **тогда́ как** = *whereas, while;* **да́же** = *even.*

12

FUGITIVE VOWELS; THE SHORT FORMS OF ADJECTIVES; RELATIVE ADJECTIVES; THE PRESENT ACTIVE PARTICIPLE

Fugitive Vowels

In preceding chapters some nouns have been used which have within them the vowel **о** or **е** in one case but not in other cases. This phenomenon of the 'fugitive vowel' or interchange of vowel and zero occurs in other parts of speech, too. A detailed description of the phenomenon, with examples, is given in the first part of Appendix III, which students should now read through.

Short Forms of Adjectives

Very many adjectives have so-called 'short forms,' such forms as have been used in previous chapters being known as the 'long forms.' They are used only in the nominative case[1] and the markers are the same as those of the nominative case of nouns:

Long Form		*Short Form*			
Nom. sing. masc.		*Masc.*	*Fem.*	*Neuter*	*Pl.*
нóвый	*new*	**нов**	**новá**	**нóво**	**нóвы**
сúний	*blue*	**синь**	**синя́**	**сúне**	**сúни**
полéзный	*useful*	**полéзен**[2]	**полéзна**	**полéзно**	**полéзны**
корóткий	*short*	**кóроток**[2]	**короткá**	**кóротко**	**коротки́**

These short forms are found only in 'predicative' usage, i.e. in such sentences as:

Вóздух чист.	*The air is clean.*
Жéнщина больнá.	*The woman is ill.*
Пóле бы́ло пýсто.	*The field was empty.*
Э́ти продýкты óчень полéзны.	*These products are very useful.*

[1] 'Fossilised' forms of other cases of the short forms are found in many adverbs (see Chapter 11).

[2] Showing the fugitive vowel phenomenon mentioned in the preceding section.

The long forms of adjectives may appear in this context too, though sometimes a difference in meaning distinguishes this usage:

Же́нщина больна́.	*The woman is ill* (i.e. *at the moment*).
Же́нщина больна́я.	*The woman is* (*permanently*) *ill,* i.e. *is a sick woman.*

Past passive participles (and some other participles) may have short forms and those with the marker **-нн-** have the peculiar feature that this marker is reduced to **-н-** in the short forms, whereas non-participial adjectives in **-нный** may retain the **-нн-** in the short form, a fugitive vowel **-е-** being inserted between the two **н**'s in the short form masculine. Thus:

Long form masculine	*Meaning*
сде́ланный	*done*
проанализи́рованный	*analysed*
унесённый	*carried off*

Short form masculine	*Short form feminine*
сде́лан	**сде́лана**
проанализи́рован	**проанализи́рована**
унесён	**унесена́**

Compare the last forms in this list with the short forms of such an adjective as **отве́тственный** *responsible,* **отве́тственен** — more commonly **отве́тствен** (masculine), **отве́тственна** (feminine), etc.

Relative Adjectives

A few adjectives have the peculiarity that the 'normal' or long forms of the nominative feminine, neuter and plural end in one vowel, not two, and therefore *look* as if they are short forms. Such are the number-adjective **тре́тий** *third* and some of the co-called 'relative' adjectives. The latter are adjectives derived from nouns denoting animals and persons, having the meaning 'belonging to a/the . . . .' or 'like a/the . . . .'s.' They do not have short forms. Examples of this type of adjective are:

Nom. sing. masc.		*Fem.*	*Neuter*	*Nom. pl.*
тре́тий	*third*	**тре́тья**	**тре́тье**	**тре́тьи**
во́лчий	*wolf's*	**во́лчья**	**во́лчье**	**во́лчьи**
медве́жий	*bear's*	**медве́жья**	**медве́жье**	**медве́жьи**

Another type of relative adjective, the 'possessive' adjective, has all the nominative case forms like short forms and some of the other case markers like those of nouns, some like those of long adjectives. Adjectives of this type are not likely to be met with very often in technical literature but a specimen is given in Appendix I for reference.

PRESENT ACTIVE PARTICIPLE (Declinable Type)

The meaning of the present active participle is that the action denoted by the participle is performed by the thing or person delimited by the participle at the time to which the sentence as a whole relates. It expresses therefore the idea common to the italicised forms in the following English sentences:

The mixture *resulting* from this operation is put into a small vessel.

Experiments *giving* good results are already being carried out in the Soviet Union.

Much of the plankton *rising* to the surface will be consumed by larger fish.

Frequently a present active participle in a Russian sentence may have to be translated into English by a clause beginning *who/which*, etc.

Thus, the phrases in italics in the following English sentences might well be rendered in Russian by a single word, a present active participle, agreeing grammatically with the noun to which it refers:

The plankton *which rises* to the surface is caught in a small sample flask.

It was noticeable that the surgeon *who was carrying out* the operation was handicapped by the absence of a competent sister.

The lighter particles *which issue* from the nucleus are then deflected by a strong magnetic field.

The marker of this participle, like the marker of the past passive participle, is non-final: it consists of the letter **щ** (preceded by **у**/**ю** or **а**/**я**) inserted between the verbal stem and the adjectival ending of the participle. While not being as common in technical literature, perhaps, as the past passive participle, the present active participle nevertheless occurs quite frequently. Here are some examples of the present active participle:

Infinitive	*Meaning*	*Present tense 3rd person pl.*	*Present active participle nom. sing. masc.*
чита́ть	*to read*	**чита́ют**	**чита́ющий**
знать	*to know*	**зна́ют**	**зна́ющий**
анализи́ровать	*to analyse*	**анализи́руют**	**анализи́рующий**
нести́	*to be bearing*	**несу́т**	**несу́щий**
идти́	*to be going*	**иду́т**	**иду́щий**
говори́ть	*to say, speak*	**говоря́т**	**говоря́щий**
лежа́ть	*to lie*	**лежа́т**	**лежа́щий**
сиде́ть	*to sit*	**сидя́т**	**сидя́щий**
вести́	*to be leading*	**веду́т**	**веду́щий**

It will be noticed that the element preceding the marker of the present active participle consists, as it were, of the third person plural of the present tense minus the final **-т.** Short forms of the present active participle are very rare.

Exercise 23

Translate into English:

1. При́нято счита́ть, что в махро́вых цветка́х не образу́ются семена́.

   при́нято = *accepted*, trans. *it is usual;* **махро́вый** = *double;* **цвето́к** (gen. **цветка́**) = *flower.*

2. Результа́ты о́пытов при pH 4,27 и 6,0 приведены́ в табл. 6.

   при trans. here *when;* **приводи́ть, привести́** = *to bring*, here = *to give.*

3. Оказа́лось, что при pH 4,27 ферме́нт практи́чески был неакти́вен в иссле́дованных систе́мах.

   ока́зываться, оказа́ться = *to turn out;* **иссле́довать** = *to investigate.*

4. Рассмо́тренную здесь магни́тную систе́му, по-ви́димому, целесообра́зно испо́льзовать и в фазотро́нах (синхроциклотро́нах).

   рассма́тривать, рассмотре́ть = *to examine;* **здесь** = *here;* **по-ви́димому** = *it seems, apparently;* **целесообра́зный** = *expedient, convenient.*

5. Нали́чие э́той ли́нии в спе́ктре герма́ния пока́зывает, что в герма́нии, находя́щемся в твёрдом состоя́нии, у́ровень $H_{II\text{-}III}$ части́чно запо́лнен электро́нами.

   нали́чие = *presence;* **пока́зывать, показа́ть** = *to show;* **находи́ться** = *to be;* **у́ровень** = *level;* **части́чно** = *partly;* **заполня́ть, -ить** = *to fill in, supplement.*

6. На рис. 1 пока́зан оди́н из рассмо́тренных вариа́нтов **систе́мы**.

   рис. = **рису́нке,** prepositional case of **рису́нок** *sketch, diagram.*

7. Постоя́нство пери́ода обраще́ния ио́нов мо́жет быть **обеспе́чено** до весьма́ бо́льших эне́ргий.

   постоя́нство = *constancy;* **обраще́ние** = *revolution;* **обеспе́чивать, обеспе́чить** = *to ensure;* **весьма́** = *very.*

8. В ка́честве рабо́чего вещества́ была́ взята́ ртуть.

   в ка́честве = *as;* **рабо́чий** = *working;* **взять** = *to take;* **ртуть** = *mercury.*

9. На ка́рте пока́зана сре́дняя биома́сса микроогани́змов в 1 $м^2$ в сло́е 0—10 м в разли́чных райо́нах Чёрного мо́ря.

   ка́рта = *map;* **сре́дний** = *average;* **разли́чный** = *various.*

10. После́дние в интерва́ле λλ300-500 мμ поглоща́ют 90% па́дающей на них радиа́ции.

    после́дний = *last, latter;* **поглоща́ть, поглоти́ть** = *to absorb;* **па́дать** = *to fall;* **них** is form of the accusative of **они́** *they* occurring after prepositions (see Chapter 17).

11. В зи́мне-весе́нний пери́од, наоборо́т, наблюда́ется сниже́ние физиологи́ческой акти́вности ко́жи, проявля́ющееся в её атони́и и анеми́и.

    зи́мне-весе́нний = *winter-spring;* **наоборо́т** = *on the other hand;* **сниже́ние** = *lowering;* **проявля́ть, -ви́ть** = *to show, manifest;* **её** = *its.*

12. Толщина́ ко́жи и слага́ющих её слоёв уменьша́ется.

    слага́ть, сложи́ть = *to compose;* **и . . . слоёв** = *and the layers composing it;* **уменьша́ть, уменьши́ть** = *to decrease.*

13. Но уже́ на после́дующих ста́диях ко́жная скла́дка постепе́нно уменьша́ется и, наконе́ц, соверше́нно исчеза́ет.

    после́дующий = *subsequent;* **скла́дка** = *fold;* **постепе́нный** = *gradual;* **соверше́нный** = *complete;* **исчеза́ть, исче́знуть** = *to disappear.*

14. Из рис. 1 и 2 ви́дно, что наибо́льшие измене́ния наблю́даются во фра́кциях белко́в, ме́дленно дви́жущихся в электри́ческом по́ле.

    рис. here is genitive plural of **рису́нок**; **ви́дно** = *it is clear;* **наибо́льший** = *greatest;* **измене́ние** = *change;* **бело́к** = *albumen;* **ме́дленный** = *slow;* **дви́гать** = *to move* (see Appendix IV).

15. О́чень интере́сны результа́ты о́пытов, проведённых с бакте́риями, вы́ращенными на бульо́не с добавле́нием глюко́зы.

    выра́щивать, вы́растить = *to rear, cultivate;* **добавле́ние** = *addition.*

16. Гемолити́ческая акти́вность вы́ражена в метаболи́тах о́рганов бе́лых крыс и кро́ликов, а та́кже в метаболи́тах ко́шек и морски́х сви́нок.

выража́ть, вы́разить = *to express;* **кры́са** = *rat;* **кро́лик** = *rabbit;* **ко́шка** = *cat;* **морска́я сви́нка** = *guinea-pig.*

17. Э́ти о́пыты я́сно показа́ли, что интоксика́ция у живо́тных мо́жет развива́ться то́лько тогда́, когда́ головно́й мозг не защищён от де́йствия токси́на.

я́сный = *clear;* **развива́ть, разви́ть** = *to develop;* **то́лько тогда́, когда́** = *only* (*then*) *when;* **головно́й мозг** = *brain, cerebrum;* **защища́ть, защити́ть** = *to protect;* **де́йствие** = *action.*

18. На́ми бы́ло пока́зано, что э́тот механи́зм интоксика́ции не явля́ется еди́нственным.

на́ми бы́ло пока́зано = lit. *by us it has been shown,* i.e. *we have shown;* **еди́нственный** = *only, single.*

19. Необходи́мо специа́льное изуче́ние адсорбцио́нных сво́йств окислённой пла́тины, что ещё не вы́полнено.

необходи́мый = *essential;* **сво́йство** = *property;* **окисля́ть, окисли́ть** = *to oxidise;* **ещё** = *yet;* **выполня́ть, -ить** = *to carry out.*

20. В настоя́щей рабо́те полу́чены результа́ты всео́бщего интере́са.

настоя́щий = *present, real;* **всео́бщий** = *general.*

13

THE CONDITIONAL PARTICLE **бы**; INDECLINABLE PRESENT PARTICIPLE

Conditional Participle

The word **бы** is associated in Russian with the past tense to convey the idea which English expresses with the verb forms *should/would* (*go, take,* etc.), *should have/would have* (*gone, taken,* etc.). It is therefore of frequent occurrence in sentences containing the word **éсли** *if*, just as the *should/would* verb forms in English occur frequently in sentences containing the word *if*.[1] Here are some examples of the usage of **бы**:

Éсли бы профéссор был там, он читáл бы лéкцию.	*If the professor had been there, he would have read the lecture.* OR *If the professor were there, he would read the lecture.*
Профéссор читáл бы лéкцию, éсли бы он был там.	*The professor would have read the lecture, if he had been there.* OR *The professor would read the lecture, if he were there.*
Я сдéлал бы э́то, éсли бы мог.	*I would have done this, if I had been able.* OR *I would do this, if I were able.*
Éсли бы мы произвели́ оперáцию, больнóй мог бы умерéть.	*If we were to carry out the operation, the patient might die* (literally: *the patient could die*). OR *If we had carried out the operation, the patient might have died.*

[1] Note that the word **éсли** is not necessarily associated with the word **бы,** just as in English the word *if* is not necessarily associated with *should/would* forms.

It will be seen that the choice between *should/would* and *should/have/would have* in translating these sentences with **бы** does not necessarily depend on the aspect of the verb in the Russian. The choice has to be made according to the context.

In general, it may be said that **бы** with the past tense expresses hypothetical or doubtful ideas, unfulfilled or unrealised situations. Thus:

Каза́лось бы, что э́то невозмо́жно.	*It might seem that this is impossible.*
Мы хоте́ли бы ви́деть э́тот аппара́т.	*We would like to see this apparatus.*

In the following two usages the word **бы** is not necessarily associated with the past tense.

1. **как бы** = *as it were, a sort of*; **бу́дто бы** = *as it were, as if.*

В середи́не аппара́та нахо́дится как бы изо́гнутая тру́ба.	*In the middle of the apparatus there is a sort of bent tube.*
Бу́дто бы сове́тские учёные не зна́ют, что э́то так.	*As if Soviet scholars do not know that this is so.*

2. **хотя́ бы** or **хоть бы** — *even though, if only, at least,* etc.

Оши́бочность тео́рии ясна́ хотя́ бы из сле́дующего фа́кта.	*The erroneousness of the theory is clear if only from the following fact (from the following fact alone).*
Результа́ты э́того иссле́дования даю́т хотя́ бы ориентиро́вочное поня́тие о структу́ре моле́кулы.	*The results of this investigation give at least an approximate idea of the structure of the molecule.*

Together with **ни** and pronouns and adverbs, **бы** expresses *-ever*:

Куда́ бы мы ни смотре́ли, всю́ду на не́бе звёзды.	*Wherever we look there are stars in the sky.*
Что бы он ни де́лал, самолёт не дви́гался.	*Whatever he did, the plane did not move.*

The conjunction **чтóбы/чтоб** is not to be confused with **что бы . . . . ни** (*whatever*). Its meaning is *in order that, so that,* etc., and it is associated with the infinitive or the past tense. Thus:

Чтóбы автомоби́ль дви́нулся, нáдо пусти́ть в ход дви́гатель.	*In order that the car should move it is necessary to set the engine in motion.*
Профéссор получи́л óтпуск, чтóбы поéхать в Москвý на конферéнцию.	*The professor has obtained leave-of-absence in order to go to Moscow on a conference.*

Sometimes the word **чтóбы** is, as it were, introduced by **для тогó** (literally *for that*) or **с тем** (literally *with that*):

Для тогó чтóбы поня́ть э́то, нáдо знать пéрвый закóн термодинáмики.	*In order to understand this, it is necessary to know the first law of thermodynamics.*
Он поéхал в Москвý с тем, чтóбы прочитáть доклáд на конферéнции.	*He has gone to Moscow in order to read a paper at a conference.*

The word **чтóбы** also occurs after certain verbs in Russian where the corresponding English does not have *in order that* or *in order to*:

Хирýрг хотéл, чтóбы все студéнты слы́шали егó.	*The surgeon wanted all the students to hear him.*
Сомневáюсь, чтóбы э́то удалóсь.	*I doubt whether this will succeed.*
Медици́нская сестрá боя́лась, чтóбы больнóй не ýмер.[1]	*The nursing sister was afraid that the patient would die.*

[1] In this last example the word **чтóбы** is associated with **не** but the meaning is positive, as given in the translation. **Чтóбы . . . не** may be compared with the English *lest.* **Как бы . . . не** may also occur in this meaning.

Indeclinable Present Participle

The two participles which were described in Chapters 11 and 12 are declinable participles—they have case-gender-number markers like adjectives and, like adjectives, are in grammatical agreement with the nouns which they delimit. There are two more declinable participles and these will be dealt with later. There are also indeclinable participles, i.e. participles which do not have adjectival markers, which remain unchanged and whose function is more purely verbal than that of the declinable participles. Indeclinable participles may refer only to the subject of a sentence or clause, whereas the declinable participles may delimit a noun which is not the subject of a clause or sentence and may thus be in the accusative, genitive, instrumental, or any other case, as well as the nominative. Indeclinable participles are not to be confused with 'gerunds' or 'gerundives,' whose function is entirely different.

There are two indeclinable participles in Russian—a present active and a past active participle; the latter will be dealt with in Chapter 16.

The indeclinable present participle denotes an action that goes on at the same time as that denoted by the main verb, the subject of both participle and verb being the same. This participle, in spite of the name given to it here, may be associated with verbs in the past, present or future tense and it expresses the idea common to the words or phrases italicised in the following English sentences:

We carried out the experiment, *knowing* that few, if any, positive results could be expected.

We are carrying out the experiment, *knowing* that few, if any, positive results can be expected.

We shall carry out this experiment, *knowing* that few, if any, positive results can be expected.

While admitting the value of his work, he does not think it should be exaggerated.

They observed certain deficiencies in the apparatus *while investigating* this problem.

The marker of the indeclinable present active participle is final **-а** or **-я**. Here are some examples of this participle:

Infinitive	*3rd person pl.*	*Declinable present participle*	*Indeclinable present participle*
чита́ть	**чита́ют**	**чита́ющий**	**чита́я**
знать	**зна́ют**	**зна́ющий**	**зна́я**
анализи́ровать	**анализи́руют**	**анализи́рующий**	**анализи́руя**
нести́	**несу́т**	**несу́щий**	**неся́**
идти́	**иду́т**	**иду́щий**	**идя́**
говори́ть	**говоря́т**	**говоря́щий**	**говоря́**
лежа́ть	**лежа́т**	**лежа́щий**	**лёжа**
сиде́ть	**сидя́т**	**сидя́щий**	**си́дя**
вести́	**веду́т**	**веду́щий**	**ведя́**

The form of the indeclinable present participle may be thought of as the declinable present participle in which the **-ущий, -ющий, -ащий** or **-ящий** element has been replaced by **-а** or **-я,** or as the 3rd person plural of the present tense in which the element **-ут, -ют, -ат** or **-ят** has been replaced by **-а** or **-я.**

EXERCISE 24

Translate into English:

1. Е́сли бы не́ было лобово́го сопротивле́ния, пласти́нка дви́галась бы в воде́ о́чень бы́стро.

   лобово́й = *frontal;* **сопротивле́ние** = *resistance;* **пласти́нка** = *plate.*

2. Значе́ние фу́нкции измени́лось бы, е́сли бы мы при́няли во внима́ние други́е фа́кторы.

   значе́ние = *value, significance;* **изменя́ть, -и́ть** = *to change;* **принима́ть, приня́ть во внима́ние** = *to take into account.*

3. Реакти́вный самолёт не мог бы лета́ть ни в пустоте́, ни да́же в высо́кой стратосфе́ре.

   ни = *nor, neither;* **да́же** = *even.*

4. В тако́м слу́чае, я бы ампути́ровал ру́ку над ло́ктем.

   в тако́м слу́чае = *in that case, in such a case;* **рука́** = *arm, hand;* **ло́коть** (fugitive vowel) = *elbow.*

5. Каза́лось бы, что мы непра́вильно рассчита́ли коэффицие́нт подъёмной си́лы.

   рассчи́тывать, рассчита́ть = *to calculate;* **подъёмная си́ла** = *lifting force.*

6. Во́здух бу́дто бы уплотня́ется пе́ред про́филем, так что сопротивле́ние увели́чивается.

   уплотня́ть, -и́ть = *to condense, to compress;* **увели́чивать, увели́чить** = *to increase.*

7. Несмотря́ на полу́ченные да́нные, бы́ло бы непра́вильно ду́мать, что соедине́ние стаби́льно.

   несмотря́ на = *in spite of;* **ду́мать** = *to think;* **соедине́ние** = *compound.*

8. Когда́ бы мы ни проводи́ли о́пыты, мы всегда́ получа́ли одина́ковые результа́ты.

   когда́ бы . . . ни = *whenever;* **всегда́** = *always;* **одина́ковый** = *identical.*

9. Доста́вкой спу́тника на орби́ту челове́к сде́лал хотя́ бы пе́рвый шаг в косми́ческое простра́нство.

   доста́вка = *delivery, placing;* **челове́к** = *man;* **шаг** = *step;* **простра́нство** = *space.*

10. Мы не хоти́м, что́бы чита́тели ду́мали, что э́то де́лается без осо́бых прибо́ров — да́тчиков, дистанцио́нных измери́телей и т.п.

    чита́тель = *reader;* **осо́бый** = *special;* **прибо́р** = *instrument;* **да́тчик** = *transducer;* **измери́тель** = *measuring instrument, gauge.*

11. Что́бы успе́шно уско́рить пучо́к части́ц до высо́кой ско́рости, тре́бовалась бы пови́димому о́чень сло́жная аппарату́ра.

    успе́шный = *successful;* **ускоря́ть, -ить** = *to accelerate;* **пучо́к** (fugitive vowel) = *beam;* **тре́бовалась бы** (+ gen.) = *there would be needed;* **пови́димому** = *apparently.*

12. Всё-таки, основно́й при́нцип тако́го ускори́теля был бы дово́льно просто́й.

    всё-таки = *yet, however;* **тако́й** = *such;* **дово́льно** = *fairly.*

13. Что́бы обнару́жить э́тот эффе́кт необходи́мо бы́ло примени́ть систе́му, кото́рая позволя́ла бы ионизи́ровать проходя́щий а́томный пучо́к.

    применя́ть, -и́ть = *to apply;* **кото́рый** = *which;* **позволя́ть, -ить** = *to allow.*

14. Э́то мо́жно обнару́жить, анализи́руя пучо́к на масс-спектро́метре.

    мо́жно = *one may, it is possible.*

15. Учи́тывая э́то, мы испо́льзовали ряд ме́тодов, применённых ра́нее для фракциони́рования желати́на.

    учи́тывать, уче́сть = *to take into account;* **испо́льзовать** = *to use;* **ряд** = *row, series;* **ра́нее** = *earlier.*

16. Полу́ченные да́нные, несмотря́ на их ориентиро́вочный хара́ктер, позволя́ют оцени́ть поря́док молекуля́рных ве́сов α- и β-компоне́нтов.

    ориентиро́вочный = *tentative, approximate;* **оце́нивать, оцени́ть** = *to evaluate;* **поря́док** = *order.*

17. Испо́льзуя коэффицие́нты седимента́ции и диффу́зии α- и β-компоне́нтов (при концентра́ции 0,3 %) и принима́я уде́льный объём V = 0,7, мы получа́ем молекуля́рный вес α-компоне́нтов о́коло 80 000 и β-компоне́нтов о́коло 130 000.

    принима́ть, приня́ть = *to take;* **уде́льный объём** = *specific volume;* **о́коло** (+ gen.) = *about, around.*

18. Га́ллоп, иссле́дуя седимента́цию прогре́того в ки́слом цитра́тном бу́ферном раство́ре ихтиоко́ла, не обнару́жил расщепле́ния э́того белка́.

    прогре́ть is a perfective of **греть**; **ки́слый** = *acid;* **расщепле́ние** = *splitting.*

19. Исходя́ из сре́дней биома́ссы микрооргани́змов в сероводоро́дной о́бласти и объёма сероводоро́дных глуби́н, мы заключи́ли, что о́бщая биома́сса микрооргани́змов в сероводоро́дной о́бласти составля́ет 17,2 млн. т.

исходя́ из = *starting from, proceeding from;* **сероводоро́дный** is derived from **се́ра** *sulphur* and **водоро́д** *hydrogen;* **о́бласть** (*f.*) = *region;* **глубина́** = *depth;* **заключа́ть, -и́ть** = *to conclude;* **составля́ть** = *to comprise;* **т.** = **тонн** (gen. pl. of **то́нна**).

20. Пови́димому, гипервитаминиза́ция, ускоря́я и уси́ливая биохими́ческие и физиологи́ческие проце́ссы, тормози́т регенерацио́нные проце́ссы соедини́тельной тка́ни.

гипер- = *hyper-;* **уси́ливать, уси́лить** = *to strengthen;* **тормози́ть, за-** = *to brake;* **соедини́тельный** = *connective;* **ткань** (*f.*) = *tissue.*

14

THE DATIVE CASE

Form of Dative Case

The marker for the dative plural of nouns and adjectives is **м**, preceded by **а/я** in nouns and by **ы/и** in adjectives. Thus:

зуб	*tooth*	**зубáм**	**лáмпа**	*lamp*	**лáмпам**
чу́вство	*feeling*	**чу́вствам**	**дóля**	*portion*	**дóлям**
твёрдый	*hard*	**твёрдым**	**зарáзный**	*infectious*	**зарáзным**
мя́гкий	*soft*	**мя́гким**	**большóй**	*big*	**больши́м**

The marker for the dative singular masculine and neuter of nouns and adjectives is **у/ю,** preceded in adjectives by **ом/ем.** Thus:

азóт	*nitrogen*	**азóту**	**строй**	*order*	**стрóю**
óлово	*tin*	**óлову**	**пóле**	*field*	**пóлю**
твёрдый	*hard*	**твёрдому**	**мя́гкий**	*soft*	**мя́гкому**
си́ний	*blue*	**си́нему**	**большóй**	*bigger*	**большóму**

Exceptions to this are **путь,** with dative **пути́,** and nouns of the type of **врéмя,** for example, with dative **врéмени.**

The marker for the dative singular of feminine nouns is **е** (for those with the nominative singular in **а/я**) or **и** (for those with the nominative singular in **ь** or **ия**). In other words, it is identical with the marker for the prepositional singular of feminine nouns. Thus:

лáмпа	*lamp*	**лáмпе**	**фáза**	*phase*	**фáзе**
дóля	*portion*	**дóле**	**кость**	*bone*	**кóсти**
ли́ния	*line*	**ли́нии**	**болéзнь**	*disease*	**болéзни**

The marker for the dative singular feminine of adjectives is **й,** preceded by **о/е,** i.e. it is identical with the genitive, prepositional and instrumental markers. Thus:

зарáзная болéзнь	*infectious disease*	**зарáзной болéзни**
си́няя лáмпа	*blue lamp*	**си́ней лáмпе**
твёрдая кость	*hard bone*	**твёрдой кóсти**
дли́нная ли́ния	*long line*	**дли́нной ли́нии**

All the case-markers have now been described. For ready reference Appendix I gives a complete set of paradigms ('declension patterns') for some typical nouns and adjectives of all three genders, singular and plural.

Exercise 25

Give the meaning of the following and say in what case are the nouns and adjectives:

1. ла́мпам, мя́гким, стро́ю, си́нему, вре́мени.

2. твёрдым вещество́м, зара́зным боле́зням, большо́му числу́, дли́нной фа́зе, кра́сному пла́мени.

3. семь фа́кторов, чи́стому сосу́ду, углу́, но́вым ме́тодам, атмосфе́ру.

4. руке́, патоло́гии, но́вым ме́тодом, твёрдым мета́ллам, много-кле́точной.

5. электри́ческому прибо́ру, сло́жными проце́ссами, бактерио-фа́гам, пять каучу́ковых дере́вьев, семена́м.

Use of Dative Case

The dative case is used in a variety of ways, some of which correspond to the usage in English of the preposition *to*, others of which are quite strange to the idiom of English. The following are the uses of the dative case:

1. With (*a*) some prepositions and (*b*) certain words functioning as prepositions.

   (*a*) **к, ко** (takes only the dative case) *to, towards*; **вопреки́** (takes only the dative case) *contrary to*; **по** (may take other cases with other meanings) *with respect to, according to.*[1]

   (*b*) **благодаря́** *thanks to*; **согла́сно** *according to*; **подо́бно** *similarly to, like.*

[1] The preposition **по** with the dative case may be translated into English in several ways, depending on the context. The examples and exercises will clarify its variety of meanings.

Examples:

движе́ние к	*movement towards*
отноше́ние х к у	*the relation of x to y*
вопреки́ жела́нию профе́ссора	*contrary to the professor's wish, desire*
по тео́рии	*according to the theory*
по изве́стной фо́рмуле	*according to the (well) known theory*
по содержа́нию	*according to the content, in content*
по дли́нным тру́бкам	*through long tubes*
по суббо́там	*on Saturdays*
благодаря́ зна́нию ру́сского языка́	*thanks to a knowledge of Russian*
согла́сно тео́риям Эйнште́йна	*according to, in accordance with Einstein's theories*
Подо́бно до́ктору, профе́ссор изуча́ет ру́сский язы́к.	*Like the doctor, the professor is studying the Russian language.*
подо́бно тому́ как[1] моле́кулы состоя́т из а́томов	*just as molecules consist of atoms*

[1] Literally *according to that how.*

2. To express the ' indirect object.' In such expressions English often has *to* where Russian simply has the dative case. Among the verbs which require the dative case to express the recipient of a thing or an action are:

дава́ть, дать and compounds	*to give*
придава́ть, прида́ть	*to add*
поддава́ться, подда́ться	*to give in, to yield*
говори́ть, сказа́ть[1]	*to tell, say*
припи́сывать, приписа́ть	*to ascribe*
сообща́ть, сообщи́ть	*to communicate*
подверга́ть, подве́ргнуть	*to subject*

[1] **сказа́ть** is the perfective to **говори́ть.**

All these verbs require a direct object as well—in the accusative case—and when these verbs are reflexive, the direct object is contained, as it were, in the reflexive particle, the indirect object being still in the dative case:

Неуда́ча припи́сывается поспе́шности.	*The failure is attributed to haste.*
Мета́лл подверга́ется нагрева́нию.	*The metal is subjected to heating.*

3. With adjectives whose English equivalents can be used with the preposition *to*:

аналоги́чный	*analogous*
пропорциона́льный	*proportional*
знако́мый	*familiar, known*
изве́стный	*known*
ра́вный	*equal*
неви́димый	*invisible*

Examples:

Учёный знако́мый америка́нским фи́зикам . . .	*A scholar known to American physicists . . .*
Факт изве́стный ру́сским хи́микам . . .	*A fact known to Russian chemists . . .*
Е́сли мы счита́ем, что x равно́ едини́це . . .	*If we consider that x is equal to unity . . .*

4. With nouns whose English equivalents can be used with the preposition *to*:

сопротивле́ние	*resistance*
сообще́ние	*communication*
прозра́чность	*transparency*
противополо́жность	*opposition*

Examples:

сопротивле́ние уда́ру	*resistance to the blow*
сообще́ние европе́йским чита́телям э́тих новосте́й	*the communication of this news to European readers*
прозра́чность ультрафиоле́товым луча́м	*transparency to ultra-violet rays*

5. With certain verbs which, for the most part, have only one object, this object being expressed in the dative case. The English equivalents of these verbs usually have a direct object, though one or two of them require the preposition *to*:

помога́ть, помо́чь	*to help*
соотве́тствовать	*to correspond to*
уступа́ть, уступи́ть	*to yield to*
спосо́бствовать	*to promote, assist*

удовлетворя́ть, удовлетвори́ть	*to satisfy*[1]
противоре́чить	*to contradict*
подлежа́ть	*to be subject to, open to*
принадлежа́ть	*to belong to*[2]
служи́ть, по-	*to serve*
учи́ть, на-	*to teach*
учи́ться, на-, вы́-	*to learn*

[1] Requires dative in one sense (see exercise).

[2] When this verb expresses possession properly speaking the dative case is used without a preposition, but when the verb expresses membership the preposition **к** is required.

6. With some so-called 'impersonal' verbs:

каза́ться, показа́ться	*to seem*
e.g. **Профе́ссору каза́лось, что э́то желе́зо.**	*It seemed to the professor/The professor thought that it was iron.*
Студе́нтам ка́жется, что э́то так.	*It seems to the students/The students think that this is so.*
удава́ться, уда́ться	*to succeed*
e.g. **Профе́ссору удало́сь проанализи́ровать жи́дкость.**	*The professor succeeded in analysing the liquid.*
Англи́йским студе́нтам никогда́ не удаётся поня́ть э́того.	*English students never succeed in understanding this.*
хоте́ться	*to want*
e.g. **Профе́ссору хо́чется поговори́ть со студе́нтами.**	*The professor wants to have a word with the students.*
Студе́нтам хоте́лось слы́шать о его́ но́вой тео́рии.	*The students wanted to hear about his new theory.*

7. In some other idiomatic expressions:

Студе́нтам тепло́ в ко́мнате.	*The students are warm in the room.*
Астроно́му хо́лодно в обсервато́рии.	*The astronomer is cold in his observatory.*
Профе́ссору 83 го́да.	*The professor is 83 years old.*

Ско́лько лет брита́нскому студе́нту?[1]	*How old is the British student?*
Студе́нтам фи́зики необходи́мо (ну́жно, на́до) знать пе́рвый зако́н термодина́мики.[2]	*Students of physics must know the first law of thermodynamics.*

[1] Literally: *How many years are there to the British student?* **лет** being genitive plural of **ле́то** *summer, year.*

[2] Literally: *To students of physics it is essential (necessary) to know,* etc.

Use of по with Numbers

The preposition **по** is used with the dative or accusative case in 'distributive' numerical expressions, i.e. to express the idea of *so many each.*

Accusative

по́ два	2 *each*
по́ три	3 *each*
по четы́ре	4 *each*
по́ сто	100 *each*
по две́сти	200 *each*
по три́ста	300 *each*
по четы́реста	400 *each*

Dative

по одному́ электро́ну[1]	*one electron each*
по одно́й ча́сти	*one part each*
по пяти́	5 *each*
по шести́	6 *each*
по десяти́	10 *each*
по двадцати́	20 *each*
по сорока́	40 *each*

[1] The numbers in these illustrations are all in the dative case (see Chapter 19 for declension of number-words).

Exercise 26

Translate into English:

1. Га́зовое освеще́ние уступи́ло ме́сто электри́ческому.

   освеще́ние = *illumination, lighting;* **ме́сто** = *place.*

2. По вне́шнему ви́ду алма́з си́льно отлича́ется от графи́та, хотя́ о́ба они́ явля́ются углеро́дами.

   вне́шний = *external;* translate **по** as *in;* **си́льный** = *strong;* **отлича́ть, -и́ть** = *to distinguish;* **хотя́** = *although;* **о́ба** = *both.*

3. Нельзя́ сказа́ть, что строе́ние моле́кулы аналоги́чно строе́нию а́тома.

   нельзя́ = *it is impossible, one cannot;* **строе́ние** = *structure.*

4. В э́том проце́ссе я́дра захва́тывают по одному́ электро́ну.

   захва́тывать, захвати́ть = *to seize, capture.*

5. Еди́нственная цель катализа́тора э́то спосо́бствовать хо́ду реа́кции; никако́го друго́го эффе́кта нельзя́ приписа́ть ему́.

   еди́нственный = *only, unique;* **цель** = *aim, purpose;* **ход** = *process, course;* **никако́й** = *no, not any;* **ему́** is dative of **он** and **оно́.**

6. Откры́тие, что причи́на ра́зных боле́зней — микро́б, существо́ неви́димое невооружённому гла́зу, яви́лось значи́тельным ша́гом вперёд в исто́рии медици́ны.

   причи́на = *cause;* **ра́зный** = *various;* **существо́** = *creature;* **невооружённый глаз** = '*unarmed*' *eye,* i.e. *naked eye;* **значи́тельный** = *considerable, significant;* **шаг** = *step.*

7. „Математи́ческие нача́ла" Нью́тона яви́лись отправно́й то́чкой рабо́т по меха́нике и небе́сной меха́нике в тече́ние после́дующих двух веко́в.

   нача́ла = *principles;* **отправно́й** = *departure;* **небе́сный** = *celestial;* **тече́ние** = *course;* **двух** is genitive of **два** and **две**; **век** = *century.*

8. Результа́т э́того о́пыта не совсе́м соотве́тствовал тео́рии, что не удиви́тельно, потому́ что э́та тео́рия всегда́ подлежа́ла сомне́нию и всё ещё подлежи́т сомне́нию.

   совсе́м = *entirely, quite;* **что не** = *which is not;* **удиви́тельный** = *surprising;* **потому́ что** = *because;* **подлежа́ть** = *to be subject to, open to;* **сомне́ние** = *doubt;* **всё ещё** = *still.*

9. Мета́лл подверга́ется нагре́ву до высо́кой температу́ры, ме́жду тем жи́дкость прохо́дит по изо́гнутым тру́бкам и, наконе́ц вытека́ет ка́плями в сосу́д.

   нагре́в = *heating;* **ме́жду тем** = *meanwhile;* **изо́гнутый** = *curved, bent;* **наконе́ц** = *finally;* **вытека́ть, -течь** = *to flow out, issue;* **ка́пля** = *drop* (**ка́плями** = *as drops, in the form of drops*).

10. То, что они́ ви́дели в лаборато́рии, соотве́тствовало фа́ктам уже́ изве́стным студе́нтам, потому́ что результа́т о́пыта удовлетворя́л теорети́ческим тре́бованиям.

    тре́бование = *demand, need.*

11. Де́йствие катала́з определя́лось по ра́нее опи́санному ме́тоду.

    де́йствие = *action, influence;* **определя́ть, -и́ть** = *to determine;* **опи́сывать, описа́ть** = *to describe.*

12. Исслéдованию подвергáлись малоуглерóдистые сплáвы, состав котóрых приведён в табл. 1.

The meaning of **малоуглерóдистый** will be evident if the word is broken down: **мало/углерóд/истый**; note that the first half of this sentence is 'inverted.'

13. Э́тим трéбованиям удовлетворя́ет триóдная манометри́ческая лáмпа ЛМ-2: с систéмой ламп (рис. 1) бы́ли проведены́ измерéния по выяснéнию врéмени насыщéния.

по here = *of, on;* **выяснéние** = *clarification* (or translate the preposition and noun thus : *in order to clarify*); **насыщéние** = *saturation.*

14. В любóе другóе врéмя таки́е услóвия для проникновéния протóнов к эквáтору не осуществля́ются.

любóй = *any;* **услóвие** = *condition;* **проникновéние** = *penetration;* **осуществля́ть, -ви́ть** = *to realise, bring about.*

15. Продýкты распáда проколлагéна по хими́ческому состáву и нéкоторым физи́ческим свóйствам напоминáют желати́н.

распáд = *decay, dissolution;* **по** here = *in;* **нéкоторые** = *several, certain;* **свóйство** = *property;* **напоминáть** = *to remind, be reminiscent of.*

16. Учи́тывались тáкже толщинá слоёв в процéнтах к óбщей толщинé кóжи и коэффициéнт соотношéния слоёв.

в here = *as,* **к** = *of;* **кóжа** = *skin;* **соотношéние** = *relation* (*ship*).

17. Настоя́щее сообщéние посвящáется разбóру разви́тия э́того óргана в онтогенéзе с задáчей, по возмóжности, вы́яснить причи́ны егó появлéния и исчезновéния.

сообщéние = *communication;* **посвящáть, посвяти́ть** = *to devote, dedicate;* **разбóр** = *analysis;* **задáча** = *task, problem;* **по возмóжности** = *as far as possible;* **появлéние** = *appearance;* **исчезновéние** = *disappearance.*

18. Укáзанные растéния отличáлись не тóлько по высотé, но и по числý цветкóв, плодóв и коли́честву семя́н.

укáзывать, указáть = *to indicate;* **высотá** = *height;* **цветóк** (fugitive **о**) = *flower;* **плод** = *fruit;* **семя́н** is gen. pl. of **сéмя** *seed* (nom. pl., **семенá**).

19. При прибавлéнии к нормáльному пищевóму рациóну витами́нов A и D и органи́ческих сóлей кáльция в оптимáльных дозирóвках кóстная ткань станóвится способóбной к нормáльной регенерáции.

прибавлéние = *addition;* **пищевóй** = *alimentary, food;* **кóстный**—adjective pertaining to **кость**; **ткань** (*f.*) = *fabric, tissue;* **станови́ться, стать** = *to become;* **способóбный** = *capable.*

20. Всё э́то пока́зывает, что откры́тые райо́ны Чёрного мо́ря (кислоро́дная зо́на) по микро́бной ма́ссе уступа́ют се́веро-за́падной его́ о́бласти, а Чёрное мо́ре в це́лом по разви́тию бактериа́льной жи́зни в слоя́х акти́вного фотоси́нтеза в ря́де слу́чаев не уступа́ет сре́днему и ю́жному Ка́спию.

всё = *all;* **откры́тый** = *open;* **се́веро-за́падный** = *north-west;* **в це́лом** = *as a whole;* **ряд** = *series;* **сре́дний** = *middle, average;* **ю́жный** = *south.*

15

THE FUTURE TENSE; EXPRESSIONS OF OBLIGATION; THE IMPERATIVE; THE THIRD PERSON PRONOUN

FUTURE TENSE

As with the past tense, there are two aspects of the future: imperfective and perfective. The imperfective future consists of an auxiliary verb and the imperfective infinitive. This auxiliary, consisting of a root **буд-** with the present tense endings, also occurs without the imperfective infinitive in the meaning *will be, shall be*. Here are some examples of the imperfective future:

бу́ду анализи́ровать	*I shall analyse*
бу́дет чита́ть	(*he/she*) *will read*
бу́дем ввози́ть	*we shall import*
бу́дете де́лать	*you will do*
бу́дут получа́ть	*they will receive*

The perfective future consists of endings identical with those of the present tense,[1] attached to perfective verbs. Examples are:

проанализи́рую	*I shall analyse*
прочита́ет	(*he*) *will read*
ввезём	*we shall import*
сде́лаете	*you will do*
полу́чат[2]	*they will receive*

The difference in meaning between the imperfective future and the perfective future is the same as that between the imperfective past and the perfective past: the perfective implies completion in some sense or other, or refers to a single point in time, whereas with the imperfective there is no such implication or reference. Thus:

Он бу́дет осма́тривать лабора-то́рии.	*He will inspect the laboratories* (i.e. he will spend some time looking, the emphasis being on looking).

[1] **дать,** its compounds and compounds of **есть** *to eat* have some anomalous forms (see Appendix IV).

[2] The infinitive associated with this is: **получи́ть** (pfv.); cf. **получа́ют,** infinitive (impfv.) **получа́ть.**

Он осмо́трит лаборато́рии.	*He will inspect the laboratories* (i.e. he will make an inspection, the emphasis being on completion).
Она́ бу́дет писа́ть бра́ту.	*She will write to her brother* (i.e. more than once).
Она́ напи́шет бра́ту письмо́.	*She will write her brother a letter* (i.e. one letter on one occasion).
Вы бу́дете анализи́ровать э́ти про́бы це́лый день.	*You will be analysing these samples the entire day* (i.e. it will take you all day).
Вы проанализи́руете э́ти про́бы за два часа́.	*You will analyse these samples in two hours* (i.e. you will complete the analysis by the end of two hours).

The 1st person plural of the perfective future is used, without a pronoun, in the sense of *let us . . .*, e.g. :

Просмо́трим отчёт.	*Let us look through the report.*
Ска́жем, два кг.[1]	(*Let us*) *say, two kilogrammes . . .*

Occasionally, the imperfective form is used in a similar way :

Не бу́дем перепи́сывать все ци́фры.	*We shall not/Let us not copy out all the figures.*

[1] **килогра́мма.**

Expressions of Obligation

A few expressions of obligation have already been used, namely, **на́до, ну́жно, прихо́дится,** all of which combine with the dative case. **На́до** and **ну́жно** may be translated as *must,* **прихо́дится** as *has, have to.* Two more expressions of obligation are **сле́дует** *ought* and **до́лжен, должна́, должно́, должны́** *must, should.*

Сле́дует is used with the dative case : **До́ктору сле́дует . . .** *the doctor ought* (*to*) . . . or on its own in the sense of *one ought* (*to*) . . . The words **до́лжен, должна́,** etc., are in fact the short forms of an adjective and therefore agree with the subject : **Профе́ссор до́лжен чита́ть . . .** *the professor must read, should read . . .,* **студе́нтка должна́ писа́ть . . .** *the student should write . . .*

All the expressions of obligation quoted above are in the present tense. The other tenses are as follows :

Past	*Future*
на́до бы́ло	**на́до бу́дет**
ну́жно бы́ло	**ну́жно бу́дет**
приходи́лось (impfv.) **пришло́сь** (pfv.)	**придётся**
сле́довало	—
до́лжен был, должна́ была́, etc.	**до́лжен, должна́, бу́ду, бу́дет,** etc.

These expressions may also occur with the particle **бы,** implying hypothetical or unfulfilled circumstances. A fairly wide variety of expressions of obligation is thus available, the finer shades of which cannot all be rendered into English. Such expressions as *must, should, should have, ought, ought to have,* etc., will usually serve to translate the Russian expressions adequately.

Сле́довать, the infinitive with which **сле́дует,** etc., are connected, also means *to follow,* when it often has with it the preposition **за** and the instrumental case.

Ну́жно is the short form neuter of an adjective **ну́жный** *necessary* : cf. **ну́жный элеме́нт** *the necessary element,* **ну́жные да́нные** *the necessary data.*

Note the expression **должно́ быть** (literally *it must be*). This expression remains constant, i.e. it is unaffected by changes of tense and person :

Он, должно́ быть, здесь.	*It must be that he is here,* i.e. *he must be here.*
Должно́ быть, она́ была́ здесь.	*It must be that she was here,* i.e. *she must have been here.*
Они́, должно́ быть, бу́дут здесь.	*It must be that they will be here,* i.e. *they must be coming/they must be going to be here.*

Imperative

The markers of the imperative are **-й,** which occurs after vowels, **-и** and **-ь,** which occur after consonants. The singular consists simply of one of the imperative markers, while the plural has the additional marker **-те,**[1] i.e. consists of **-йте, -ите, -ьте.** The imperative does not occur very frequently in technical literature. It is most likely to occur in instructions for procedures:

Возьми́те два гр.	*Take two grammes.*
Нале́йте ещё воды́.	*Add ('pour in') more water.*

[1] Compare the marker **-те** for the 2nd person plural of the present and future perfective tenses.

The following are examples of imperatives:

Infinitive		*Imp. sing.*	*Imp. pl.*
узна́ть	*to find out*	**узна́й**	**узна́йте**
смотре́ть	*to look*	**смотри́**	**смотри́те**
повтори́ть	*to repeat*	**повтори́**	**повтори́те**
поста́вить	*to put*	**поста́вь**	**поста́вьте**
встать	*to stand/get up*	**вста́нь**	**вста́ньте**
нама́зать	*to grease*	**нама́жь**	**нама́жьте**

Note the following imperative forms:

Infinitive		*Singular*	*Plural*
лить	*to pour*	**лей**	**ле́йте**
пить	*to drink*	**пей**	**пе́йте**
вить	*to weave*	**вей**	**ве́йте**
бить	*to strike*	**бей**	**бе́йте**

The imperative **дава́йте** (**дава́ть** *to give*) is used with 1st person plural verb forms or with the infinitive in the sense *let us*. Thus:

Дава́йте бу́дем рабо́тать вме́сте.	*Let us work together.*
Дава́йте перепи́шем все ци́фры.	*Let us copy out all the figures.*
Дава́йте чита́ть как мо́жно бо́льше[1] материа́ла на э́ту те́му.	*Let us read as much material as possible on this subject.*

[1] For this construction see Chapter 16 'Comparative Adjective and Adverb.'

Third Person Pronoun

The pronouns in Russian may be divided into two groups, according to the nature of their declensions, viz. a non-adjectival and an adjectival group. The adjectival group has a declensional pattern very similar to that of the adjectives and the commonest member of this group is the 3rd person pronoun, some of the forms of which have been used in previous lessons. The nominative of the 3rd person pronoun has a stem or base which is quite different from the stem or base in the other cases. Here is a complete table of the declension of the 3rd person pronoun:

	Masculine (*he, it*)	*Neuter* (*it*)	*Feminine* (*she, it*)	*Plural* (*they*)
Nom.	**он**	**оно́**	**она́**	**они́**
Gen.	**его́**		**её**	**их**
Dat.	**ему́**		**ей**	**им**
Acc.	**его́**		**её**	**их**
Inst.	**им**		**ей/е́ю**	**и́ми**
Prep.	**нём**		**ней**	**них**

It will be seen at a glance that, in the oblique cases (genitive onwards), this pronoun has no stem,[1] except in the prepositional, where the stem is **н-**. This stem occurs *whenever* the 3rd person pronoun is preceded by a preposition, whatever the case, and since the prepositional case is always preceded by a preposition it exists only in the form with initial ('prosthetic') **н-**. With this proviso, then, almost all the forms of the 3rd person pronoun are identical in spelling with the case-endings of adjectives (see Appendix I for full declension patterns of adjectives). The **г** in **его́,** as in the adjective endings, is pronounced as a **в**. This form serves as genitive and accusative to both **он** and **оно́,** there being no animate-inanimate distinction in the accusative of this pronoun (see Chapter 9). Similarly, **её** is both genitive and accusative to **она́,** and **их** is genitive and accusative to **они́.** **её,** unlike the other non-nominative forms, does not look like an adjective ending and therefore special note should be made of this form. The instrumental feminine has the alternative form **е́ю,** which is, however, less common than **ей.** The genitive forms **е́го, её, их** are also used to express *his, its* (**его́**), *her, hers* (**её**), *their, theirs* (**их**).

The following are some simple examples of the use of the 3rd person pronoun, both with and without the prosthetic **н-** :

я дал ему́	*I gave (to) him*
я шёл к нему́	*I was going towards him*
по́льзоваться им	*to make use of it*
пе́ред ним	*in front of him/it*
кора́ де́рева — его́ кора́	*the bark of the tree—its bark*
стетоско́п до́ктора — его́ стетоско́п	*the doctor's stethoscope—his stethoscope*
ядро́ а́тома — его́ ядро́	*the nucleus of the atom—its nucleus*
по́льзоваться ей	*to make use of it (f.)*
пе́ред ней	*in front of her/it*
он сообщи́л ей	*he informed her*
он подошёл к ней	*he went up to her*
я ви́дел её	*I saw her/it*
её кни́га	*her book*
от неё	*from her/it*
с ни́ми	*with them*
их тео́рия	*their theory*
от них	*from them*
мы ви́дели их	*we saw them*

[1]No written stem, that is: in pronunciation, forms such as **его**, etc., have an initial **у** sound (like *y* in *yield*), which is optional in the plural (**их**, etc.).

Exercise 27

Translate into English:

1. В результа́тс а́льфа-распа́да радиоакти́вный изото́п хими́ческого элеме́нта преврати́тся в изото́п друго́го хими́ческого элеме́нта с ме́ньшим а́томным но́мером.

   превраща́ть, преврати́ть = *to convert;* **ме́ньший** = *smaller.*

2. Кровь бу́дет вытека́ть из ра́ны до того́ как, благодаря́ коагуля́ции, ра́на покро́ется то́нким сло́ем студени́стого вещества́.

   вытека́ть, вы́течь = *to flow out;* **ра́на** = *wound;* **до того́ как** = *until;* **покрыва́ть, покры́ть** = *to cover;* **то́нкий** = *fine, thin;* **студени́стый** = *jelly-like.*

3. Ско́рость движе́ния раке́ты, под влия́нием си́лы тя́жести, бу́дет коне́чно уменьша́ться до того́ как она́ уменьши́тся до ноля́.

   движе́ние = *movement;* **си́ла тя́жести** = *force of gravity;* **коне́чно** = *of course;* **уменьша́ть, -и́ть** = *to decrease;* **ноль** (*m.*) = *zero.*

4. Результа́ты измере́ния сече́ний бу́дут опублико́ваны в сле́дующих статья́х.

   сече́ние = *section;* **статья́** = *article.*

5. При́мем, что в о́бщем слу́чае $N_{AA} = N^1{}_{AA}(1 - x)$, где x бу́дет пара́метром корреля́ции.

   принима́ть, приня́ть (приму́, при́мешь, при́мет, etc.) = *to take, receive, assume;* **о́бщий** = *general;* **слу́чай** = *case;* **где** = *where.*

6. Дета́льное изуче́ние хими́ческих и фи́зико-хими́ческих свойств э́тих компоне́нтов должно́ быть предме́том дальне́йших иссле́дований.

   сво́йство = *property;* **дальне́йший** = *further.*

7. Десо́рбция анио́нов должна́, согла́сно вышеска́занному, привести́ к сниже́нию адсо́рбции катио́нов.

   согла́сно = *according to;* **вышеска́занное** = *the above-said;* **сниже́ние** = *lowering.*

8. Сле́дует име́ть в виду́, что фо́рма кривы́х бу́дет зави́сеть не то́лько от коэффицие́нта поглоще́ния вещества́.

   име́ть в виду́ = *to have in view, bear in mind;* **крива́я** = *curve* **зави́сеть** = *to depend;* **поглоще́ние** = *absorption.*

9. Э́то зна́чит, что из о́бщей ма́ссы живо́го вещества́ в Чёрном мо́ре на до́лю микроорга́низмов прихо́дится приме́рно 20-25%.

зна́чит = (*it*) *means;* **живо́й** = *live, living;* **приме́рно** = *approximately;* in this sentence **прихо́дится** does not mean *has to*—the meaning is *to the portion of micro-organisms 'falls' approximately* 20-25%, i.e. *the micro-organisms make up about* 20-25%.

10. Сле́довательно, электростати́ческая адсо́рбция катио́нов должна́ была́ бы наблюда́ться то́лько при отрица́тельных заря́дах пове́рхности.

сле́довательно = *consequently;* **должна́ была́ бы наблюда́ться** = *should be/should have been observed* (implying *but it is/was not*); **отрица́тельный** = *negative;* **заря́д** = *charge.*

11. Пре́жде всего́ сле́дует уче́сть, что в о́бласти иониза́ции существу́ет молекуля́рное тече́ние па́ра рту́ти, а не а́томный пучо́к.

пре́жде всего́ = *first of all;* **учи́тывать, уче́сть** = *to take into account;* **тече́ние** = *current;* **пар** = *steam, vapour;* **ртуть** (*f.*) = *mercury.*

12. Необходи́мо отме́тить, что опи́санное явле́ние мо́жет яви́ться исто́чником серьёзных системати́ческих оши́бок при то́чных масс-спектрометри́ческих измере́ниях.

отмеча́ть, отме́тить = *to note;* **исто́чник** = *source;* **то́чный** = *precise.*

13. На основа́нии э́того мо́жно счита́ть, что у́ровень N_{I} в герма́нии до́лжен быть запо́лнен и, сле́довательно, перехо́ды $L_{\mathrm{III}} \rightarrow N_{\mathrm{I}}$ и $L_{\mathrm{II}} \rightarrow N_{\mathrm{I}}$ должны́ име́ть ме́сто.

основа́ние = *basis;* **у́ровень** = *level;* **заполня́ть, -ить** = *fill up, supplement;* **име́ть ме́сто** = *to take place.*

14. Ио́ны, попада́ющие на като́д, бу́дут реиспаря́ться, а ио́ны, попада́ющие на ано́д, бу́дут остава́ться на нём, что вы́зовет ослабле́ние проходя́щего пучка́ и измене́ние его́ соста́ва.

попада́ть, попа́сть = *to fall on, to strike;* **реиспаря́ться, -и́ться** = *to re-evaporate;* **остава́ться, оста́ться** = *to remain;* **вызыва́ть, вы́звать** (**вы́зову, вы́зовешь, вы́зовет,** etc.) = *to provoke;* **ослабле́ние** = *weakening;* **измене́ние** = *change.*

15. Для нагля́дности проиллюстри́руем ска́занное вы́ше графи́чески; вы́делим в криста́лле лине́йную цепо́чку узло́в, в кото́рой узлы́ кла́сса 1 и 2 бу́дут чередова́ться друг с дру́гом.

нагля́дность = *clarity;* **вы́ше** = *above;* **графи́чески** here = *in the form of a graph;* **выделя́ть, -ить** = *to single out, isolate, allot;* **цепо́чка** = *chain;* **у́зел** (fugitive vowel) = *knot, node, ganglion;* **чередова́ться** = *to alternate;* **друг с дру́гом** = *one with the other.*

16. Таки́м о́бразом мы никогда́ не смо́жем получи́ть хоро́ших результа́тов; оши́бки бу́дут постоя́нно возника́ть. Одна́ко, измене́ние дета́лей систе́мы непреме́нно принесёт удовлетвори́тельные результа́ты.

таки́м о́бразом = *in that way;* **никогда́** = *never ;* **смо́жем** is future perfective of the verb 'to be able', translate *we shall never manage;* **постоя́нно** = *constantly;* **возника́ть, возни́кнуть** = *to arise;* **одна́ко** = *however;* **непреме́нно** = *definitely.*

17. Е́сли исходи́ть из тако́го предположе́ния, то ста́нет поня́тным, почему́ при ра́зных коли́чествах перхлора́тов наблюда́ется одина́ковая полимеризу́ющая спосо́бность их.

исходи́ть из = *to start from;* **предположе́ние** = *supposition;* **станови́ться, стать (ста́ну, ста́нет,** etc.) = *to become;* **поня́тный** = *understandable;* **одина́ковый** = *identical;* **спосо́бность** = *ability.*

18. Е́сли усло́вно приня́ть гемолити́ческую акти́вность метаболи́тов селезёнки за 100 %, то акти́вность метаболи́тов други́х о́рганов вы́разится сле́дующими величи́нами (табл. 2).

усло́вно = *conditionally, conventionally;* **селезёнка** = *spleen;* **за** = *as;* **то** = *then;* **выража́ть, вы́разить** = *to express;* **величина́** = *magnitude, value;* **табл.** (= **табли́ца**) = *table.*

19. Доба́вим к э́тому, что нагрева́ние раство́ров проколлаге́на ведёт к необрати́мому распа́ду нати́вной структу́ры э́того белка́, и поэ́тому объясне́ние Ма́тьюса, Куло́нена и До́рфмана нельзя́ призна́ть обосно́ванным.

добавля́ть, доба́вить = *to add;* **необрати́мый** = *irreversible;* **нати́вный** = *native;* **объясне́ние** = *explanation;* **нельзя́** = *one cannot;* **признава́ть, призна́ть** = *to admit;* **обосно́вывать, обосновá́ть** = *to found.*

20. Таки́м о́бразом, в слу́чае идеа́льной Земли́ в любо́й то́чке се́верного полуша́рия должны́ бы́ли бы наблюда́ться четы́ре относи́тельных ма́ксимума интенси́вности и частоты́ нерегуля́рных магни́тно-ионосфе́рных возмуще́ний и поля́рных сия́ний.

любо́й = *any;* **то́чка** = *point;* **полуша́рие** = *hemisphere;* **относи́тельный** = *relative;* **частота́** = *frequency;* **возмуще́ние** = *disturbance;* **сия́ние** = *aurora.*

16

THE COMPARATIVE AND SUPERLATIVE

Comparative Adjective

There are two types of comparative adjective in Russian—a complex type and a simple type. The complex type is formed with the word **бóлее** *more,* thus:

бóлее корóткий	*shorter*
бóлее длúнный	*longer*
бóлее красúвый	*more beautiful*

(The converse of **бóлее** is **мéнее** *less*:

мéнее гóрький	*less bitter*
мéнее красúвый	*less beautiful*)

The words **бóлее** and **мéнее** are indeclinable but the adjectives accompanying them are declined in the normal way:

бóлее длúнная фáза	*a longer phase*
бóлее тяжёлым молéкулам	*heavier molecules* (dat.)
мéнее гóрькой жúдкости	*less bitter liquid* (gen., dat., prep.)

This type of comparative is productive, i.e. new comparative adjectives of this type can be and are continually formed.

The simple type occurs in two variants. Variant (*a*) has as its marker **-ee,**[1] which is attached to the adjective stem. This type is indeclinable and is productive. Examples are:

длиннéе	*longer*
красúвее	*more beautiful*
краснéе	*redder*

Variant (*b*) has as its marker **-e,** added to the adjective stem, with consonant interchange according to the patterns given in Appendix II. This type is indeclinable and non-productive (i.e. the number of this type is strictly limited and no new ones are formed). Altogether, there are about sixty adjectives forming a

[1] The alternative **-ей** is sometimes found, though this is hardly likely to occur in technical literature.

comparative in this manner and the following lists, while not being exhaustive, include all those comparatives of this type which are likely to be met with in technical literature. It is not suggested that the student should commit all these to memory at once but that he should read through the lists a few times, testing his memory after the first reading(s) by covering the central and right-hand columns, thereafter using the lists as ready reference tables. The lists are arranged with the left-hand column (the comparatives) in alphabetical order; the central column gives the nominative singular masculine of the adjective, and the right-hand column gives the basic meaning of the adjective.

1. **к** alternates with **ч**:

вя́зче	**вя́зкий**	*viscous*
го́рче	**го́рький**[1]	*bitter*
гро́мче	**гро́мкий**	*loud*
е́дче	**е́дкий**	*corrosive, caustic,* etc
жа́рче	**жа́ркий**	*hot*
жёстче	**жёсткий**	*hard*
зво́нче	**зво́нкий**	*sonorous*
кра́тче	**кра́ткий**	*short*
кре́пче	**кре́пкий**	*firm, strong*
ле́гче	**лёгкий**	*light; easy*
ме́льче	**ме́лкий**	*fine; shallow*
мя́гче	**мя́гкий**	*soft*
ре́зче	**ре́зкий**	*sharp; strident; harsh,* etc.
те́рпче	**те́рпкий**	*tart, sharp*
хру́пче	**хру́пкий**	*brittle*
я́рче	**я́ркий**	*vivid, bright*

N.B.—No **ь** in the comparative.

2. **ст** alternates with **щ**:

гу́ще	**густо́й**	*thick, dense*
про́ще	**просто́й**	*simple, easy*
то́лще	**толсто́й**	*fat, thick*
ча́ще	**ча́стый**	*frequent, fine,* etc.[1]

[1] Literally = *occurring at frequent intervals, temporally or spatially,* e.g. **ча́стое повторе́ние** *frequent repetition,* **ча́стая сеть** *fine network,* **ча́стый лес** *dense wood,* **ча́стая ткань** *close fabric.*

3. **г** alternates with **ж**:

доро́же	**дорого́й**	*dear, expensive*
стро́же	**стро́гий**	*strict, severe*
ту́же	**туго́й**	*tight, stiff*

4. **д** alternates with **ж**:

моло́же	**молодо́й**	*young*
твёрже	**твёрдый**	*hard, firm*

5. **т** alternates with **ч**:

бога́че	**бога́тый**	*rich*
кру́че	**круто́й**	*steep, abrupt*

6. **х** alternates with **ш**:

су́ше	**сухо́й**	*dry*
ти́ше	**ти́хий**	*quiet, calm*

7. **в** alternates with **вл**:

деше́вле	**дешёвый**	*cheap*

8. In this group the **к** found in other forms of the adjective is missing from the comparative, the last consonant of the adjective stem showing one or other of the alternations listed above:

гла́же	**гла́дкий**	(д ~ ж)[1]	*smooth*
жи́же	**жи́дкий**	(д ~ ж)	*liquid*
ре́же	**ре́дкий**	(д ~ ж)	*rare*
коро́че	**коро́ткий**	(т ~ ч)	*short*

also

бли́же	**бли́зкий**	(з ~ ж)	*near*
ни́же	**ни́зкий**	(з ~ ж)	*low*
у́же	**у́зкий**	(з ~ ж)	*narrow*

[1] The sign ~ means 'alternates with.'

9. The two adjectives in this group lose a suffix **-ок** in the comparative, one of them showing an alternation **с ~ ш**:

вы́ше	**высо́кий**	*high*
ши́ре	**широ́кий**	*broad*

10. In the following group the comparative has the letter **ш** in front of **е,** i.e. the entire marker consists of **ше**:

бо́льше (and **бо́лее**)	{ **большо́й**	*big*
	{ **вели́кий**[1]	*big, great*
да́льше (and **да́лее**)	**далёкий**[2]	*distant, far*
до́льше (and **до́лее**)	**до́лгий**[3]	*long (in time)*
лу́чше	**хоро́ший**[1]	*good*
ме́ньше (and **ме́нее**)	{ **ма́лый**[1]	*small, little*
	{ **ма́ленький**[1]	,, ,,
ста́рше	**ста́рый**	*old*
то́ньше (**ь** occurs only in the comparative)	**то́нкий**	*fine, thin*

[1] The comparative of these adjectives is formed, as can be seen, from a different root. Compare English *good, better; bad, worse,* etc.
[2] N.B. loss of **-ёк-** in comparative.
[3] N.B. loss of **-г-** in comparative.

11. The following anomalous forms should be noted:

глу́бже	**глубо́кий**	*deep*
сла́ще	**сла́дкий**	*sweet*
ху́же	**плохо́й**[1]	*bad*

Superlative Adjective

The complex consisting of the word **са́мый** plus an adjective, in which both **са́мый** and the adjective are in grammatical agreement with the noun which they delimit, is the Russian expression of the superlative degree of comparison, corresponding to the English *most, -est.* Thus:

са́мый высо́кий у́ровень	*the highest level*
са́мая сло́жная тео́рия	*the most complicated theory*
в са́мых глубо́ких моря́х	*in the deepest seas*

Adjectival forms in **-е́йший** or **-а́йший**, which may be called 'superlatives' in some grammars, are now commonly used in the sense of *most* (as well as *the most*), *very, exceedingly*, etc.:

важне́йший вопро́с	*a most important question*
тонча́йшая нить	*a very fine filament*
до мельча́йших подро́бностей	*down to the finest details*
кратча́йший срок	*an exceedingly short period, the shortest period*

The prefix **наи** added to comparatives or superlatives implies a superlative with added emphasis:

наибо́лее	*the most*
наилу́чший[1]	*the very best*
наиспосо́бнейший	*the most capable*

[1] See below for the form **лу́чший**.

Comparative and Superlative Adverb

The indeclinable comparative adjectives may also function as comparative adverbs and the complex consisting of **бо́лее** plus an ordinary adverb is also an expression of a comparative adverb. Thus:

идти́ вы́ше	*to go higher*
ча́ще варии́руется	*it varies more frequently*
бо́лее механи́чески	*more mechanically*

The complex **са́мым . . . о́бразом** is a superlative adverbial phrase, as in

са́мым жела́тельным о́бразом	*in the most desirable manner*
са́мым бы́стрым о́бразом	*in the quickest manner*

Use of Comparative Forms

Corresponding to some of the indeclinable comparative adjectives in **-e,** given in the first part of this chapter, there are declinable adjectives ending in **-ший,** most of which no longer have purely comparative meaning:

(*a*) **бо́льший** (cf. **бо́льше**) means *greater, larger, major*; **бо́льшей ча́стью** means either *for the greater part* or *for the most part.*

(*b*) **ме́ньший** (cf. **ме́ньше**) means *lesser, smaller, minor*; **по ме́ньшей ча́сти** means *at least, to say the least.*

(*c*) **лу́чший** (cf. **лу́чше**) and **ху́дший** (cf. **ху́же**) are used as comparatives or superlatives (the use of the word **са́мый** with these and other declinable simple comparatives emphasises the superlative degree):

Лу́чшего результа́та нельзя́ ожида́ть.	*A better result cannot be expected.*[1]
Э́то всё к лу́чшему.	*It is all for the best.*
са́мый лу́чший тип	*the very best type*
переме́на к ху́дшему	*a change for the worse*
в ху́дшем слу́чае	*in the worst event, at worst*
са́мый ху́дший ме́тод	*the very worst method*

[1] Literally: *it is impossible to expect a better result.*

(*d*) **ста́рший** (cf. **ста́рше**), **вы́сший** (cf. **вы́ше**), **ни́зший** (cf. **ни́же**) and **мла́дший** (a form of Church Slavonic origin corresponding to the Russian indeclinable **моло́же**) are used in limited contexts, as illustrated by the following examples :

ста́рший нау́чный сотру́дник[1]	*Senior Scientist*
мла́дший нау́чный сотру́дник	*Junior Scientist*
ста́ршая дочь	*eldest or elder daughter* (i.e. born first)
мла́дший сын	*youngest or younger son* (i.e. born last)
вы́сшая матема́тика	*higher mathematics*
вы́сшая то́чка	*highest point, acme*
ни́зший слой	*lower layer*
ни́зший тип живо́тных	*lower type of animals*
ни́зшая то́чка	*lowest point, nadir*

[1] **сотру́дник** = *collaborator, assistant, fellow-worker, employee.*

The genitive or the word **чем** used in conjunction with the comparative is equivalent to the English *than*. Thus:

Профе́ссор ста́рше до́ктора	*The professor is older than the doctor.*
Втора́я фа́за коро́че пе́рвой.	*The second phase is shorter than the first.*
У́ровень вы́ше, чем ожида́лось бы.	*The level is higher than would be expected.*

Comparatives plus **всего́** or **всех**[1] are equivalent to the English usage *most, best,* etc., *of all,* as in

Ча́ще всего́ живо́тное продолжа́ет спать.	*Most often the animal goes on sleeping* (literally : *continues to sleep*).
Лу́чше всего́, э́то взять кусо́к мета́лла . . .	*Best of all is to take a piece of metal . . .*
Э́та гора́ вы́ше всех.	*This mountain is highest of all.*
Э́та фа́за коро́че всех.	*This phase is the shortest of all.*

[1] **всего́** is genitive singular of **всё** *all*, **всех** is genitive plural of **всё** *all.*

The complex ' **чем** plus comparative . . ., **тем** plus comparative ' is the equivalent of the English *the more . . . the more . . .* Thus :

чем скоре́е, тем лу́чше	*the quicker the better*
Чем быстре́е он рабо́тает, тем ча́ще он де́лает оши́бки.	*The faster he works, the more often does he make mistakes.*
Чем вы́ше мы поднима́емся на́ гору, тем ре́же стано́вится во́здух.	*The higher we climb up a mountain, the more rarefied the air becomes.*

The complex ' **как мо́жно** plus comparative ' is the equivalent of the English *as . . . as possible.* Thus:

как мо́жно скоре́е	*as quickly as possible*
как мо́жно бо́льше	*as much/many as possible*

Exercise 28

Translate into English:

1. Необходи́мо отме́тить, что все изме́ренные величи́ны бо́льше рассчи́танных.

   необходи́мый = *essential;* **отмеча́ть, отме́тить** = *to note;* **измеря́ть, -ить** = *to measure;* **рассчи́тывать, рассчита́ть** = *to calculate.*

2. Гуммиара́бик снижа́ет акти́вность катала́зы да́же в бо́льшей сте́пени, чем желати́н.

   снижа́ть, сни́зить = *to lower;* **сте́пень** (*f.*) = *degree.*

3. Э́тот о́рган, в проце́ссе онтогене́за, стано́вится всё у́же и у́же.

   всё here is an adverb and with the comparative is equivalent to *more and more . . . .*; here it could be omitted in translation.

4. В э́той ста́дии о́рганы достига́ют наибо́льшего относи́тельного разви́тия.

   достига́ть, дости́гнуть/дости́чь (+ gen.) = *to reach, achieve;* **относи́тельный** = *relative.*

5. Э́та гру́ппа веще́ств регули́рует тонча́йшие синтети́ческие биохими́ческие реа́кции.

6. В 3-ей генера́ции образова́лось лишь немно́гим ме́ньше семя́н по сравне́нию с контро́льными расте́ниями.

   3-ей is an abbreviation of **тре́тьей** *third;* **лишь** = *only;* **немно́гим** (+ comp.) = *a little, a few . . . .* (here *a few less*); **семя́н** is gen. pl. of **се́мя** *seed;* **по сравне́нию** = *in comparison.*

7. Таки́м о́бразом, молоды́е целлюло́зы облада́ют наиме́ньшей одноро́дностью соста́ва, а межледнико́вые наибо́льшей.

облада́ть (+ inst.) = *to possess, to have;* **одноро́дность** = *homogeneity;* **межледнико́вый** = *interglacial.*

8. Осуществля́ется э́то че́рез опти́ческую приспосо́бленность листово́го, точне́е, пигме́нтного аппара́та расте́ния.

осуществля́ть, -ви́ть = *to realise, to bring about;* **че́рез** (+ acc.) = *through, by way of;* **приспосо́бленность** = *adaptation;* **листово́й** —adjective pertaining to **лист** *leaf;* **то́чный** = *precise.*

9. Отклоне́ния изме́ренных да́нных от рассчи́танных наибо́лее заме́тно при выключе́нии всех ламп одновре́менно.

отклоне́ние = *deviation;* **заме́тный** = *noticeable;* **выключе́ние** = *switching off;* **всех** is genitive of **все.**

10. С ро́стом давле́ния ни́же то́чки Кюри́ диэлектри́ческая проница́емость уменьша́ется, а вы́ше увели́чивается.

рост = *growth;* **давле́ние** = *pressure;* **то́чка** = *point;* **проница́емость** = *penetrability.*

11. Южне́е Ка́менец-Подо́льска изоги́псы —100, —400 м., характеризу́ющие кристалли́ческое основа́ние, изменя́ют своё направле́ние на широ́тное.

южне́е is comparative of **ю́жный** *south;* **основа́ние** = *base, basis;* **изменя́ть, -и́ть** = *to change;* **направле́ние** = *direction;* **широ́тный** = *latitudinal.*

12. О́коло 20 лет наза́д в райо́не Ка́ра-та́у бы́ло откры́то одно́ из крупне́йших месторожде́ний фосфори́тов.

о́коло (+ gen.) = *about;* **наза́д** = *ago;* **открыва́ть, откры́ть** = *to discover;* **кру́пный** = *large;* **месторожде́ние** = *deposit.*

13. Ра́нее, тако́го ти́па месторожде́ния не́ были изве́стны не то́лько в Казахста́не, но и вообще́ на террито́рии СССР.

ра́нее is comparative of **ра́но** *early;* **изве́стный** = *known;* **то́лько** = *only;* **вообще́** = *in general;* **СССР**[1] = U.S.S.R.

[1]Pronounced **эсэсэсэ́р.**

14. Наибо́льшая акти́вность катала́зы наблюда́ется в коацерва́тах при 43°, а в бу́ферном раство́ре катала́за акти́внее всего́ при 37°.

наблюда́ть = *to observe.*

15. Акти́вностьферме́нта в бу́ферном раство́ре во всех слу́чаях вы́ше, чем в коацерва́тах и коацерва́тных ка́плях.

ка́пля = *drop.*

16. Четвёртая зо́на, лежа́щая бли́же к по́люсу дипо́ля, мо́жет быть вы́черчена так же, как и три бо́лее ю́жные зо́ны.

лежа́ть = *to lie;* **мо́жет быть** = *may be;* **вычё́рчивать, вы́чертить** = *to trace;* **так же, как** = *just as, in the same way as.*

17. Из рис. 1 ви́дно, что на изохро́нах-спира́лях от 12 до 17 час. и от 04 до 08 час. о́бласть А должна́ занима́ть всё бо́лее и бо́лее се́верное положе́ние.

ви́дно = *visible, it can be seen;* **о́бласть** (*f.*) = *region;* **занима́ть, заня́ть** = *to occupy;* **всё**—see sentence 3 above ; **положе́ние** = *position.*

18. Кре́мний в двойно́й систе́ме Cu — Si слабе́е повыша́ет жаропро́чность твёрдого раство́ра, чем ни́кель в двойно́й систе́ме Cu — Ni.

кре́мний = *silicon;* **двойно́й** = *double;* **сла́бый** = *weak;* **повыша́ть, повы́сить** = *to raise.*

19. Сравне́ние позволя́ет установи́ть, что во второ́м слу́чае углеро́д бо́лее интенси́вно „оттеснён" к грани́цам ноля́, чем в пе́рвом.

устана́вливать, установи́ть = *to establish;* **оттесня́ть, -и́ть** = *to force back;* **грани́ца** = *border;* **ноль** (*m.*) = *zero.*

20. Ка́жется вероя́тным, что перестро́йка биохими́ческих проце́ссов внутри́ расте́ний позволя́ет полне́е испо́льзовать эне́ргию со́лнца.

ка́жется = *it seems;* **вероя́тный** = *probable;* **перестро́йка** = *rebuilding, reorganisation;* **внутри́** (+ gen.) = *within;* **по́лный** = *full;* **испо́льзовать** = *to use.*

17

PARTICIPLES

Three participles have been introduced in previous chapters (11, 12 and 13). Three more participles remain to be considered.

Past Active Participle (Declinable Type)

The past active participle, like the past tense, may be imperfective or perfective. The meaning of the imperfective form is that the action denoted by the participle was being performed by the thing or person delimited by the participle. It expresses, therefore, the idea common to the words italicised in the following English sentences:

We easily overcame the difficulties *arising* from time to time in this investigation.

It was noticeable that the substances *passing* through the tubes condensed rapidly.

Particles *issuing* with low velocity were repulsed from the metal.

This participle is limited to sentences which relate to the past, whereas the present active participle is not so limited: in spite of its name it may occur in sentences which refer to the past, present or future (see Chapter 12). For this reason the past active participle is much less common than the present active participle.

The meaning of the perfective form of the past active participle of the declinable type is that the action denoted by the participle has been performed by the thing or person delimited by the participle. It expresses, therefore, the idea common to the words or phrases italicised in the following English sentences:

We easily overcame the difficulties *which had arisen.*

The particles *which had issued* with low velocity were repulsed from the metal.

The particles *which have issued* with low velocity are repulsed from the metal.

The particles *which have issued* with low velocity will be repulsed from the metal.

The last three examples make it clear that the perfective form of this past participle, in spite of the name given to it here, is not limited to sentences in which the main verb is in the past tense—the point to notice is that the action denoted by the participle has been completed before the action denoted by the main verb.

The marker of this participle (imperfective and perfective) is non-final: it consists of **-вш-** (which occurs after vowels) or **-ш-** (which occurs after consonants) and is followed by adjectival endings. Here are some examples:

Infinitive	*Meaning*	*Past tense*	*Past active participle*
чита́ть	*to read*	**чита́л**	**чита́вший**
анализи́ровать	*to analyse*	**анализи́ровал**	**анализи́ровавший**
проанализи́ровать		**проанализи́ровал**	**проанализи́ровавший**
унести́	*to carry off*	**унёс**	**унёсший**
выходи́ть	*to come out*	**выходи́л**	**выходи́вший**
переводи́ть	*to translate*	**переводи́л**	**переводи́вший**
перевести́		**перевёл**	**переве́дший**
производи́ть	*to produce*	**производи́л**	**производи́вший**
произвести́		**произвёл**	**произве́дший**

Notice that **переве́дший** and **произве́дший** show the **д** which is found in the future perfective tenses of **переведу́**, etc., **произведу́**, etc. This is in general the case with verbs which have **д** or **т** in their present (or future perfective) tense but not in their past tense.

The verb **идти́** and its (perfective) compounds form this participle from a different root. Thus:

Infinitive	*Meaning*	*Past tense*	*Past active participle*
идти́	*to be going*	**шёл**	**ше́дший**
вы́йти	*to come out*	**вы́шел**	**вы́шедший**
пройти́	*to pass through*	**прошёл**	**проше́дший**

We may now illustrate the usage of this participle by giving the Russian equivalents of the English sentences quoted above.

Imperfective

Мы легко́ преодоле́ли затрудне́ния, возника́вшие вре́мя от вре́мени при э́том иссле́довании.

Замéтно бы́ло, что веществá, проходи́вшие по трýбкам, бы́стро сгущáлись.

Части́цы, выходи́вшие с ни́зкой скóростью, оттáлкивались от метáлла.

Perfective

Мы легкó преодолéли возни́кшие затруднéния.

Части́цы, вы́шедшие с ни́зкой скóростью, оттолкнýлись от метáлла.

Части́цы, вы́шедшие с ни́зкой скóростью, отталкивáются от метáлла.

Части́цы, вы́шедшие с ни́зкой скóростью, оттолкнýтся от метáлла.

Indeclinable Past Active Participle

Like its declinable counterpart, this participle may be imperfective or perfective and its meaning is identical with that of the declinable past active participle. Like the indeclinable present participle, however, it can refer only to the subject of the sentence or clause in which it occurs. The imperfective form is not very common, the present active participle being used instead.

There are two sets of markers for this participle : (1) final **-в** (or **-вши,** which is less common) and **-ши** ; (2) **-а** and **-я.** The former set is found with imperfective and perfective forms, the latter set only with perfective forms. The latter markers are, of course, identical with the markers of the indeclinable *present* participle but, since they are associated only with perfective forms and the present participle markers cannot be associated with perfective forms, confusion is not likely to arise. Here are some examples of imperfective and perfective forms of this participle :

	Infinitive	*Meaning*	*Indeclinable past active participle*
Impfv.	**читáть**	*to read*	**читáв(ши)**
,,	**анализи́ровать**	*to analyse*	**анализи́ровав(ши)**
Pfv.	**прочитáть**	*to read*	**прочитáв**
,,	**проанализи́ровать**	*to analyse*	**проанализи́ровав**
,,	**заперéть**	*to lock*	**зáперши/заперéв**
,,	**унести́**	*to carry off*	**унеся́**
,,	**перевести́**	*to translate*	**переведя́**
,,	**вы́йти**	*to come out*	**вы́йдя**
,,	**пройти́**	*to pass through*	**пройдя́**

The following sentences illustrate the usage of this participle:

(*a*) **Анализи́ровав (Анализи́руя) вещество́, мы бы́ли убеждены́,**[1] **в том, что**[2] **оно́ не металли́ческое.**
While analysing the substance, we were convinced that it was non-metallic.

(*b*) **Проанализи́ровав вещество́, мы убеди́лись, что оно́ не металли́ческое.**
Having analysed the substance, we became convinced that it was non-metallic.

(*c*) **Пройдя́ по аппара́ту, жи́дкость пото́м подверга́ется центрифуги́рованию.**
Having passed through the apparatus, the liquid is then subjected to centrifuging.

(*d*) **Живо́тное, унеся́ добы́чу, не сра́зу пожира́ет её.**
The animal, having carried off its prey, does not devour it at once.

(*e*) **Вы́йдя из тру́бок вещество́ бы́стро засты́нет.**
Having issued from the tubes, the substance will rapidly harden.

[1] Past passive participle, short form, plural, of **убежда́ть, убеди́ть** *to convince.*
[2] Notice the construction, equivalent to *were convinced of the fact that.*

Present Passive Participle

The meaning of this declinable participle is that the action it denotes is being performed on the thing or person delimited by it at the time to which the sentence relates. Whereas the past passive participle denotes a completed action and is therefore perfective, the present passive participle implies that the action is still going on at the time of the main action, be it past, present or future. It expresses, therefore, the idea common to the words or phrases italicised in the following English sentences:

The liquid (*which is*) *being analysed* is undoubtedly alkaline.

We were unable to find the *desired* relationship (i.e. which was 'being desired' at that time).

The *ejected* particles (i.e. which are 'being ejected') will have low velocity.

The process *being investigated* turned out to be adiabatic.

The marker of this participle is non-final and consists of the letter **м** (preceded by **е** or **и**), which is followed by adjectival endings. This participle, therefore, looks like the 1st person plural of the present tense endowed with adjectival endings. Thus:

Infinitive	*Meaning*	*1st person plural present tense*	*Present passive particle*
чита́ть	*to read*	**чита́ем**	**чита́емый**
жела́ть	*to desire*	**жела́ем**	**жела́емый**
анализи́ровать	*to analyse*	**анализи́руем**	**анализи́руемый**
выделя́ть	*to secrete*	**выделя́ем**	**выделя́емый**
вводи́ть	*to introduce*	**вво́дим**	**вводи́мый**

The Russian equivalent of the English sentences quoted above would be:

> **Нет сомне́ния, что[1] анализи́руемая жи́дкость щелочна́я.**
> **Мы не могли́ найти́ жела́емое соотноше́ние.**
> **Выта́лкиваемые части́цы бу́дут владе́ть[2] ни́зкой ско́ростью.**
> **Иссле́дуемый проце́сс оказа́лся адиабати́ческим.**

[1] *There is no doubt that . . .*
[2] *Possess, own;* governs instrumental case.

This participle also occurs in the short form, e.g. **чита́ем, чита́ема, чита́емо, чита́емы.**

Since this participle is passive in meaning it is normally formed only from transitive verbs (i.e. verbs which denote the performance of an action on something or somebody and govern the accusative case). A few examples of this participle have, however, been formed from intransitive verbs (i.e. verbs which do not govern the accusative case), e.g. **предше́ствуемый** (from **предше́ствовать** *to precede*, governing the dative case), **угрожа́емый** (from **угрожа́ть** *to threaten*, also governing the dative case).

From participles of this type nouns are formed by means of the suffix **-ость,** e.g. **непроница́емость** *impenetrability* (cp. **проница́ть** *to pierce, penetrate*). Such nouns are fairly widely used in technical literature.

Reflexive Participles

Active participles may be reflexive in form. Such participles are usually derived only from transitive verbs or from verbs which are 'formally' (i.e. permanently) reflexive. The following are examples of reflexive participles:

Infinitive	*Meaning*	*Participle*	*Meaning*
нести́сь / **нести́сь**	*to be carried* / *to sweep along*	**несу́щийся** (pres. act.) **неся́сь** (pres. act. indecl.)	*being carried, sweeping along*
боя́ться	*to fear*	**боя́сь** (pres. act., indecl.)	*fearing*
произво-ди́ться	*to be produced*	**производи́вшийся** (past act., impfv.)	(*being*) *produced*
соедини́ться	*to be joined*	**соедини́вшийся** (past act., pfv.)	(*having been*) *joined*
унести́сь	*to be carried off*	**унеся́сь** (past act., pfv., indecl.)	(*having been*) *carried off*
отверну́ться	*to turn away*	**отверну́вшись** (past act., pfv., indecl.)	*having turned away, turning away*

Exercise 29

Translate into English:

1. Образова́вшийся оса́док был отделён центрифуги́рованием.

   оса́док = *deposit;* **отделя́ть, -и́ть** = *to separate.*

2. Аналоги́чные да́нные полу́чены та́кже Е. П. Панфи́ловой, изуча́вшей ко́жу ягня́т.

   изуча́ть, изучи́ть = *to study;* **ко́жа** = *skin, hide;* **ягня́т** is genitive plural of **ягнёнок** *lamb*, which has nominative plural **ягня́та.**

3. В. О. Клер, изуча́вший гистологи́ческое строе́ние ко́жи крыс при дли́тельном голода́нии, установи́л, что це́лостность ко́жи, как о́ргана, сохраня́ется.

   кры́са = *rat;* **дли́тельный** = *prolonged;* **голода́ние** = *fasting, starving;* **це́лостность** = *wholeness, entirety;* **сохраня́ть, -и́ть** = *to preserve.*

4. Ацетиле́н подава́лся из балло́на с регули́руемой ско́ростью.

   подава́ть, пода́ть = *to serve, deliver;* **балло́н** = *gas-cylinder, gas-container;* **регули́ровать** = *to regulate.*

5. Предполага́емое схемати́чное расположе́ние зо́ны А в це́лом представлено на рис. 3.

   предполага́ть, -ложи́ть = *to (pre)suppose, to conjecture;* **расположе́ние** = *distribution;* **в це́лом** = *as a whole;* **представля́ть, -вить** = *to present.*

6. Осо́бое значе́ние име́ют предлага́емые магни́тные систе́мы для микротро́нов.

   осо́бый = *special, particular;* **предлага́ть, -ложи́ть** = *to propose, suggest.*

7. Примене́ние систе́мы рассма́триваемого ти́па позво́лит значи́тельно уменьши́ть расстоя́ние ме́жду по́люсами микротро́нного магни́та.

   примене́ние = *application;* **рассма́тривать, рассмотре́ть** = *to examine;* **значи́тельно** = *considerably;* **расстоя́ние** = *distance;* **ме́жду** (+ inst.) = *between.*

8. На рис. 1 пока́зана систе́ма, состоя́щая из пяти́ после́довательно соединённых ламп, кото́рая была́ испо́льзована для обнару́жения и иссле́дования опи́санного явле́ния.

   пока́зывать, показа́ть = *to show;* **состоя́ть из** = *to consist of;* **пяти́**—genitive of **пять**; **после́довательно** = *successively, in sequence;* **соединя́ть, -и́ть** = *to join, link;* **испо́льзовать** = *to use;* **обнару́жение** = *discovery;* **опи́сывать, описа́ть** = *to describe.*

9. Объясне́ние э́тому фа́кту сле́дует иска́ть в фа́зовом соста́ве рассма́триваемого спла́ва.

   объясне́ние = *explanation;* **иска́ть** = *to seek;* **фа́зовый**—adjective pertaining to **фа́за**; **соста́в** = *composition;* **сплав** = *alloy.*

10. Соста́в коне́чного проду́кта рассчи́тывался по объёму вы́делившегося га́за.

    коне́чный = *final, end;* **рассчи́тывать, рассчита́ть** = *to calculate;* **по** here = *from;* **объём** = *volume;* **выделя́ть, -ить** = *to secrete, give off.*

11. Ацета́т ко́бальта, применя́вшийся в ка́честве инициа́тора автоокисле́ния, дополни́тельной очи́стке не подверга́лся.

    применя́ть, -и́ть = *to apply, use;* **в ка́честве** = *as;* **авто-** = *auto-, self;* **окисле́ние** = *oxidisation;* **дополни́тельный** = *supplementary;* **очи́стка** = *cleansing;* **подверга́ть, -гнуть** = *to subject to* (+ dat.).

12. Раствори́мость ни́келя и кре́мния в ме́ди си́льно уменьша́ется с пониже́нием температу́ры.

    раствори́мость = *solubility;* **кре́мний** = *silicon;* **медь** (*f.*) = *copper;* **си́льно** = *strongly, considerably;* **пониже́ние** = *lowering, drop.*

13. Как изве́стно (парадо́кс Даламбе́ра), те́ло при движе́нии в идеа́льной несжима́емой жи́дкости не испы́тывает сопротивле́ния.

    как изве́стно = *as is known;* **движе́ние** = *movement;* **сжима́ть, сжать** = *to compress;* **испы́тывать** = *to experience, undergo;* **сопротивле́ние** = *resistance.*

14. Не исключенó, что наблюдáемые разли́чия мóгут быть свя́заны с изменéниями в секрéции бактéрией белкá в культурáльную средý.

исключáть, -и́ть = *to exclude;* **наблюдáть** = *to observe;* **разли́чие** = *difference;* **свя́зывать, связáть** = *to connect;* **изменéние** = *change;* **белóк** = *albumen;* **средá** = *medium* (N.B. **в** + acc. = *into*).

15. Изучáя механи́змы разви́тия интоксикáции при разли́чных заболевáниях, А. Д. Сперáнский и егó сотрýдники ужé давнó отмéтили óчень интерéсное явлéние.

изучáть, -и́ть = *to study;* **разви́тие** = *development;* **заболевáние** = *illness, disease;* **сотрýдник** = *collaborator ;* **ужé давнó** = *a long time ago;* **отмечáть, отмéтить** = *to note.*

16. Проникáя в центрáльную нéрвную систéму, токси́н окáзывает своё патогéнное дéйствие на жи́зненно-вáжные цéнтры вы́сших отдéлов нéрвной систéмы.

проникáть, прони́кнуть = *to penetrate;* **окáзывать, оказáть** = *to exert;* **дéйствие** = *action;* **жи́зненно-вáжный** = ' *life-important,*' i.e. *vital;* **отдéл** = *section.*

17. Так назывáемая óбщая интоксикáция органи́зма не всегдá действи́тельно свя́зана с циркуля́цией в органи́зме тогó и́ли инóго токси́на.

так назывáемый = *so-called;* **óбщий** = *general;* **всегдá** = *always;* **действи́тельно** = *actually;* **инóй** = *other,*—**тогó или инóго** = *of one or the other, some . . . or other.*

18. Применéние предлагáемых магни́тных систéм с соприкасáющимися траектóриями ускоря́емых части́ц в циклотрóнах позвóлит замени́ть дуáнты небольши́м ускоря́ющим элемéнтом, располóженным вне магни́тного пóля.

предлагáть, -ложи́ть = *to propose;* **соприкасáться, соприкоснýться** = *to touch, to be adjacent;* **ускоря́ть, -ить** = *to accelerate;* **заменя́ть, -и́ть** = *to replace;* **вне** (+ gen.) = *outside.*

19. Числó возмóжных резонáнсов, спосóбных раскачáть бетатрóнные колебáния, в предлагáемой магни́тной систéме горáздо меньше, чем в систéмах ти́па Тóмаса.

числó = *number;* **возмóжный** = *possible;* **спосóбный** = *capable;* **раскáчивать, раскачáть** = *to swing;* **колебáние** = *oscillation;* **горáздо мéньше** = *much smaller.*

20. Морфологи́ческие изменéния, возни́кшие в индивидуáльном разви́тии растéний, соглáсно проведённым óпытам, мóгут передавáться по наслéдству.

возникáть, возни́кнуть = *to arise* (many verbs with infinitive in **-нуть** have the past active participle without the syllable **-ну-**); **соглáсно** (+ dat.) = *according to;* **проведённый** is past passive participle of **провестѝ** = *carried out;* **передава́ть, -да́ть** = *to transfer, transmit;* **насле́дство** = *inheritance, heritage;* **мо́гут передава́ться по насле́дству** = *may be transmitted by way of heredity, may be transmitted from one generation to another.*

21. Получи́вший в после́дние го́ды дово́льно широ́кое примене́ние ме́тод прямо́го микроскопи́рования на мембра́нных ультрафи́лтрах дал возмо́жность получи́ть представле́ние о населённости микрооргани́змов ря́да море́й.

после́дний = *last, latter;* **дово́льно** = *fairly;* **широ́кий** = *wide;* **прямо́й** = *direct;* **возмо́жность** = *possibility;* **представле́ние** = *concept, idea;* **населённость** = *population* (literally '*populatedness*'); **ряд** = *series.*

22. Обнару́женную зави́симость адсо́рбции катио́нов от потенциа́ла пла́тины мо́жно объясни́ть, учи́тывая специфи́ческую адсо́рбцию анио́нов.

обнару́живать, обнару́жить = *to discover;* **зави́симость** = *dependence;* **объясня́ть, -и́ть** = *to explain;* **учи́тывать, уче́сть** = *to take into account.*

23. Менеги́ни и Дельви́че, а та́кже Ко́ммонер и др., изуча́вшие э́тот вопро́с с по́мощью азо́та N^{15}, счита́ют, что для построе́ния ви́руса норма́льные белки́ кле́тки не испо́льзуются.

вопро́с = *question;* **по́мощь** (*f.*) = *help;* **счита́ть** = *to consider;* **построе́ние** = *construction, building-up;* **кле́тка** = *cell.*

24. Иде́я „опти́ческой приспособля́емости" расте́ний, вы́двинутая К. А. Тимиря́зевым, подтверждённая и разраба́тываемая, в ча́стности, астробота́никой, послужи́л исхо́дным моме́нтом для организа́ции и осуществле́ния иссле́дований опти́ческих свойств расте́ний, произраста́ющих в разли́чных температу́рных усло́виях во́здуха и по́чвы с це́лью установле́ния закономе́рности в восприя́тии све́та расте́ниями, воспи́тываемыми при ре́зко отлича́ющихся вне́шних усло́виях.

This sentence illustrates the extent to which participles are used in Russian technical literature. The translation, which should be compared with the orginal, is as follows:

'The idea of the "optical adaptability" of plants, put forward by K. A. Timiryazev, confirmed and elaborated by astrobotanics in particular, has served as the departure point for the organisation and realisation of researches (into) the optical properties of plants growing in various temperature conditions of air and soil, with the object of establishing (some) regularity in the perception[1] of light by plants reared in sharply differing external conditions.'

[1] *sic.*

18

PRONOUNS

A number of pronouns have been used in previous chapters and in Chapter 13 the complete declensions of the 3rd person pronoun were given. The present chapter gives all the other pronouns and the patterns of their case markers. Some of the material will be found to be familiar and much of it will be found to be readily comprehensible because of its similarity to the material given in previous chapters on the noun and adjective. It is not expected that the student should try to absorb all the material in this chapter at once but rather that he should read it through and then, by referring back where necessary to the contents of this chapter, try to do the exercises. Thereafter, he should read through the chapter once again and then use it as a reference chapter.

From the point of view of their case markers, pronouns may be divided into two types: those with markers similar to adjective case markers and those with their own peculiar markers. The former may be called 'adjectival type' and the latter 'non-adjectival type.'

Pronouns of the Non-Adjectival Type

The one most likely to be found in technical literature is the reflexive pronoun. This has no nominative case, since it always expresses the object of a verb or is used with prepositions. It refers *only* to the subject of the sentence or clause. The stem is:

себ-/соб- (cf. **сóбственный** *own*)

and the endings are:

Gen. and acc.	**-я́**
Dat. and prep.	**-é**
Inst.	**-ой** (sometimes **-бю**)

Thus:	Gen., acc.	**себя́**
	Dat., prep.	**себé**
	Inst.	**собóй/собóю**

Examples of the use of the reflexive pronoun are:

Дóктор ви́дел себя в фи́льме. *The doctor saw himself in a film.*
Она ви́дела себя́ в фи́льме. *She saw herself in a film.*

представля́ть, предста́вить себе́	*to imagine, to 'figure to oneself'*
Коме́та тя́нет за собо́й дли́нный хвост.	*A comet trails a long tail behind itself.*

The endings of the 1st person singular pronoun (*I, me*) are like those of the reflexive pronoun:

Nom.	**я**
Gen., acc.	**меня́**
Dat., prep.	**мне**
Inst.	**мной/мно́ю**

Note the change in the stem: **мен-/мн-.**

The pronoun **ты** *thou, you* (sing.) has the same endings and shows the same vowel-change in the stem as does the reflexive pronoun: **ты, тебя́, тебе́, тобо́й/тобо́ю.** It is hardly likely to be found in technical literature.

The 1st and 2nd person plural pronouns have, respectively, the following declension patterns:

	1st person plural (*we*)	*2nd person plural* (*you*)
Nom.	**мы**	**вы**
Gen., acc., prep.	**нас**	**вас**
Dat.	**нам**	**вам**
Inst.	**на́ми**	**ва́ми**

In technical literature the order of frequency of these pronouns is **себя́,** etc., **мы** and **я,** with **вы** occurring only rarely.

Pronouns of the Adjectival Type

The endings of the adjective declension were originally derived from the endings of the pronouns of this type, hence the similarity between the two types of declension pattern. The main difference is in the nominative case.

The pronouns of this type are:

Masc.	*Fem.*	*Neuter*	*Pl.*	
он	**она́**	**оно́**	**они́**	'3rd person': *he, she, it, they*
сам	**сама́**	**само́**	**са́ми**	*self*
э́тот	**э́та**	**э́то**	**э́ти**	*this*
тот	**та**	**то**	**те**	*that*
весь	**вся**	**всё**	**все**	*all*

ваш	**ва́ша**	**ва́ше**	**ва́ши**	*your, yours*
наш	**на́ша**	**на́ше**	**на́ши**	*our, ours*
мой	**моя́**	**моё**	**мои́**	*my, mine*
твой	**твоя́**	**твоё**	**твои́**	*thy, thine*
свой	**своя́**	**своё**	**свои́**	'belonging to subject of verb'
чей	**чья**	**чьё**	**чьи**	*whose*

also **кто** *who* (masc. or fem.)
что *what*

Since all the case-markers have been given in previous chapters it is convenient here merely to set out some typical paradigms (declension patterns) of the pronouns pointing out anomalies and features which are to be noted specially. The paradigms of the 3rd person pronoun have already been given. The remaining adjectival-type pronouns will be described in two groups.

The first group comprises **сам, э́тот, ваш, наш, мой, твой, свой** and **чей.** The declension of **свой,** for example, is as follows:

	Masc.	*Neuter*	*Fem.*	*Plural*
Nom.	**свой**	**своё**	**своя́**	**свои́**
Gen.	**своего́**		**свое́й**	**свои́х**
Dat.	**своему́**		**свое́й**	**свои́м**
Acc.	like nom. or gen.	**своё**	**свою́**	like nom. or gen.
Inst.	**свои́м**		**свое́й**	**свои́ми**
Prep.	**своём**		**свое́й**	**свои́х**

The declension of **э́тот,** which, be it noted, has the element **-от** only in the nominative singular masculine, is as follows:

	Masc.	*Neuter*	*Fem.*	*Plural*
Nom.	**э́тот**	**э́то**	**э́та**	**э́ти**
Gen.	**э́того**		**э́той**	**э́тих**
Dat.	**э́тому**		**э́той**	**э́тим**
Acc.	like nom. or gen.	**э́то**	**э́ту**	like nom. or gen.
Inst.	**э́тим**		**э́той**	**э́тими**
Prep.	**э́том**		**э́той**	**э́тих**

From these two sets of paradigms it is clear that the declensions of pronouns of this group are identical with the declensions of adjectives, with the exception of the nominative and, in part, the accusative. The nominative markers are like those of nouns or short forms of adjectives and the accusative feminine markers are like those of nouns (cf. **ли́нию, фа́зу,** etc.). These feminine accusative markers are typical of all the adjectival-type pronouns, whichever group they belong to. The pronoun **сам,** however, has an anomalous form **самоё,** which is more common than **самý.** The pronoun **чей** has the distinctive feature that the **е** is replaced in all other forms by **ь,** thus: **чьегó** (gen. sing. masc. and neuter), **чью** (acc. sing. fem.), **чьúми** (inst. plural), etc.

The second group of adjectival type pronouns comprises **тот, весь, кто** and **что.** The declension of **тот,** which has the element **-от** only in the nominative singular masculine, is as follows:

	Masc.	*Neuter*	*Fem.*	*Plural*
Nom.	**тот**	**то**	**та**	**те**
Gen.	**тогó**		**той**	**тех**
Dat.	**томý**		**той**	**тем**
Acc.	like nom. or gen.	**то**	**ту**	like nom. or gen.
Inst.	**тем**		**той**	**тéми**
Prep.	**том**		**той**	**тех**

Note the letter **е** in certain cases where pronouns of the first group have **и.** The pronoun **весь** is declined in a similar way, the **е** being a fugitive vowel and the **ь** not being found in the other forms. Thus: **всегó** (gen. sing. masc. and neuter), **всем** (inst. sing. masc. and neuter, and dat. plural), **всем** (prep. sing. masc. and neuter), **всю** (acc. sing. fem.), **всех** (gen. and loc. plural), etc. The pronouns **кто** and **что** have the element **-то** only in the nominative (and accusative of **что**) and have a singular declension only:

Nom.	**кто**	**что**
Gen.	**когó**	**чегó**
Dat.	**комý**	**чемý**
Acc.	**когó**	**что**
Inst.	**кем**	**чем**
Prep.	**ком**	**чём**

Pronominal Adjectives

There are some pronominal adjectives, having markers like those of ordinary adjectives even in the nominative case, such as:

кáждый	*each*
котóрый	*which*
какóй	*what sort of, which*
такóй	*such*
вся́кий	*each, every*
сáмый	*very*

The last in the above list is used in the following way:

са́мый факт, что ...	*the very fact that ...*
с са́мого нача́ла ...	*from the very beginning ...*

and it is also used to form the superlative adjective (see Chapter 16):

са́мая дли́нная ли́ния	*the longest line*
са́мое высо́кое де́рево	*the highest tree*
са́мый плохо́й проводни́к	*the worst conductor*

The word **са́мый** does NOT mean *same*. This is expressed in Russian by the pronoun meaning *that* (**тот, та,** etc.), together with the emphatic particle **же**:[1]

то же расте́ние	*the same plant*
одно́ и то же	*one and the same thing*
с того́ же де́рева	*from the same tree*
с тем же коли́чеством на́трия	*with the same quantity of sodium*

The word **са́мый** may be found with such expressions as these for purposes of emphasis (*the very same*):

в то же са́мое вре́мя	*at the very same time*
в том же са́мом сосу́де	*in the very same vessel*
при той же са́мой фа́зе	*during the very same phase*

[1] Also by **э́тот, э́та,** etc., plus **же.**

COMPOUND PRONOUNS

The pronouns **кто** and **что** form a number of compounds, some of which are of frequent occurrence:

(1)	**кто́-то**	*somebody*
	что́-то	*something*
	кто́-нибудь	*anybody, somebody*
	что́-нибудь	*anything, something*
	кто́-либо	*anybody, somebody*
	что́-либо	*anything, something*

The first element of these words declines, the second element remaining unaltered, e.g.:

кого́-нибудь, че́м-то, кому́-то, чему́-нибудь, ке́м-либо.

(2)	**не́кто**	*somebody*
	не́что	*something*

Notice that the prefix **не** does NOT have negative meaning in these words, which have only a nominative case.

(3) **никтó** *nobody*
ничтó *nothing*

These two words are declined like **кто** and **что** respectively:
никтó, никогó, никомý, etc.
ничтó, ничегó, ничемý, etc.

A peculiar feature of these pronouns is that, when they are used with a preposition, the original parts of the words are separated and the preposition occurs between the parts:

Ни у когó нет карандашá.	*Nobody has a pencil.*
ни с чем	*not with anything, with nothing*
Э́то ни к чемý не пригóдно.	*This is useless for anything,* i.e. *This is of no use whatever.*

The same phenomenon affects the pronominal adjective **никакóй** *no, not any, none*:

Никакóй астронóм никогдá не ви́дел таки́х явлéний.	*No astronomer has ever seen such phenomena.*
Ни в какóм слýчае нельзя́ сказáть э́того.	*In no case can one say this.*
Ни у какóй планéты нет такóй истóрии.	*No planet has such a history.*

Notice that there is no negation of a negative in Russian, as there is in English: no matter how many negative words a sentence or phrase contains, the sentence or phrase remains in general negative.

(4) **нéкого** (gen./acc.), **нéкому** (dat.), etc. *nobody*
нéчего (gen./acc.), **нéчему** (dat.), etc. *nothing*

These are not case forms of the words given under (2) above, as their meaning shows. Their parts are separated when they are used with prepositions (compare (3) above) and they are used only in a special construction, thus:

Нéкого послáть.	*There is nobody to send.*
Нé с кем говори́ть.	*There is nobody to talk to.*
Нéчего дéлать.	*There is nothing to do* (usually in the sense *There's nothing one can do, We'll have to accept it*).
Нé о чём писáть.	*There is nothing to write about.*

If a logical subject is expressed it is used in the dative case:

Мне не́ с кем говори́ть. *I have nobody to talk to.*
Вам не́ о чём писа́ть. *You have nothing to write about.*

EXERCISE 30

State in what case the following pronouns are and what the meaning of each pronoun is:

1.	меня́ вам себя́ себе́ нам	2.	мной на́ми собо́й нас мне	3.	мы вас ва́ми его́ им
4.	ей сама́ своего́	5.	её ему́ тех	6.	кого́ чем э́тому
7.	все́ми ту чего́	8.	на́шим чьих э́ту	9.	вся его́ тем
10.	сами́х им свою́	11.	всю их самоё	12.	свои́ми на́шу чью
13.	кого́-то че́м-нибудь ни у кого́ не́что	14.	не́чего кто́-либо чему́-то ничего́	15.	никако́му не́ с кем кто́-нибудь ни в како́м

EXERCISE 31

Translate into English:

1. Предвари́тельно бы́ло прове́рено, что никако́й режи́м ла́мпы кро́ме тако́го, когда́ име́ет ме́сто ионизация га́за, не изменя́ет изото́пного соста́ва пото́ка рту́ти.

   предвари́тельный = *preliminary;* **проверя́ть, -ить** = *to verify;* **кро́ме** (+ gen.) = *except;* **пото́к** = *flow;* **ртуть** (*f.*) = *mercury.*

2. При э́том мы бу́дем исходи́ть из изве́стных фа́ктов о географи́ческом распределе́нии э́тих явле́ний.

   при э́том = *in this;* **исходи́ть из** = *to proceed from, to take as a basis;* **изве́стный** = *known;* **распределе́ние** = *distribution.*

3. Алкили́рование проводи́лось в реа́кторе, в кото́ром помеща́лся раство́р нафто́ла в 50 мл эти́лового или бути́лового спи́рта и катализа́тор H_3PO_4.

   помеща́ть, помести́ть = *to place.*

4. Одновре́менно с лаборато́рными иссле́дованиями на́ми вели́сь наблюде́ния и непосре́дственно на само́м водоёме.

   одновре́менный = *simultaneous;* **вести́** here = *to conduct;* **непосре́дственный** = *immediate, direct;* **водоём** = *water-basin, reservoir.*

5. Конста́нты, вы́численные по да́нным лаборато́рных иссле́дований, даю́т величи́ны одного́ и того́ же поря́дка.

   вычисля́ть, -ить = *to calculate;* **величина́** = *magnitude, value;* **одного́ и того́ же поря́дка** (gen. of **поря́док**) = *of one and the same order.*

6. Бли́зки ме́жду собо́ю та́кже и конста́нты, вы́численные по да́нным измене́ния содержа́ния кислоро́да.

   бли́зкий = *near;* **измене́ние** = *change, alteration;* **содержа́ние** = *content(s).*

7. Во всех слу́чаях вме́сто 0,1 мл раство́ра лиза́та бра́лся тако́й же объём печёночной катала́зы.

   слу́чай = *case, incident;* **вме́сто** = *instead of;* **брать** = *to take;* **печёночный** = *hepatic, of the liver.*

8. В лу́чшем слу́чае нам удава́лось вы́делить тот и́ли друго́й компоне́нт с уменьшённым содержа́нием второ́го компоне́нта.

   удава́лось, удало́сь, удаётся, уда́стся is a verb used in the 3rd person singular or the neuter past tense only, together with the dative of a noun or pronoun, and the meaning of **нам удава́лось,** for example, is *we succeeded;* **выделя́ть, -ить** = *to isolate.*

9. Расте́ния, для кото́рых светово́й день сокраща́лся, пе́рвое вре́мя отстава́ли в ро́сте и разви́тии, но в дальне́йшем достига́ли бо́льших разме́ров по сравне́нию с те́ми, кото́рые росли́ в усло́виях есте́ственного дня.

   светово́й день = *light-day;* **сокраща́ть, сократи́ть** = *to curtail;* **пе́рвое вре́мя** = *at first;* **отстава́ть** = *to lag behind;* **рост** = *growth;* **в дальне́йшем** = *subsequently;* **разме́р** = *dimension;* **сравне́ние** = *comparison;* **расти́** = *to grow* (past tense is **рос, росла́, росло́, росли́**) ; **есте́ственный** = *natural.*

10. Та́кую же карти́ну наблюда́ла Н. В. Моро́зова-Водяни́цкая в распределе́нии биома́ссы фитопланкто́на в зави́симости от глубины́.

    карти́на = *picture;* **глубина́** = *depth.*

11. По всему́ Чёрному мо́рю в слоя́х 0—50 и 0—200 м биома́сса фитопланкто́на составля́ет 3,6 и 4,8 млн. тонн.

    по всему́ = *throughout;* **слой** = *layer;* **составля́ть** = *to comprise.*

12. В центра́льной и восто́чной частя́х Чёрного мо́ря сре́дняя биома́сса микрооргани́змов колеба́лась приблизи́тельно в тех же преде́лах, что и в се́веро-за́падном райо́не.

восто́чный = *eastern;* **сре́дний** = *average;* **колеба́ться** = *to fluctuate;* **приблизи́тельный** = *approximate;* **преде́л** = *limit;* **что и** = *as;* **се́веро-за́падный** = *north-western.*

13. Ещé до настоя́щего вре́мени под интоксика́цией понима́ют тако́й проце́сс, при кото́ром име́ет ме́сто распростране́ние токси́на по всему́ органи́зму и ча́ще всего́ че́рез кровь.

ещё = *still, even;* **настоя́щий** = *present;* **под** (+ inst.) = *under* (translated here as *by*); **понима́ть, поня́ть** = *to understand;* **распростране́ние** = *expansion, diffusion;* **по** here = *through;* **ча́ще всего́** = *most often;* **че́рез** (+ acc.) = *through, by way of.*

14. Всего́ под о́пытом в э́тих се́риях находи́лось 30 крыс.

всего́, gen. of **всё,** is used in numerical expressions in the sense of *altogether;* **находи́ться** = *to be, to be situated;* **кры́са** = *rat.*

15. Циркули́рующий в крови́ токси́н в усло́виях защи́ты от него́ мо́зга сам по себе́ не мо́жет оказа́ть патоге́нного де́йствия на омыва́емые им о́рганы.

усло́вие = *condition;* **защи́та** = *defence, protection;* **мозг** = *brain;* translate down to **мо́зга** as follows : *The toxin circulating in the blood when the brain is protected from it* (i.e. the toxin) ; **сам по себе́** = *of itself* (' *itself by itself* '); **омыва́ть, омы́ть** = *to wash;* **им** refers to **токси́н.**

16. При э́том, вся́кий раз для ка́ждого усло́вия получа́лись соотве́тсвенно одни́ и те же результа́ты.

раз = *time;* **соотве́тственно** = *correspondingly.*

17. Для выясне́ния хара́ктера зави́симости на́ми был произведён предвари́тельный ка́чественный теорети́ческий её ана́лиз.

выясне́ние = *clarification;* **ка́чественный** = *qualitative;* **её** refers to **зави́симость** (*dependence*).

18. Для прове́рки э́тих положе́ний, вы́веденных на́ми теорети́чески, одно́й из нас бы́ли проведены́ измере́ния ско́рости.

прове́рка = *verification;* **положе́ние** = 1. *position,* 2. *thesis;* **выводи́ть, вы́вести** (past passive participle **вы́веденный**) = *to arrive at, draw;* **одно́й**—instrumental feminine because one of the authors is a woman ; **измере́ние** = *measurement.*

19. Тем са́мым бы́ло пока́зано, что нача́льный каталити́ческий ко́мплекс име́ет непосре́дственное отноше́ние к ка́ждому элемента́рному а́кту ро́ста це́пи.

нача́льный = *initial;* **непосре́дственный** = *immediate;* **отноше́ние** = *relation(ship);* **цепь** (*f.*) = *chain.*

19

NUMERALS AND KINDRED EXPRESSIONS

Much of the material in this chapter is introduced for the first time but the amount to be learnt is not as much as may appear at first sight. The basic number-elements are soon learnt; there remain then such elements as **-кратный, -еро,** a few individual words and some aspects of the syntax of numerals. Bearing in mind that he is merely asked to recognise and understand number-expressions in Russian, as a result of which much of the difficulty associated with them disappears, the student should read this chapter slowly, learning to recognise new words, then perhaps re-read the chapter before attempting the exercise. He should in any case allow himself to refer to this chapter when attempting the exercise and should thereafter use this chapter as a reference-chapter. In reading technical literature he will find that at least the larger numbers are usually written in Arabic symbols, just as they are in English technical literature but he must be prepared to find numbers written out in full. This chapter is therefore essential.

Cardinal Numbers

The cardinal numbers 1 to 10 in Russian are: **оди́н, два, три, четы́ре, пять, шесть, семь, во́семь, де́вять, де́сять.** The element **-надцать** is used to form the 'teens,' thus: **оди́ннадцать** (11), **двена́дцать**[1] (12), **трина́дцать** (13), **пятна́дцать** (15), etc. With two exceptions the tens, from 20 to 90, end in **-дцать** or **-десят,** thus: **два́дцать, три́дцать, со́рок** (40, N.B.!), **пятьдеся́т, шестьдеся́т, се́мьдесят, во́семьдесят, девяно́сто** (90, N.B.!).

The hundreds are: **сто** (100), **две́сти** (200), **три́ста** (300), **четы́реста** (400), thereafter 5 to 9 plus **сот** (genitive plural of **сто**), thus: **пятьсо́т, шестьсо́т,** etc. **Ты́сяча** means 1,000, while the meaning of **миллио́н, миллиа́рд, биллио́н** is self-evident. **Биллио́н** seems to be used largely in the American and French sense (1,000,000,000) though the British and German sense (1,000,000,000,000) is not excluded.

All the above numbers are simple numbers. Compound numbers —21, 45, 358, 596, etc.—consist simply of the appropriate number words written down in sequence, thus: **два́дцать оди́н, со́рок**

[1] Showing the alternative (feminine) form of 2: **две** (see below).

пять, три́ста пятьдеся́т во́семь, пятьсо́т девяно́сто шесть, etc.

All cardinal numbers are declined.

Оди́н is declined like an adjectival-type pronoun, the **и** occurring only in the nominative singular masculine:

	Masc.	*Neuter*	*Fem.*	*Plural*[1]
Nom.	**оди́н**	**одно́**	**одна́**	**одни́**
Gen.	**одного́**		**одно́й**	**одни́х**
Dat.	**одному́**		**одно́й**	**одни́м**
Acc.	like nom. or gen.	**одно́**	**одну́**	like nom. or gen.
Inst.	**одни́м**		**одно́й/о́ю**	**одни́ми**
Prep.	**одно́м**		**одно́й**	**одни́х**

The number 2 has a form **два,** used with masculine and neuter nouns, and a form **две,** used only with feminine nouns. **два, три** and **четы́ре** have a unique declension system, which is, in part, similar to that of adjectival pronouns:

Nom.	**два — две**	**три**	**четы́ре**
Gen.	**двух**	**трёх**	**четырёх**
Dat.	**двум**	**трём**	**четырём**
Acc.	like nom. or gen.	like nom. or gen.	like nom. or gen.
Inst.	**двумя́**	**тремя́**	**четырьмя́**
Prep.	**двух**	**трёх**	**четырёх**

Numbers ending in **-ь** are declined like feminine nouns of the same type (e.g. **кость**):

Nom.	**пять, во́семь,**[2] **пятна́дцать**
Gen., dat., prep.	**пяти́, восьми́,**[2] **пятна́дцати**
Inst.	**пятью́, восьмью́,**[2] **пятна́дцатью**

The numbers 50, 60, 70, 80 decline both parts like feminine nouns ending in the nominative singular in **ь,** thus:

	50	80
Nom.	**пятьдеся́т**	**во́семьдесят**
Gen., dat., prep.	**пяти́десяти**	**восьми́десяти**
Inst.	**пятью́десятью**	**восьмю́десятью**

Со́рок, девяно́сто and **сто** have a marker **а** for all cases other than the nominative/accusative:

[1] Having the meaning *some.*

[2] Note the fugitive vowel **е,** replaced by **ь** in the other cases.

Nom./acc.	**сóрок**	**девянóсто**	**сто**
Gen., dat., inst., prep.	**сорокá**	**девянóста**	**ста**

The number 100, however, also has plural cases, which are like those of a neuter noun ending in the nominative singular in **-о.** Thus:

	200	700
Nom./acc.	**двéсти**	**семьсóт**
Gen.	**двухсóт**	**семисóт**
Dat.	**двумстáм**	**семистáм**
Inst.	**двумястáми**[1]	**семьюстáми**
Prep.	**двухстáх**	**семистáх**

Ты́сяча, миллиáрд, биллиóн are declined exactly like nouns, though there is the anomaly that **ты́сяча** used in purely numerical expressions has the instrumental singular **ты́сячью,** whereas when it is used as a noun it has the instrumental singular **ты́сячей.**

[1] Has a secondary accent or stress on the first element.

Ordinal Numbers

The ordinal numbers 1st to 10th in Russian are **пéрвый** (1st), **вторóй** (2nd), **трéтий** (3rd), **четвёртый, пя́тый, шестóй, седьмóй, восьмóй, девя́тый, деся́тый.**

Note that **седьмóй** (7th) has a **д** which does not appear in the cardinal **семь** (7) and that the nominative forms of 3rd, other than the masculine, are **трéтье** (neuter), **трéтья** (feminine), **трéтьи** (plural).[1]

All these and all the other ordinal numbers in Russian are simply number-adjectives, having adjectival declensions.

The element **-надцат-** plus adjective endings is used to form the ordinals of the teens—**оди́ннадцатый, двенáдцатый,** etc.—and the ordinals of the tens (20 to 90) are: **двадцáтый, тридцáтый, сороковóй, пятидеся́тый, шестидеся́тый, семидеся́тый, восьмидеся́тый, девянóстый.**

The ordinals of the hundreds are: **сóтый** (100th), **двухсóтый** (200th), **трёхсóтый, четырёхсóтый, пятисóтый, шестисóтый,** and so on. The ordinals of the thousands are similar in structure: **ты́сячный, двухты́сячный, трёхты́сячный, пятиты́сячный, шеститы́сячный,** and so on. Higher simple numbers, like **миллиóн,** form their ordinals in **-ный**: **миллиóнный, биллиóнный.**

[1] See Chapter 12.

In compound ordinals only the last element has adjectival form : **два́дцать пе́рвый** (21st), **со́рок пя́тый** (45th), **шестьсо́т девяно́сто восьмо́й** (698th), and so on.

Ordinals may appear in technical literature in the form of Arabic figures with appropriate case-ending attached : **к** 1245**ому** *to the* 1,245*th*, **с** 566**ого** *from the* 566*th*, **в** 1959**ом году́** (or simply **в** 1959 **г.**, or **в** 1959) *in* (*the year*) 1959.

Other Number-Expressions

The following forms are known as ' collectives ' and express the idea ' a group of two . . three . . four . . .etc.' : **дво́е** (2), **тро́е** (3), **че́тверо** (4), **пя́теро, ше́стеро, се́меро, во́сьмеро, де́вятеро, де́сятеро.** They are declined, after the nominative case, like adjectives in the plural :

	2	5
Nom.	**дво́е**	**пя́теро**
Gen.	**двои́х**	**пятеры́х**
Dat.	**двои́м**	**пятеры́м**
Acc.	like nom. or gen.	like nom. or gen.
Inst.	**двои́ми**	**пятеры́ми**
Prep.	**двои́х**	**пятеры́х**

Of these collectives the forms for 2 to 5 (especially 2 and 3) are fairly common, the others much less so.

The following are the forms of the word **оба,** meaning *both* :

	Masc.		*Neuter*	*Fem.*
Nom.	**о́ба**		**о́ба**	**о́бе**
Gen.		**обо́их**		**обе́их**
Dat.		**обо́им**		**обе́им**
Acc.	like nom. or gen.		**о́ба**	like nom. or gen.
Inst.		**обо́ими**		**обе́ими**
Prep.		**обо́их**		**обе́их**

The word **полтора́** (masculine and neuter) means *one and a half* : it has a feminine form **полторы́** and all its cases (masculine, neuter and feminine) after the nominative are identical—**полу́тора.**

The names of fractions are as follows : $\frac{1}{2}$, **полови́на** ; $\frac{1}{3}$, **треть** ; $\frac{1}{4}$, **че́тверть.** All these are feminine nouns and are treated as such. To express smaller fractions the appropriate ordinal number-adjective is used in the feminine form : $\frac{1}{5}$, **одна́ пя́тая** ; $\frac{1}{7}$, **одна́ седьма́я** ; $\frac{1}{8}$, **одна́ восьма́я** ; $\frac{2}{5}$, **две пя́тых** ;[1] $\frac{7}{8}$, **семь восьмы́х** ;[1] $\frac{3}{16}$, **три шестна́дцатых.**[1]

[1] See ' Usage of Numerals ' in this chapter.

Decimal fractions are written with a comma and not with a point: 5,6 = 5.6, 0,25 = 0.25, etc.

There are several words expressing 'indefinite quantity' in Russian. They are: **мнóго** *many, much*; **немнóго** *a few, a little*; **скóлько** *how many, how much*; **стóлько** *so/as many, so/as much*; **нéсколько** *a few, several*; **мáло** *few, little*; **немáло** *much, many.*

Of these the last two have no other case-forms. The others have plural case-forms exactly like those of adjectives:

Nom.	**мнóго**	**нéсколько**
Gen.	**мнóгих**	**нéскольких**
Dat.	**мнóгим**	**нéскольким**
Acc.	like nom. or gen.	like nom. or gen.
Inst.	**мнóгими**	**нéсколькими**
Prep.	**мнóгих**	**нéскольких**

Forms such as **немнóгим** and **(во) мнóгом** are case-forms of the adjectives **немнóгий** (*little*), **мнóгий** (*much*).

The names of the digits are as follows:

единúца	*unity, unit* or *figure* 1
двóйка	*figure* 2
трóйка	,, 3
четвёрка	,, 4
пятёрка	,, 5
шестёрка	,, 6
семёрка	,, 7
восьмёрка	,, 8
девя́тка	,, 9
ноль, нуль (*m.*)	,, 0 or *zero*

The element **-ной** attached to the 'stems' of the collectives means *-fold, -le*:

двойнóй	*twofold, double*
тройнóй	*threefold, triple*
четвернóй	*fourfold, quadruple*
пятернóй	*fivefold, quintuple*
шестернóй	*sixfold, sextuple,* etc.

The words **двоя́кий** and **троя́кий** also occur in the sense of *double* and *triple,* respectively.

Note also the adverbs **вдвóе** *double, twice*; **вдвоём** (*the*) *two* *together* **вдвойнé** *twice, twofold*; **врóе** *three times*; **втроём** (*the*) *three together*; **втройнé** *thrice, threefold.*

'Number of times' is expressed by the appropriate numeral prefix with the element **-кратный** (for adjectives) and **-кратно** (for adverbs):

однокрáтный	**однокрáтно**	*once*
двукрáтный	**двукрáтно**	*twice*
троекрáтный	**троекрáтно**	*thrice*
пятикрáтный	**пятикрáтно**	*five times*
стокрáтный	**стокрáтно**	*hundred times*
многокрáтный	**многокрáтно**	*many times*

The adverbs are also expressed by means of the word **раз**:

(**оди́н**) **раз**	*once*
два рáза	*twice*
пять раз[1]	*five times*

Some basic arithmetical terms are:

умножéние	*multiplication*
умножáть, умнóжить на	*to multiply by*
делéние	*division*
дели́ть, раздели́ть на	*to divide by*
сложéние	*addition*
склáдывать, сложи́ть	*to add up*
вычитáние	*subtraction*
вычитáть, вы́честь	*to subtract*

This last verb has the following parts in the perfective aspect: (future) **вы́чту, вы́чтет,** etc.; (past) **вы́чел, вы́чла,** etc.; (past active participle) **вы́четший**; (past passive participle) **вы́чтенный.**

[1] Gen. pl. of **раз.**

Numeral Prefixes

Most of the numeral prefixes in Russian look like the genitive case of the corresponding cardinal numeral. Here are some examples of words with numeral prefixes:

двухднéвный	*two-day* (cf. **двухты́сячный,** etc.)
трёхчасовóй	*three-hour*
пятилéтка	*five-year plan*
десятилéтний	*ten-year, ten years old*

двадцатидвухле́тний	*22-year, 22 years old*
тридцатитрёхдне́вный	33-*day*

The numeral prefix 2 also appears as **дву-,** as in **двугра́нный** *two-facetted,* **двуро́гий** *two-horned* and as **двóе,** as in **двоежéнство** *bigamy,* **двоему́жие** *biandry.*

The numeral prefix 3 also appears as **тре-,** as in **трезу́бый** *three-toothed,* **трено́гий** *three-legged,* and as **трое-** in a very few words.

Other numeral prefixes are :

одно-	*one-, mono-, uni-*
сто-	*hundred-, centi-*
тысяче-	*thousand-, kilo-*
много-	*many-, multi-, poly-*
пол-/полу	*half-, semi-, demi-, hemi*

The prefix **полу-** remains constant but the prefix **пол-** becomes **полу-** in cases other than the nom., acc. sing., thus :

	Singular		*Plural*	
Nom.	**полчаса́**	*half-an-hour, half-hour*	**получа́сы**	*half-hours*
Gen.	**получа́са**		**получа́сов**	
Dat.	**получа́су**		**получа́сам**	
Acc.	**полчаса́**		**получа́сы**	
Inst.	**получа́сом**		**получа́сами**	
Prep.	**получа́се**		**получа́сах**	

The borrowed numeral prefixes **санти-, кило-, мега-, поли-, геми-,**[1] **деми-** are also found. Note that the numeral prefix **семи-** means *seven-, hepta-,* except in **семиполя́рный** *semi-polar.*

[1] = *hemi-.*

Syntax of Numerical Phrases

The usage of cases in numerical phrases in Russian is somewhat complicated and, though the student of this book is not expected to construct numerical phrases himself, the usage is described below to avoid his being confused when reading Russian.

If the number itself is in the nominative case (or the accusative case, when it is identical with the nominative), the following points are to be observed :

(*a*) With the number **оди́н** and compounds ending in **оди́н** the entire phrase is in the nominative singular—**оди́н электро́н, два́дцать оди́н электро́н, со́рок одна́ тяжёлая части́ца** (41 heavy particles).

(*b*) With the number **два/две, три, четы́ре** and compounds ending in **два/две, три, четы́ре** the noun is in the genitive *singular*, while the adjective is in the nominative or genitive plural—**два а́тома, три электро́на, четы́ре изото́па, два́дцать две тяжёлые части́цы, три́дцать четы́ре лёгких элеме́нта.**

Similarly with **о́ба** and **полтора́—о́ба изото́па, о́ба радиоакти́вных изото́па, полтора́ го́да, полторы́ коро́ткие фа́зы.**

Masculine and neuter adjectives used as nouns are in the genitive plural after these numbers, feminine adjectives used as nouns may be in the genitive or nominative plural—**два учёных** (*two scholars*), **четы́ре насеко́мых** (*four insects*), **две пя́тых** ($\frac{2}{5}$), **три седьмы́е/седьмы́х** ($\frac{3}{7}$).

(*c*) After other numbers (including collectives) both noun and adjective are in the genitive plural—**пять электро́нов, два́дцать шесть тяжёлых части́ц, семь девя́тых** ($\frac{7}{9}$), **де́вять деся́тых** ($\frac{9}{10}$).

If the number itself is in some case other than the nominative, then the entire phrase is in the same case—**с двумя́ электро́нами, от э́тих двадцати́ двух тяжёлых части́ц, к обо́им радиоакти́вным элеме́нтам, с тремя́ пя́тыми** (*with* $\frac{3}{5}$).

This applies also to **оди́н** and compounds ending in **оди́н,** though the entire phrase remains in the singular—**одного́ изото́па, с одни́м изото́пом, двадцати́ одно́й тяжёлой части́цы, с тридцатью́ одни́м лёгким элеме́нтом.**

The rules given in the preceding two paragraphs also apply to **мно́го, немно́го, ско́лько, не́сколько.** They also apply to *two and a half, three and a half,* etc. : **два с полови́ной го́да** *two and a half years,* **пять с полови́ной гра́дусов** *five and a half degrees,* **в тече́ние двух с полови́ной часо́в** *in the course of two and a half hours.*

Exercise 32

Translate into English:

1. Таки́м о́бразом, ма́ксимум жаропро́чности на лучевы́х разре́зах тройно́й систе́мы нахо́дится и́ли в двухфа́зной (а та́кже трёхфа́зной) о́бласти, и́ли в о́бласти ненасы́щенного твёрдого раство́ра.

таки́м о́бразом = *thus;* **жаропро́чность** = *heat-resistance;* **лучево́й** = *radial;* **разре́з** = *section;* **и́ли** = *either, or;* **о́бласть** (*f.*) = *region;* **ненасы́щенный** = *unsaturated;* **раство́р** = *solution.*

2. Э́ти вещества́ ли́бо диамагни́тны, ли́бо облада́ют магни́тным моме́нтом, соотве́тствующим одному́, двум и́ли, ма́ксимум, трём неспа́ренным электро́нам.

   ли́бо . . . ли́бо = *either . . . or;* **облада́ть** (+ inst.) = *to possess, to have;* **соотве́тствовать** (+ dat.) = *to correspond to;* **неспа́ренный** = *unpaired;* translate **ма́ксимум** as *at the most.*

3. В лаборато́рных усло́виях на́ми проводи́лись десятидне́вные инкуба́ции.

   -дневный = *-day.*

4. К концу́ а́вгуста (на двена́дцатые су́тки по́сле устано́вки прибо́ра) наблюда́лась стабилиза́ция.

   коне́ц = *end;* **су́тки** = *day* (i.e. *twenty-four hours*); **устано́вка** = *setting-up;* **прибо́р** = *instrument.*

5. По́сле прогрева́ния при 30° в тече́ние десяти́ мину́т, на́ми бы́ло обнару́жено, что э́тот бело́к распада́ется на два компоне́нта.

   прогрева́ние = *heating;* **в тече́ние** = *in the course of, during, for;* **распада́ться, распа́сться** = *to disintegrate;* **на** here = *into.*

6. Все три полу́ченных таки́м о́бразом оса́дка бы́ли растворены́ в фосфа́тном бу́ферном раство́ре.

   оса́док = *deposit;* **растворя́ть, -и́ть** = *to dissolve.*

7. В результа́те проведённых о́пытов с пятна́дцатью ви́дами расте́ний, представи́телями восьми́ семе́йств, была́ устано́влена така́я связь.

   вид = *species;* **представи́тель** = *representative;* **семе́йство** = *family* **устана́вливать, установи́ть** = *to establish;* **связь** (*f.*) = *connection.*

8. Магни́тная систе́ма таки́х ускори́телей состои́т из трёх и́ли бо́льшего числа́ се́кторов с одноро́дными магни́тными поля́ми.

   ускори́тель (*m.*) = *accelerator;* **состоя́ть из** = *to consist of;* **одноро́дный** = *homogeneous.*

9. Магни́т состои́т из четырёх се́кторов, име́ющих одина́ковую напряжённость магни́тного по́ля.

   име́ть = *to have;* **одина́ковый** = *identical;* **напряжённость** = *intensity.*

10. Измере́ния проводи́лись поочерёдно на ка́ждой из пяти́ ламп и при включе́нии всех ламп после́довательно.

    поочерёдно = *in turn;* **включе́ние** = *switching-on* (**при включе́нии . . .** = *when . . . were switched on*); **после́довательно** = *in succession.*

11. Нельзя́ не отме́тить, что и э́та зо́на по свое́й фо́рме о́чень похо́жа на три бо́лее ю́жные зо́ны, и больша́я ось второ́й зо́ны отклоня́ется к восто́ку ещё бо́льше.

нельзя́ не отме́тить = *it is impossible not to notice;* **похо́жий на** = *like;* **ю́жный** = *southern, southerly;* **ось** = *axis;* **отклоня́ться, -и́ться** = *to deviate;* **восто́к** = *east.*

12. Относи́тельная интенси́вность ка́ждого из э́тих четырёх ма́ксимумов зави́села бы от расположе́ния ста́нции по отноше́нию к четырём кольцевы́м зо́нам А, Б, В и Г.

относи́тельный = *relative;* **зави́сеть** = *to depend;* **расположе́ние** = *disposition;* **по отноше́нию к** = *in relation to;* **кольцево́й** = *annular.*

13. Определе́ние коли́чества водоро́да производи́лось паралле́льно тремя́ ме́тодами.

определе́ние = *definition, determination;* **коли́чество** = *quantity.*

14. Зави́симость соста́ва гидри́да це́рия от температу́ры была́ изу́чена при двух разли́чных режи́мах веде́ния о́пыта.

гидри́д = *hydride;* **це́рий** = *cerium;* the last six words, translated literally, read: *under two different régimes of conduct of* (i.e. *ways of conducting*) *the experiment.*

15. Из приведённых ни́же да́нных ви́дно та́кже, что биома́сса микрооргани́змов в кислоро́дной зо́не Чёрного мо́ря составля́ет приме́рно четвёртую часть биома́ссы фитопланкто́на.

. . . приведённых ни́же = *. . . given below;* **ви́дно** = *it can be seen;* **приме́рно** = *approximately.*

16. Авитамино́з у живо́тных вызыва́лся путём их постано́вки в тече́ние одного́-полу́тора ме́сяцев на специа́льную дие́ту.

живо́тное = *animal;* **вызыва́ть, вы́звать** = *to call forth, to produce;* **путём** = *by means of;* **постано́вка** = *placing;* **одного́-полу́тора** = *one to one-and-a-half months*—Russian usually places the two numbers together in such 'approximate' expressions as *two or three* (**два-три**), *three or four* (**три-четы́ре**), etc. **ме́сяц** = *month.*

17. Иссле́довались гемолити́ческие сво́йства метаболи́тов восьми́ о́рганов у четырёх ви́дов живо́тных.

иссле́довать = *to investigate;* **сво́йство** = *property, attribute.*

18. Реа́кцию прекраща́ли добавле́нием семикра́тного коли́чества абсолю́тного эти́лового спи́рта.

прекраща́ть, прекрати́ть = *to curtail, to stop;* **добавле́ние** = *addition.*

19. Настоя́щее иссле́дование отно́сится к изуче́нию приро́ды фа́зовых превраще́ний в двойны́х металли́ческих спла́вах.

относи́ться к = *to relate to, to refer to, to concern;* **приро́да** = *nature;* **превраще́ние** = *conversion;* **сплав** = *alloy.*

APPENDIX I

NOUN AND ADJECTIVE DECLENSIONS

The following tables of typical noun and adjective declensions are given for purposes of revision and reference:

Masculine Nouns[1]

(*a*) Nominative ending in a consonant letter:

	Singular	*Plural*
Nom.	**áтом** *atom*	**áтомы**
Gen.	**áтома**	**áтомов**
Dat.	**áтому**	**áтомам**
Acc.	**áтом**	**áтомы**
Inst.	**áтомом**	**áтомами**
Prep.	**áтоме**	**áтомах**

(*b*) Nominative ending in **-ь**:[2]

	Singular	*Plural*
Nom.	**зверь** *wild beast*	**звéри**
Gen.	**звéря**	**зверéй**
Dat.	**звéрю**	**зверя́м**
Acc.	**звéря**	**зверéй**
Inst.	**звéрем**	**зверя́ми**
Prep.	**звéре**	**зверя́х**

(*c*) Nominative ending in **-й**:[3]

	Singular	*Plural*
Nom.	**слу́чай** *case*	**слу́чаи**
Gen.	**слу́чая**	**слу́чаев**
Dat.	**слу́чаю**	**слу́чаем**
Acc.	**слу́чай**	**слу́чаи**
Inst.	**слу́чаем**	**слу́чаями**
Prep.	**слу́чае**	**слу́чаях**

[1] Accusative of nouns denoting animate beings is identical with genitive, of those denoting inanimate objects is identical with nominative.

[2] Except **путь** (see below).

[3] Nouns with nom. sing. **-ий** have prep. sing. **-ии**, e.g. **рáдий—рáдии.**

(*d*) With fugitive vowel:

	Singular	*Plural*
Nom.	**день** *day*	**дни**
Gen.	**дня**	**дней**
Dat.	**дню**	**дням**
Acc.	**день**	**дни**
Inst.	**днём**	**дня́ми**
Prep.	**дне**	**днях**

(*e*) With nominative plural in **-ья**:

	Singular	*Plural*
Nom.	**лист** *leaf*	**ли́стья**
Gen.	**ли́ста**	**ли́стьев**
Dat.	**ли́сту**	**ли́стьям**
Acc.	**лист**	**ли́стья**
Inst.	**ли́стом**	**ли́стьями**
Prep.	**ли́сте**	**ли́стьях**

NEUTER NOUNS

(*a*) Nominative ending in **-о**:

	Singular	*Plural*
Nom.	**сло́во** *word*	**слова́**
Gen.	**сло́ва**	**слов**
Dat.	**сло́ву**	**слова́м**
Acc.	**сло́во**	**слова́**
Inst.	**сло́вом**	**слова́ми**
Prep.	**сло́ве**	**слова́х**

(*b*) Nominative ending in **-е**:

	Singular	*Plural*
Nom.	**по́ле** *field*	**поля́**
Gen.	**по́ля**	**поле́й**
Dat.	**по́лю**	**поля́м**
Acc.	**по́ле**	**поля́**
Inst.	**по́лем**	**поля́ми**
Prep.	**по́ле**	**поля́х**

(*c*) Nominative ending in **-ие**:

	Singular	*Plural*
Nom.	**мне́ние** *opinion*	**мне́ния**
Gen.	**мне́ния**	**мне́ний**
Dat.	**мне́нию**	**мне́ниям**
Acc.	**мне́ние**	**мне́ния**
Inst.	**мне́нием**	**мне́ниями**
Prep.	**мне́нии**	**мне́ниях**

(*d*) Nominative ending in **-мя**:[1]

	Singular	*Plural*
Nom.	**вре́мя** *time*	**времена́**
Gen.	**вре́мени**	**времён**
Dat.	**вре́мени**	**времена́м**
Acc.	**вре́мя**	**времена́**
Inst.	**вре́менем**	**времена́ми**
Prep.	**вре́мени**	**времена́х**

[1] Nine other nouns have this type of declension : **бре́мя** *burden*, **вы́мя** *udder*, **зна́мя** *banner*, **и́мя** *name*, **пла́мя** *flame*, **пле́мя** *tribe*, **се́мя** (gen. pl. **семя́н**) *seed*, **стре́мя** *stirrup*, **те́мя** *occiput*.

Feminine Nouns[1]

(*a*) Nominative ending in **-а**:

	Singular	*Plural*
Nom.	**фа́за** *phase*	**фа́зы**
Gen.	**фа́зы**	**фаз**
Dat.	**фа́зе**	**фа́зам**
Acc.	**фа́зу**	**фа́зы**
Inst.	**фа́зой/ою**	**фа́зами**
Prep.	**фа́зе**	**фа́зах**

(*b*) Nominative ending in **-я**:

	Singular	*Plural*
Nom.	**земля́** *earth*	**зе́мли**
Gen.	**земли́**	**земе́ль**
Dat.	**земле́**	**зе́млям**
Acc.	**зе́млю**	**зе́мли**
Inst.	**землёй/ёю**	**зе́млями**
Prep.	**земле́**	**зе́млях**

[1] In the plural only the accusative of nouns denoting animate beings is identical with the genitive, that of nouns denoting inanimate objects is identical with the nominative.

(*c*) Nominative ending in **-ь**:[1]

	Singular	*Plural*
Nom.	**кость** *bone*	**ко́сти**
Gen.	**ко́сти**	**косте́й**
Dat.	**ко́сти**	**костя́м**
Acc.	**кость**	**ко́сти**
Inst.	**ко́стью**	**костя́ми**
Prep.	**ко́сти**	**костя́х**

(*d*) Nominative ending in **/ия**:

	Singular	*Plural*
Nom.	**ли́ния** *line*	**ли́нии**
Gen.	**ли́нии**	**ли́ний**
Dat.	**ли́нии**	**ли́ниям**
Acc.	**ли́нию**	**ли́нии**
Inst.	**ли́нией/ею**	**ли́ниями**
Prep.	**ли́нии**	**ли́ниях**

(*e*) The noun **дочь**:[2]

	Singular	*Plural*
Nom.	**дочь** *daughter*	**до́чери**
Gen.	**до́чери**	**дочере́й**
Dat.	**до́чери**	**дочеря́м**
Acc.	**дочь**	**дочере́й**
Inst.	**до́черью**	**дочерьми́**
Prep.	**до́чери**	**дочеря́х**

[1] The masculine noun **путь** is declined like a feminine noun ending in **ь** in the nominative, with the sole exception that the instrumental singular is **путём.**

[2] **мать** *mother* is declined like **дочь** except for the instrumental plural **матеря́ми.**

ADJECTIVES

(*a*) Masculine and neuter singular:

	'Hard'		'Soft'	
	Masc.	*Neuter*	*Masc.*	*Neuter*
Nom.	**кра́сный** *red*	**кра́сное**	**си́ний** *blue*	**си́нее**
Gen.	**кра́сного**		**си́него**	
Dat.	**кра́сному**		**си́нему**	
Acc.	like nom. or gen.	**кра́сное**	like nom. or gen.	**си́нее**
Inst.	**кра́сным**		**си́ним**	
Prep.	**кра́сном**		**си́нем**	

'Mixed' Type

	Masc.	*Neuter*
Nom.	**широ́кий** *broad*	**широ́кое**
Gen.	**широ́кого**	
Dat.	**широ́кому**	
Acc.	like nom. or gen.	**широ́кое**
Inst.	**широ́ким**	
Prep.	**широ́ком**	

Adjectives with the stress on the end have endings identical with those of **кра́сный** or **широ́кий,** except for the nominative singular masculine, e.g. **второ́й, большо́й.**

(*b*) Feminine singular:

	'Hard'	*'Soft'*
Nom.	**кра́сная**	**си́няя**
Gen.	**кра́сной**	**си́ней**
Dat.	**кра́сной**	**си́ней**
Acc.	**кра́сную**	**си́нюю**
Inst.	**кра́сной/ою**	**си́ней/ею**
Prep.	**кра́сной**	**си́ней**

(*c*) Plural, all genders:

	'Hard'	*'Soft'*
Nom.	**кра́сные**	**си́ние**
Gen.	**кра́сных**	**си́них**
Dat.	**кра́сным**	**си́ним**
Acc.	like nom. or gen.	like nom. or gen.
Inst.	**кра́сными**	**си́ними**
Prep.	**кра́сных**	**си́них**

Adjectives such as **тре́тий** *third* have endings like those of **си́ний,** both singular and plural, except for the nominative singular neuter and feminine and the nominative plural, which are respectively **тре́тье, тре́тья** and **тре́тьи.** The soft sign in these forms occurs in all cases except the nominative singular masculine.

(*d*) Relative adjectives of the type **сéстрин** *sister's* :

	Masc.		*Neuter*	*Feminine*
Nom.	**сéстрин**		**сéстрино**	**сéстрина**
Gen.		**сéстрина**		**сéстриной**
Dat.		**сéстрину**		**сéстриной**
Acc.	like nom. or gen.		**сéстрино**	**сéстрину**
Inst.		**сéстриным**		**сéстриной/ою**
Prep.		**сéстрином**		**сéстриной**

	Plural
Nom.	**сéстрины**
Gen.	**сéстриных**
Dat.	**сéстриным**
Acc.	like nom. or gen.
Inst.	**сéстриными**
Prep.	**сéстриных**

Since all the markers of this type of adjective are like those of nouns or ' ordinary ' adjectives, the recognition of the case-forms should present no difficulty.

APPENDIX II

CONSONANT INTERCHANGES

Forms of what is historically the same root may have different final consonants. Such consonant interchanges are particularly frequent in verb-forms, especially in the present tense. A knowledge of these interchanges will help students to recognise the roots to which various forms belong and may be summed up in the following tables, which are intended for ready reference:

(1)	**б**	interchanges	with	**бл**
	в	,,	,,	**вл**
	м	,,	,,	**мл**
	п	,,	,,	**пл**
	ф	,,	,,	**фл**

Examples:

б ~ бл: **люби́ть** *to love*, **люблю́** *I love*, **влюблённый** *in love*; **гребу́** *I row*, **гре́бля** *rowing*.

в ~ вл: **лови́ть** *to catch*, **ловлю́** *I catch*, **ло́вля** (*act of*) *catching*.

м ~ мл: **корм** *fodder*, **корми́ть** *to feed*, **кормлю́** *I feed*, **рас-ко́рмленный** *fattened up*, **кормле́ние** *feeding*.

п ~ пл: **топи́ть** *to melt*, *heat*, **топлю́** *I heat*, **расто́пленный** *melted*, **отопле́ние** *heating*.

ф ~ фл: **графа́** *column*, **графи́ть** *to rule* (*lines*), **графлю́** *I rule*, **разгра́фленный** *ruled*, **разграфле́ние** *ruling*.

(2)	**с**	interchanges	with	**ш**
	с	,,	,,	**х**
	х	,,	,,	**ш**
	ц	,,	,,	**ч**
	з	,,	,,	**ж**

Examples:

с ~ ш: **носи́ть** *to bear*, **ношу́** *I bear*, **но́ша** *burden*, **произ-носи́ть** *to pronounce*, **произноше́ние** *pronunciation*.

с ~ х: **потряса́ть** *to shake*, **встряхну́ть** *to shake up*.

х ~ ш: **дух** *spirit*, **душа́** *soul*, **духота́** *stuffiness*, **душный** *stuffy*; **мох** *moss*, **мши́стый** (with loss of *o*) *mossy*.

ц ~ ч: **оте́ц** *father*, **оте́ческий** *father's*, **оте́чество** *fatherland*.

з ~ ж: **вози́ть** *to bring* (*in a vehicle*), **вожу́** *I bring*; **ре́зать** *to cut*, **ре́жу** *I cut*; **ма́зать** *to smear*, **ма́жу** *I smear*, **мазь** *grease*.

(3) **г** interchanges with **ж** and **з**
к ,, ,, **ч** and **ц**
д ,, ,, **ж** and **жд**
т ,, ,, **ч** and **щ**

Examples:

г ~ ж ~ з: **друг** *friend*, **дру́жба** *friendship*, **друзья́** *friends*, **дру́жеский** *friendly*.

к ~ ч ~ ц: **рука́** *hand*, **ручно́й** *manual*; **кли́кнуть** *to call*, **клич** *a call*, **восклица́ние** *exclamation*; **о́блик** *countenance*, **ли́чный** *personal*, **лицо́** *face, person*.

д ~ ж ~ жд: **роди́ть** (pfv.) *to give birth to*, **ро́ды** *parturition*, **рожа́ть/рожда́ть** (impfv.) *to give birth to*; **ходи́ть** *to go*, **хожу́** *I go*, **находи́ть** *to find*, **нахожу́** *I find*, **нахожде́ние** *finding*.

т ~ ч ~ щ: **свет** *light*, **свети́ть** *to light*, **свечу́** *I light*, **освеща́ть, освети́ть** *to illuminate*, **освеще́ние** *illumination*, **свеча́** *candle*.

(4) **ск** interchanges with **щ** and **ст**

Examples: **иска́ть** *to seek*, **ищу́** *I seek*, **исте́ц** *plaintiff*.

Note that some consonants appear in more than one interchange. However, any of these interchanging consonants can be a member of only one interchange within any one root.

APPENDIX III

THE FUGITIVE VOWEL

The vowels **о** and **е** appear in some forms of certain roots and suffixes in Russian but not in other forms of the same roots and suffixes. This phenomenon, which in this book has been called the phenomenon of the fugitive vowel, is sometimes known as the phenomenon of the inserted vowel. The following lists, while not being exhaustive, include the commoner examples of the phenomenon:

(1) The Fugitive Vowel **о**

(*a*) Masculine noun suffix **-ок**:[1]

кусо́к — куска́	*piece*	**бело́к — белка́**	*albumen*
обло́мок — обло́мка	*fragment*	**деся́ток — деся́тка**	*ten*
плато́к — платка́	*cloth*		

(*b*) Short form masculine of some adjectives:

вя́зкий — вя́зок	*viscous*	**у́зкий — у́зок**	*narrow*
гла́дкий — гла́док	*smooth*	**лёгкий — лёгок**	*light, easy*
коро́ткий — ко́роток	*short*		

(*c*) Genitive plural of some feminine and neuter nouns:

кишка́ — кишо́к	*gut*	**стекло́ — стёкол**	(*pane of*) *glass*
бе́лка — бе́лок	*squirrel*	**окно́ — о́кон**	*window*
доска́ — досо́к	*board*		

(*d*) Roots:[2]

у́гол — угла́	*corner, angle*	**шов — шва**	*seam, suture*
у́голь — у́гля	*coal, carbon*	**рот — рта**	*mouth*
лоб — лба	*forehead*	**ко́готь — ко́гтя**	*claw*

[1] The **о** of an ending **ок** does not disappear when the ending is not a suffix or when such disappearance would lead to a difficult consonant combination: **уро́к—уро́ка** *lesson*, **чесно́к—чеснока́** *garlic*.

[2] Strictly speaking, the **о** is from a historical point of view part of a suffix in some of these examples but since the suffix is 'fossilised,' i.e. no longer productive, it is convenient here to include it in the root

мох — мха	*moss*	**но́готь — но́гтя**	*nail* (*on finger or toe*)
сон — сна	*sleep*	**ло́коть — ло́ктя**	*elbow*

(*e*) **о** interchanging with zero and **ы** :
называ́ть, назва́ть *to call, name,* **назову́** *I will call, name,* **призы́в** *call, appeal,* **вы́зов** *challenge ;* **посыла́ть, посла́ть**[1] *to send,* **отсыла́ть, отосла́ть**[1] *to send away,* **посо́л** *ambassador* (gen. **посла́**).

(2) The Fugitive Vowel **е**[2]

(*a*) Masculine noun suffixes **-ек** and **-ец** :

мотылёк — мотылька́	*moth, butterfly*	**саме́ц — самца́**	*male*
бара́шек — бара́шка	*young ram*	**оте́ц — отца́**	*father*
вдове́ц — вдовца́	*widower*		

(*b*) Short form masculine of some adjectives :

тя́жкий — тя́жек	*heavy*	**больно́й — бо́лен**	*ill*
го́рький — го́рек	*bitter*	**жи́рный — жи́рен**	*fat, greasy*

(*c*) Genitive plural of some feminine and neuter nouns :

земля́ — земе́ль	*land*	**письмо́ — пи́сем**	*letter*
десна́ — дёсен	*gum* (in mouth)	**ребро́ — рёбер**	*rib*
сосна́ — со́сен	*pine tree*	**ядро́ — я́дер**	*nucleus*
число́ — чи́сел	*number*		

(*d*) Genitive plural of neuter nouns having a suffix **-ко, -це** or **-цо** :

зёрнышко — зёрнышек	*small seed*	**се́рдце — серде́ц**	*heart*
яичко — яичек	*egg ; testicle*	**кольцо́ — коле́ц**	*ring*

(*e*) Roots :[3]

о́кисел — о́кисла	*oxide*	**лёв — льва**	*lion*
пе́пел — пе́пла	*ash*	**лёд — льда**	*ice*
у́зел — узла́	*knot, node ganglion*	**пёс — пса**	*dog*
котёл — котла́	*boiler*	**ве́тер — ве́тра**	*wind*
ка́шель — ка́шля	*cough*	**ка́мень— ка́мня**	*stone*
день — дня	*day*	**мураве́й — муравья́**	*ant*

[1] Compounds of **слать,** which has an anomalous conjugation : **шлю, шлёшь,** etc.

[2] In some words **е** interchanges not with zero but with **ь.**

[3] Note 2, page 166, applies her e*mutatis mutandis*.

Note also the past tense forms : **шёл, шла, шло, шли** from **идти́** *to be going*, **ушёл, ушла́, ушло́, ушли́** from **уйти́** *to go away* (and other compounds) ; **жёг, жгла, жгло, жгли** from **жечь** *to burn*, **сжёг, сожгла́**, etc., from **сжечь** *to burn down* (and other compounds).

(*f*) A variant of this alternation, after vowels, is **е ~ й** :

дво́йка, gen. pl. **дво́ек** *figure* 2 — **наём — на́йма** *hiring*
тро́йка, gen. pl. **тро́ек** *figure* 3 — **заём — за́йма** *loan*

(*g*) **е** interchanging with zero and **о, и** :

вытира́ть, вы́тереть *to wipe out*, **вы́тру** *I will wipe out*, **тре́ние** *friction* (also other compounds of the same root verb) ; **беру́** *I take*, **брать** *to take*, **выбира́ть, вы́брать** *to select*, **вы́бор** *selection, choice* (also other compounds of the same root verb) ; **умира́ть, умере́ть** *to die*, **умрёт** *he will die*, **у́мер** *died*, **мор** *plague*.

APPENDIX IV

TABLE OF VERBS

Verbal roots are particularly subject to modification in the deriving of verb forms, especially with regard to the final consonant of the roots. The patterns of these consonant modifications are given in Appendix II. Most students, however, will find it an additional convenience to have at their disposal a ready-reference list of verb forms and it is for this reason that the following table has been compiled. It is a select list and does not contain verbs which are not likely to be met in technical literature.

In this table Column 1 gives the infinitives, which are imperfective, unless marked with an asterisk, when they are perfective. A hyphen preceding an infinitive form means that the form always occurs with a prefix. Column 2 gives a general indication of the meaning of the infinitive.

Column 3 shows the form of the infinitive in the corresponding compound verbs. All forms in this column, therefore, are to be understood to have a prefix. Nearly all these corresponding forms are imperfective: those which are perfective are marked with an asterisk. Normally, the perfective compounding forms corresponding to the imperfective compounding forms in this column are, of course, the infinitives in Column 1, since a simple verb when prefixed becomes perfective in most instances. A dash in Column 3 means either that the verb in Column 1 forms no compounds or is already compound.

Column 4 gives the present tense (or, in a few instances, the perfective future, which is marked with an asterisk), which is associated with the infinitive in Column 1. Except in the few instances marked with a dagger, these present tense forms may also function as future perfective forms in some compound or other. This column gives in most cases only the 1st and 3rd persons singular: other forms are to be understood to have the same final letter in the root as the 3rd person singular. Anomalous conjugations are given in greater detail.

Column 5 gives the past tense associated with the infinitive in Column 1: masculine form only, unless the masculine form has no -л or forms other than the masculine have a fugitive vowel, when the feminine form is given as a model of the others. These past tenses are imperfective, unless marked with an asterisk, and may also function as past perfective in some compound or other, unless they are marked with a dagger. Column 6 gives the past passive participle. Some of these forms may occur without a prefix as well as with a prefix, though most of them occur only with a prefix. Those marked § in this column are either already compound (prefixed) or do not form compounds. A dash in this column means that the verb has no past passive participle

The stress shifts to **вы-** in all *pfv.* forms with this prefix.

Column 1 is in alphabetical order. Columns 3 to 6 are more or less in alphabetical order, since it is impossible to keep all the columns in strict alphabetical order.

Here are two examples of the usage of the table:

(i) **пересéк**: clearly a past tense masculine of the **л**-less type. Remove the prefix, leaving **-сек.** This is found in Column 5 as the past tense masculine of **сечь** *to chop*. A glance across the line shows that imperfective compounds associated with this are formed in **-секáть** (e.g. **пересекáть**), that the present tense of **сечь** is **секý, сечёт . . . секýт** (and the perfective future is, e.g., **пересекý,** etc.), and that the past passive participle is **(пере-)сечённый.**

(ii) **сни́мем**: clearly a present tense or a future perfective. There is no entry **сним-** under present tense (Column 4), therefore we assume that **с-** is a prefix, remove it and look for **-ниму.** This is found in Column 4 with a reference to the infinitive ***-нять** *to take*, which has a number of future perfective forms, among them **-ниму,** etc. The form **сни́мем,** therefore, is 1st person plural, future perfective of **снять** and means *we shall/let us take away/off* or *we shall/let us take* (*a photograph*) the past tense is **снял** and the past passive participle is **сня́тый.**

It needs only a few such references to fix in the memory entire patterns such as the ones quoted and the student soon begins to recognise verb forms or to work them out for himself without referring to the table.

1 Infinitive (* = Pfv.)	2 Meaning	3 Compounds in (* = Pfv.)	4 Present or Future Perfective (* = Fut. Pfv., † = never Fut. Pfv.)	5 Past Tense (* = Pfv., † = never Pfv.)	6 Past Passive Participle (§ = no compound forms)
берéчь	*guard*	**берегáть**	**берегý, бережёт, берегýт**	**берёг, береглá**	**бережённый**
бить	*strike*	**бивáть**	**бью, бьёт**	**бил**	**бúтый**
брать	*take*	**бирáть**	**берý, берёт**	**брал**	**брáнный**
брить	*shave*	**бривáть**	**брéю, брéет**	**брил**	**брúтый**
везтú	*transport*	**возúть (*везтú)**	**везý, везёт**	**вёз, везлá**	**везённый**
вестú	*lead*	**водúть (*вестú)**	**ведý, ведёт**	**вёл**	**ведённый**
***взять**	*take*	——	**возьмý, возьмёт**	**взял**	**§взя́тый**
вить	*twine*	**вивáть**	**вью, вьёт**	**вил**	**вúтый**
влечь	*draw*	**влекáть**	**влекý, влечёт, влекýт**	**влёк, влеклá**	**влечённый**
водúть	*lead*	**водúть (*вестú)**	**вожý, вóдит**	**водúл**	**ведённый**
возúть	*transport*	**возúть (*везтú)**	**вожý, вóзит**	**возúл**	**везённый**
***-вратúть** (impfv. **вращáть**)	*turn*	——	***-вращý, -вратúт**	***-вратúл**	**-вращённый**
вставáть	*rise*	——	**†встаю́, встаёт**	**†вставáл**	——
***встать**	*rise*	——	***встáну, встáнет**	***встал**	——
***вы́нуть** (impfv. **вынимáть**)	*take out*	——	***вы́ну, *вы́нет**	***вы́нул**	**вы́нутый**
вязáть	*bind*	**вя́зывать**	**вяжý, вя́жет**	**вязáл**	**вя́занный**
вя́нуть	*fade*	**вядáть**	**вя́ну, вя́нет**	**вя́нул** and **вял**	——
гасúть	*extinguish*	**гашáть**	**гашý, гáсит**	**гасúл**	**гáшенный**
гáснуть	*be extinguished*	**гасáть**	**гáсну, гáснет**	**гас, гáсла**	——
глодáть	*gnaw*	**глáдывать**	**гложý, глóжет**	**глодáл**	**глóданный**
гнать	*chase*	**гоня́ть**	**гоню́, гóнит**	**гнал**	**гнáнный**
гнестú	*press*	**гнетáть**	**гнетý, гнетёт**	**(гнёл)**	**гнетённый**
гнить	*rot*	**гнивáть**	**гнию́, гниёт**	**гнил**	——
грестú	*row; dig*	**гребáть**	**гребý, гребёт**	**грёб, греблá**	**гребённый**
давáть	*give*	**давáть**	**†даю́, даёт**	**†давáл**	**дáнный**
***дать**	*give*	***дать**	***дам, дашь, даст, дадúм, дадúте, дадя́т**	***дал**	**дáнный**
двúгать	*move*	**двигáть, *двúгать**	**двúгаю, двúгает** and **движý, двúжет**	**двúгал**	**двúнутый**
***двúнуть**	*move*	***двúнуть**	***двúну, двúнет**	***двúнул**	**двúнутый**
***деть** (impfv. **девáть**)	*put*	**девáть**	***дéну, дéнет**	***дел**	**дéтый**

***достигнуть** *достичь (impfv. **достигать**)	*reach*	——	***достигну, достигнет**	***достиг, достигла** and **достигнул**	§**достигнутый**
драть	*tear, rip*	**дирать**	**деру, дерёт**	**драл**	**дранный**
ездить	*go*	**езжать**	**езжу, ездит**	**ездил**	**езженный**
ехать	*go*	***ехать**	**еду, едет**	**ехал**	
есть	*eat*	**едать**	**ем, ешь, ест, едим, едите, едят**	**ел**	**еденный**
жать	*press*	**жимать**	**жму, жмёт**	**жал**	**жатый**
жать	*reap*	**жинать**	**жну, жнёт**	**жал**	**жатый**
ждать	*wait*	**жидать**	**жду, ждёт**	**ждал**	**жданный**
жечь	*burn*	**жигать**	**жгу, жжёт, жгут**	**жёг, жгла**	**жжённый**
жить	*live*	**живать**	**живу, живёт**	**жил**	**житый**
запереть (impfv. **запирать**)	*lock*	——	***запру, запрёт**	***запер, -ла**	§**запертый**
звать	*call*	**зывать**	**зову, зовёт**	**звал**	**званный**
идти (see also **-йти**)	*go*	**ходить** (***-идти, *-йти**)	**иду, идёт**	**шёл, шла**	
изобрести (impfv. **изобретать**)	*invent*	——	***изобрету, изобретёт**	***изобрёл**	§**изобретённый**
искать	*seek*	**йскивать** (***-искать -ыскать**)	**ищу, ищет**	**искал**	**-йсканный** / **-ысканный**
***-йти** (compounding form of **идти**)	*go*	**ходить**	***-йду, -йдёт**	***-шёл, -шла**	**-йденный**
(see ***-нять**)	'*take*'	——	***-йму, -ймёт**	(see **-нял**)	(see ***-нятый**)
***изъять** (impfv. **изымать**)	*take out*	——	***изыму, изымет**	***изъял**	§**изъятый**
***-казать**	'*show*', etc.	**-казывать**	***-кажу, -кажет**	**-казал**	**-казанный**
класть	*put*	**кладывать** (***ложить**)	†**кладу, кладёт**	†**клал**	**ложенный**
клевать	*peck*	**клёвывать**	**клюю, клюёт**	**клевал**	**клёванный**
ковать	*forge*	**ковывать**	**кую, куёт**	**ковал**	**кованный**
колебать	*agitate*	——	**колеблю, колеблет**	**колебал**	§**поколебленный**
колоть	*pierce*	**калывать**	**колю, колет**	**колол**	**колотый**
***-кратить** (impfv. **-кращать**)	*shorten*	**-кращать**	***-кращу, -кратит**	***-кратил**	**-кращённый**
крыть	*cover*	**крывать**	**крою, кроет**	**крыл**	**крытый**
***лечь** (impfv. **ложиться**)	*lie down*	**легать**	***лягу, ляжет, лягут**	***лёг, легла**	——

лить	*pour*	лива́ть	лью, льёт	лил	ли́тый
*-ложи́ть	*put*	-кла́дывать and -лага́ть	*-ложу́, -ло́жит	*-ложи́л	-ло́женный
ма́зать	*smear*	ма́зывать	ма́жу, ма́жет	ма́зал	ма́занный
моло́ть	*grind*	ма́лывать	мелю́, ме́лет	моло́л	мо́лотый
мочь	*be able*	мога́ть	могу́, мо́жет, мо́гут	мог, могла́	——
мыть	*wash*	мыва́ть	мо́ю, мо́ет	мыл	мы́тый
мять	*crush*	мина́ть	мну, мнёт	мял	мя́тый
*нача́ть (impfv. начина́ть)	*begin*	——	*начну́, начнёт	*на́чал	§на́чатый
нести́ (see *-ня́ть)	*bear*	носи́ть	несу́, несёт *-ниму́, -ни́мет	нёс, несла́	несённый
носи́ть	*bear*	[1]носи́ть (*нести) [2]на́шивать (*носи́ть)	ношу́, но́сит	носи́л	[1]несённый [2]но́шенный
*-ня́ть	*'take'*	-нима́ть	(1) *-иму́, -и́мёт (with до-, на-, за-, пере-, по-, про-, у-) (2) *-ниму́, -ни́мет (with с-, под-, об-, раз-, от-) (3) *-му́, -мет (with при-)	*-нял	-нятый
*отпере́ть (impfv. отпира́ть)	*unlock*	——	*отопру́, отопрёт	*о́тпер, отперла́	о́тпертый
*пасть	*fall*	пада́ть	*паду́, падёт	*пал	——
па́хнуть	*smell*	——	па́хну, па́хнет	па́хнул and пах, па́хла	——
петь	*sing*	пева́ть	пою́, поёт	пел	пе́тый
печь	*bake*	пека́ть	пеку́, печёт, пеку́т	пёк, пекла́	печённый
пить	*drink*	пива́ть	пью, пьёт	пил	пи́тый
писа́ть	*write*	пи́сывать	пишу́, пи́шет	писа́л	пи́санный
пла́вать	*swim*	плыва́ть	пла́ваю, пла́вает	пла́вал	——
плести́	*plait, weave*	плета́ть	плету́, плетёт	плёл, плела́	плетённый
плыть	*swim*	плыва́ть	плову́, пловёт	плыл	——
*поги́бнуть (impfv. погиба́ть)	*perish*	——	*поги́бну, поги́бнет	*поги́б, поги́бла	——
*помо́чь (impfv. помога́ть)	*help*	——	*помогу́, помо́жет, помо́гут	*помо́г, помогла́	——
пря́тать	*hide*	пря́тывать	пря́чу, пря́чет	пря́тал	пря́танный
рвать	*tear*	рыва́ть	рву, рвёт	рвал	рва́нный

ре́зать	*cut*	ре́зывать and реза́ть	ре́жу, ре́жет	ре́зал	ре́занный
рыть	*dig*	рыва́ть	ро́ю, ро́ет	рыл	ры́тый
*сесть (impfv. сади́ться)	*sit down*	седа́ть	*ся́ду, ся́дет	*сел	——
сечь	*chop*	сека́ть	секу́, сечёт, секу́т	сек, секла́	сечённый
*сказа́ть	*say*	ска́зывать	*скажу́, ска́жет	*сказа́л	§ска́занный
слать	*send*	сыла́ть	шлю, шлёт	слал	сла́нный
*сова́ть	*push*	со́вывать	сую́, суёт	сова́л	су́нутый
со́хнуть	*dry up*	сыха́ть	со́хну, со́хнет	сох, со́хла	——
спать	*sleep*	сыпа́ть	сплю, спит	спал	——
*стать (impfv. станови́ться)	*become*	става́ть	*ста́ну, ста́нет	стал	——
стлать	*spread*	стила́ть	стелю́, сте́лет	стлал	стла́нный
стыть	*grow cold*	стыва́ть	сты́ну, сты́нет	стыл	——
*су́нуть	*push*	со́вывать	*су́ну, су́нет	*су́нул	су́нутый
сы́пать	*strew, pour*	сыпа́ть	сы́плю, сы́плет	сы́пал	сы́панный
*сыска́ть (impfv. иска́ть)	*seek out*	——	*сыщу́, сы́щет	*сыска́л	§сы́сканный
тере́ть	*rub*	тира́ть	тру, трёт	тёр, тёрла	тёртый
течь	*flow*	тека́ть	теку́, течёт, теку́т	тёк, текла́	——
узнава́ть }	*recognise,*	——	†узнаю́, узнаёт	†узнава́л }	у́знанный
*узна́ть }	*come to know*	——	*узна́ю, узна́ет	*узна́л }	
умере́ть (impfv. умира́ть)	*die*	——	*умру́, умрёт	*у́мер, умерла́	——
ходи́ть	*go*	{ [1]ходи́ть (*-йти́- идти́) [2]ха́живать (*ходи́ть)	хожу́, хо́дит	ходи́л	[1]-йдённый [2]хо́женный
хоте́ть	*want*	——	хочу́, хо́чешь, хо́чет, хоти́м, хоти́те, хотя́т	хоте́л	——
чеса́ть	*scratch*	чёсывать	чешу́, чёшет	чеса́л	чёсанный
*честь	(various)	чита́ть, чи́тывать	*-чту, -чтёт	*-чёл	-чтённый
*-шиби́ть	'*knock*'	шиба́ть	*-шибу́, -шибёт	*-ши́б, -ши́бла	ши́бленный
(see слать)			шлю, шлёт		
шить	*sew*	шива́ть	шью, шьёт	шил	ши́тый

GENERAL VOCABULARY

The General Vocabulary contains (if only in their basic forms) all the words used in the exercises, whether or not they are given in the individual vocabularies, together with some of the words which occur in the grammatical explanations. Imperfective and perfective pairs of infinitives are given together, the imperfective being placed first. If, however, a verb has only 'specialised' perfectives and no 'general' perfective, then the imperfective only is given, unless the perfective has been used in the exercises, when it is given too. Perfectives used in the exercises are listed separately, with a reference to the imperfective, unless, as often happens, the two infinitives are in immediate alphabetical sequence, in which case they are given as a pair only and not as separate items. In the pairs of imperfective-perfective infinitives such entries as **писáть, на-** are to be read as **писáть, написáть** and such entries as **уменьшáть, -ить** are to be read as **уменьшáть, уменьшить.**

а, *and, but, while*
абсолютный, *absolute*
абсорбировать, *to absorb*
аберрáция, *aberration*
áвгуст, *August*
авитаминóз, *avitaminosis*
авто-, *auto-, self-*
автомáт, *automaton; sub-machine gun*
автоматический, *automatic*
автомобиль (*m.*), *automobile, car*
автоокислéние, *auto-oxidation*
адсорбциóнный, *adsorption* (*adj.*)
адсóрбция, *adsorption*
азóт, *nitrogen*
акадéмия, *academy*
аккумулятор, *accumulator, battery*
акролейн, *acrolein(e), acrylaldehyde*
акт, *act*
активность (*f.*), *activity*
активный, *active*
алкилáт, *alkylate*
алкилирование, *alkylation*
алмáз, *diamond*
áльфа-распáд, *alpha-decay*
áльфа-частица, *alpha-particle*
аммóний, *ammonia*
амплитýда, *amplitude*
ампутировать, *to amputate*
анáлиз, *analysis*
анализировать, про-, *to analyse*
аналогичный, *analogous*
анатóмия, *anatomy*
ангина, *tonsillitis, quinsy*
английский, *English*
анемия, *anaemia*
аниóн, *anion*
анóд, *anode*
антисептический, *antiseptic*

аппара́т, *apparatus, instrument*
аппарату́ра, *apparatus, gear*
асимптоти́ческий, *asymptotic*
астробота́ника, *astrobotanics*
астроно́м, *astronomer*
астроно́мия, *astronomy*
атмосфе́ра, *atmosphere*
а́том, *atom*
атоми́стика, *atomism, atomic theory*
а́томный, *atomic*
атони́я, *atony*
ацета́т, *acetate*
ацетиле́н, *acetylene*
ацето́н, *acetone*

бакели́т, *bakelite*
бактериа́льный, *bacterial*
бактериологи́ческий, *bacteriological*
бактериофа́г, *bacteriophage*
бакте́рия, *bacterium*
баллисти́ческий, *ballistic*
балло́н, *gas-cylinder, gas-container*
ба́рий, *barium*
баци́лла, *bacillus*
без (+ gen.), *without*
бело́к (gen. **белка́**), *albumen*
бе́лый, *white*
бензи́н, *petrol, gasoline*
бензо́л, *benzene, benzol(e)*
бере́чь (берегу́, бережёт . . . берегу́т), *to take care of*
беспозвоно́чный, *invertebrate*
бе́та-распа́д, *beta-decay*
бетатро́нный, *betatron (adj.)*
бе́та-части́ца, *beta-particle*
био́лог, *biologist*
бioма́сса, *biomass*
биохими́ческий, *biochemical*
бить, *to beat, to strike*
благодаря́ (+ dat.), *thanks (to)*
бли́же, *nearer*
бли́зкий, *near*
бо́лее, *more, greater*
боле́знь (*f.*), *disease, illness*
боль (*f.*), *pain*
больно́й, *sick, ill;* as noun = *patient*
бо́льше, *more, greater*
бо́льший, *bigger;* **бо́льшей ча́стью,** *for the most/greater part*
большинство́, *majority*
большо́й, *big*
бомбардирова́ть, *to bombard*
борьба́, *struggle*
боя́ться (+ gen.), *to fear, to be afraid*
брать, взять, *to take*
буд-, stem of the future auxiliary verb (see Chapter 15)
бу́дто бы, *as it were, as if*
бульо́н, *broth, soup*
бути́ловый, *butyl;* **бути́ловый спирт,** *butyl alcohol*
бу́ферный, *buffer (adj.)*
бы, conditional particle (see Chapter 13)
бы́стро, *swiftly*
быстрота́, *rapidity*
бы́стрый, *rapid, fast, swift*
быть, *to be*

в(во) (+ acc. or prep.), *in, into,* etc.
ва́жность (*f.*), *importance*
ва́жный, *important*
вариа́нт, *variant, version*
вариа́ция, *variation*
ва́та, *cotton-wool, wadding*
ватт, *watt*
ваттме́тр, *watt-meter*
вводи́ть, ввести́, *to bring in, to introduce*
ввози́ть, ввезти́, *to import*

веде́ние, *conduct*
везде́, *everywhere*
век, *century*
ве́ко, *eye-lid*
вели́кий, *great*
величина́, *magnitude, size, value, quantity*
вероя́тный, *probable*
ве́рхний, *upper*
вес, *weight;* **уде́льный вес,** *specific gravity*
весе́нний, *spring, vernal*
вести́, *to be leading, to lead, to bring*
весь (*f.* **вся,** *n.* **всё,** *pl.* **все**), *all* (see Chapter 18)
весьма́, *very*
вещество́, *matter, substance*
взаимоде́йствие, *interaction*
взлета́ть, взлете́ть, *to take off*
взять, see **брать**
вид, *species; form, shape; view;* **в виду́,** *in view (of);* **име́ть в виду́,** *to have in mind*
ви́деть, *to see*
ви́дно, *it is clear, it can be seen*
ви́дный, *visible*
ви́рус, *virus*
витами́н, *vitamin*
вить, *to twine*
включе́ние, *switching-on*
вкус, *taste*
вла́га, *moisture*
влить, *to pour in*
влия́ние, *influence*
вме́сто (+ gen.), *instead of*
вне (+ gen.), *outside*
вне́шний, *external*
внима́ние, *attention;* **принима́ть/приня́ть во внима́ние,** *to take into account*
вноси́ть, внести́, *to bring in*
вну́тренний, *internal, inner*
внутри́ (+ gen.), *within, inside*
вода́, *water*
води́ть, *to lead*
водоём, *water-basin, reservoir*
водоро́д, *hydrogen*
водоро́дный, *hydrogen (adj.)*
возвра́тный, *recurring;* **возвра́тный тиф,** *relapsing fever (typhoid)*
во́здух, *air*
во́зле (+ gen.), *by, beside, past*
возмо́жность (*f.*), *possibility;* **по возмо́жности,** *as far, as much, etc., as possible*
возмо́жный, *possible*
возмуще́ние, *disturbance*
возника́ть, возни́кнуть, *to arise*
войти́, see **входи́ть**
волна́, *wave*
волново́й, *wave (adj.)*
вообще́, *in general*
вопро́с, *question*
воро́нка, *funnel*
во́семь, *eight*
воспале́ние, *inflammation*
воспи́тывать, воспита́ть, *to rear, to bring up, to cultivate*
восприя́тие, *perception*
восто́к, *east*
восто́рг, *rapture, delight*
восто́чный, *eastern*
впервы́е, *first, for the first time*
вперёд, *forward, forwards*
врач, *doctor (medical or dental)*
вре́менный, *temporary*
вре́мя (*n.*, gen. **вре́мени**), *time;* **тем вре́менем,** *meanwhile*; **во вре́мя** (+ gen.), *during*
все, *all (pl.)*
всё, *all, everything; (adv.) always, continually;* **всё ещё,** *still;* **всё** + comparative = *more and more . . .*

всегда́, *always*
всего́ (gen. of **всё**), *altogether*
всеми́рный, *universal*
всео́бщий, *general*
всё-таки, *however, though, and yet, nevertheless*
всплеск, *splash, burst*
вспы́шка, *flare*
всю́ду, *everywhere*
вся́кий, *each, any*
вторже́ние, *intrusion, irruption*
второ́й, *second*
вулканизи́рованный, *vulcanised*
входи́ть, войти́, *to enter, to come in, to go in*
вы, *you*
выбира́ть, вы́брать, *to select, to choose*
вы́вести, see **выводи́ть**
вы́вод, *conclusion*
выводи́ть, вы́вести, *to bring out, to draw, to arrive at (conclusion, etc.)*
вы́глядеть, *to look, to seem*
выдвига́ть, вы́двинуть, *to advance, to put/move/bring forward*
выделя́ть, вы́делить, *to distinguish, to isolate, to allot; to secrete*
вызыва́ть, вы́звать, *to call forth, to produce*
вы́йти, see **выходи́ть**
выключе́ние, *switching-off*
вылива́ть, вы́лить, *to pour out*
выноси́ть, вы́нести, *to take out, to bring out*
вы́пить, see **пить**
выполня́ть, вы́полнить, *to carry out*
выража́ть, вы́разить, *to express*
выра́щивать, вы́растить, *to rear, to cultivate*
выска́зывать, вы́сказать, *to express*
высо́кий, *high*
высота́, *height*
вы́сший, *upper, higher, supreme, highest*
вытека́ть, вы́течь, *to flow out, to issue, to exude*
выходи́ть, вы́йти, *to go out, to come out*
вычё́рчивать, вы́чертить, *to trace*
вычисля́ть, вы́числить, *to calculate*
вычища́ть, вы́чистить, *to clean out*
вы́ше, *higher, above*
вышеска́занное, *the above-said*
выясне́ние, *clarification*
выясня́ть, вы́яснить, *to clarify, to examine, to find out*

газ, *gas*
га́зовый, *gaseous, gas (adj.)*
га́снуть, по-, *to go out, to fade*
где, *where*
гексаэ́др, *hexahedron*
ге́лий, *helium*
гемолити́ческий, *haemolitic*
генера́ция, *generation*
гениа́льный, *of genius*
географи́ческий, *geographic(al)*
геометри́ческий, *geometric(al)*
герма́ний, *germanium*
гидри́д, *hydride*
гинеколо́гия, *gynaecology*
гипервитаминиза́ция, *hypervitaminisation*
гистологи́ческий, *histological*
гла́вный, *main, principal;* **гла́вным о́бразом,** *for the most part, principally*

глаз, *eye*
глубина́, *depth*
глюко́за, *glucose*
говори́ть, сказа́ть, *to say, to speak*
год, *year*
голова́, *head*
головно́й, *head* (*adj.*); **головно́й мозг,** *brain, cerebrum*
голода́ние, *fasting, starving*
голубо́й, *blue, sky-blue*
гора́, *mountain*
гора́здо (+ comparative), *much*
горе́ть, *to burn, to be on fire*
гото́вить, при-, *to prepare*
гра́мм, *gramme*
грани́т, *granite*
грани́ца, *border*
графи́т, *graphite*
графи́чески, *graphically; in the form of a graph*
грести́, *to row, to paddle*
греть, *to warm, to heat*
грибо́к (gen. **грибка́**), *fungus*
гру́ппа, *group*
гу́бка, *sponge*
гуммиара́бик, *gum* (*arabic*)
густо́й, *thick, dense*

дава́ть, дать, *to give*
давле́ние, *pressure*
давно́, *long ago*
да́же, *even*
да́лее, *further*; **и так д—,** *and so on*
далеко́, *far*; **далеко́ не,** *far from*
дальне́йший, *further, future;* **в дальне́йшем,** *in the future, subsequently*
да́нный, *given;* **да́нные,** *data*
да́тчик, *transducer*
дать, see **дава́ть**
два (*m.* and *n.*), **две** (*f.*), *two*
две, see **два**
двенадца́тый, *twelfth*
дви́гатель (*m.*), *engine*
дви́гать, дви́нуть, *to move*
движе́ние, *movement*
дви́нуть, see **дви́гать**
двойно́й, *double, twofold*
двухфа́зный, *two-phase*
де́вять, *nine*
дегенера́ция, *degeneration*
де́йствие, *action, influence*
действи́тельно, *actually, in fact*
де́лать, с-, *to do, to make*
дели́тель (*m.*), *divisor*
дендри́т, *dendrite*
день (*m.*, gen. **дня**), *day*
де́рево, *tree*
десо́рбция, *desorption*
десятидне́вный, *ten-day*
де́сять, *ten*
дета́ль (*f.*), *detail, part*
дета́льный, *detailed*
диабе́т, *diabetes*
диамагни́тный, *diamagnetic*
дие́новый, *diene*
дина́мика, *dynamics*
дипо́ль (*m.*), *dipole*
дире́ктор, *director*
диск, *disc*
дистанцио́нный, *distance* (*adj.*), *remote, remote-control*
дистилли́рованный, *distilled*
дифтери́т, *diphtheria*
дифференциа́льный, *differential*
диффу́зия, *diffusion*
диэлектри́ческий, *dielectric*
дие́та, *diet*
длина́, *length*
дли́нный, *long*
дли́тельный, *prolonged*
для (+ gen.), *for;* **для того́, что́бы,** *in order that, in order to*

до (+ gen.), *before, until, to, up to, about;* **до того́ как,** *until*
добавле́ние, *addition*
добавля́ть, доба́вить, *to add*
доводи́ть, довести́, *to bring* (*to*), *to lead, to reduce* (*to*)
дово́льно, *enough, fairly, rather*
до́за, *dose*
дозиме́тр, *dosimeter*
дозиметри́ческий, *dosimetric*
дозиро́вка, *dosage*
дока́зывать, доказа́ть, *to prove, to show*
докла́д, *lecture, paper*
до́ктор, *doctor*
до́лжен (должна́, должно́, должны́), *must, should* (see Chapter 15)
до́ля, *lot, portion, part*
дом, *house, home, building*
до́мна, *blast-furnace*
дополни́тельный, *supplementary*
доста́вка, *delivery, placing*
достига́ть, дости́гнуть (+ gen.) *to achieve, to reach*
досто́йный, *worthy, deserving*
доходи́ть, дойти́, *to go up to, to reach*
друг, *friend* ; *one . . . the other* as in **друг с дру́гом,** *one with the other* ; **друг от дру́га,** *one from the other,* etc.
друго́й, *other*
дуа́нт, *duant*
ду́мать, *to think*
дуть, *to blow*

его́, *him, it; his, its*
еди́нственный, *only, unique*
её, *her, it; hers, its*
е́сли, *if*
есте́ственный, *natural*
есть, съесть, *to eat*
есть, *is, are, there is, there are*
е́хать, *to go* (*in a vehicle*)
ещё, *still, even, yet;* **всё ещё,** *still*

жар, *heat*
жаропро́чность (*f.*), *heat-resistance*
же, emphatic particle ; with **тот, та,** etc. = *the same*
жева́ть, *to chew*
желати́н, *gelatine*
желе́зо, *iron*
же́нщина, *woman*
жечь, *to burn* (transitive verb)
живо́й, *living, live, lively*
живо́тный, *animal* (*adj.*) ; **живо́тное,** *animal* (*n.*)
жи́дкость (*f.*), *liquid*
жи́зненно-ва́жный, *vital*
жизнь (*f.*), *life*
жир, *fat*

за (+ acc. or inst.), *beyond, behind; for; during; in*
заболева́ние, *illness, disease*
зави́симость (*f.*), *dependence*
зави́сеть, *to depend*
зада́ча, *task, problem*
зака́ливать, закали́ть, *to temper*
заключа́ть, заключи́ть, *to conclude*
зако́н, *law*
закономе́рность (*f.*), *regularity, rule; mechanism*
заложи́ть, *to lay*
заменя́ть, замени́ть, *to replace*
заме́тный, *noticeable*
занима́ть, заня́ть, *to occupy*
занима́ться, заня́ться (+ inst.), *to be engaged* (*in*), *to study, to occupy oneself* (*with*)

за́пах, *smell*
заполня́ть, запо́лнить, *to fill (up), to supplement, to make up*
зара́зный, *infectious*
заря́д, *charge*
заставля́ть, заста́вить, *to compel, to make*
затуха́ние, *fading, damping*
захва́тывать, захвати́ть, *to seize, to capture*
защи́та, *defence*
защища́ть, защити́ть, *to protect*
звезда́, *star*
звёздный, *stellar*
здесь, *here*
зелёный, *green*
земля́, *earth, land*
зерка́льный, *mirror (adj.)*
зима́, *winter*
зи́мне-весе́нний, *winter-spring*
зна́ние, *knowledge*
знать, *to know*
значе́ние, *meaning, value*
зна́чит, *means, signifies; so*
значи́тельный, *considerable, significant*
зной, *heat*
зоб, *crop, goitre*
зо́на, *zone*
зонд, *probe*
зо́олог, *zoologist*
зуб, *tooth*

и, *and, too, also;* is sometimes used to emphasise the following word or phrase ; **и . . . и** = *both . . . and*
и́ва, *willow*
игра́ть, *to play*
идеа́льный, *ideal*
иде́я, *idea*
идти́, итти́, *to be going*
из (+ gen.), *out of, from*
избега́ть, избежа́ть (+ gen.), *to avoid*
избира́ть, избра́ть, *to elect*
избы́точный, *surplus (adj.)*
изве́стность (*f.*), *fame, reputation*
изве́стный, *known, well-known; a certain*
излуче́ние, *radiation*
измене́ние, *change, alteration*
изменя́ть, -и́ть, *to change*
измере́ние, *measurement*
измери́тель (*m.*), *measuring instrument, gauge*
измеря́ть, изме́рить, *to measure*
изоги́пс, *isogyps*
изо́гнутый, *curved, bent*
изоли́ровать, *to isolate*
изоме́р, *isomer*
изото́п, *isotope*
изото́пный, *isotope (adj.)*
изохро́н, *isochron*
изуча́ть, -и́ть, *to study*
изуче́ние, *study*
и́ли, *or;* **и́ли . . . и́ли,** *either . . . or*
иллюстри́ровать, про-, *to illustrate*
име́ть, *to have;* **име́ется,** *there is,* **име́ются,** *there are*
иммуните́т, *immunity*
иммуноло́гия, *immunology*
индивидуа́льный, *individual*
инди́го, *indigo*
ине́рция, *inertia*
инициа́тор, *initiator*
инкуба́ция, *incubation*
ино́й, *other, some*
институ́т, *institute*
инструме́нт, *instrument*
интегра́льный, *integral*
интенси́вность (*f.*), *intensivity*

интенси́вный, *intensive*
интерва́л, *interval*
интере́с, *interest*
интере́сный, *interesting*
интересова́ться, за-, (+ inst.), *to be interested* (*in*)
интоксика́ция, *intoxication*
ио́н, *ion*
иониза́ция, *ionisation*
ионизи́ровать, *to ionise*
ио́нный, *ionic*
ионосфе́рный, (*pertaining to the*) *ionosphere*
иска́ть, *to seek*
исключа́ть, -и́ть, *to exclude*
иску́сственный, *artificial*
испо́льзовать, *to use*
испуска́ть, испусти́ть, *to emit*
испы́тывать, испыта́ть, *to experience, to undergo*
иссле́дование, *research, investigation*
иссле́довать, *to investigate*
исто́рия, *history*
исто́чник, *source*
исходи́ть, изойти́ (из), *to issue, to proceed* (*from*)
исхо́дный, *initial;* **исхо́дный моме́нт,** *departure point*
исчеза́ть, исче́знуть, *to disappear*
исчезнове́ние, *disappearance*
исче́знуть, see **исчеза́ть**
итти́, see **идти́**
их, *them; of them; their*(*s*)
ихтиоко́л, *ichthyocol*

к (+ dat.), *to, towards*
ка́жется, see **каза́ться**
каза́ться, *to seem, to appear*
как, *how, as;* **как бы,** *as it were, 'a sort of'*
ка́ждый, *each, every*
ка́лий, *potassium*
ка́льций, *calcium*
ка́пля (gen. pl. **ка́пель**), *drop*
ка́рта, *map*
карти́на, *picture*
Ка́спий, *Caspian*
катала́за, *catalase*
катализа́тор, *catalyst*
каталити́ческий, *catalytic*
катио́н, *cation*
като́д, *cathode*
каучу́к, *rubber, caoutchouc*
каучу́ковый, *rubber* (*adj.*)
ка́чественный, *qualitative*
ка́чество, *quality;* **в ка́честве,** *in the capacity, as*
квадра́т, *square*
ква́нтовый, *quantum* (*adj.*)
ква́рцевый, *quartz* (*adj.*)
кероси́н, *kerosene, paraffin*
кинotéхника, *cinetechnics*
кислоро́д, *oxygen*
кислоро́дный, *oxygenous, oxygen* (*adj.*)
кислота́, *acid*
ки́слый, *acid, sour*
кишка́, *gut, intestine*
класс, *class*
класси́ческий, *classical*
класть, положи́ть, *to put*
клева́ть, клю́нуть, *to peck*
кле́тка (gen. pl. **кле́ток**), *cell*
кни́га, *book*
коагуля́ция, *coagulation*
коацерва́т, *coacervate*
коацерва́тный, *coacervate* (*adj.*)
ко́бальт, *cobalt*
кова́ть, *to forge, to beat, to hammer*
когда́, *when*
когда́-то, *at some time*
ко́жа, *skin*

ко́жный, *skin* (*adj.*), *cutaneous*
колеба́ние, *oscillation*
колеба́ться, по-, *to fluctuate, to oscillate*
кольцево́й, *annular*
коли́чество, *quantity, amount, number*
коммута́тор, *commutator*
ко́мплекс, *complex, group*
компоне́нт, *component*
конденса́торный, *condenser* (*adj.*)
коне́ц (gen. **конца́**), *end*
коне́чно, *of course*
коне́чный, *final, end*
конста́нта, *constant*
констру́кция, *construction, structure*
контро́льный, *control* (*adj.*)
ко́нтур, *circuit*
ко́нус, *cone*
конфере́нция, *conference*
концентра́ция, *concentration*
кора́бль (*m.*), *ship*
коренно́й, *fundamental, radical*
коро́ва, *cow*
короле́вский, *royal*
коро́ткий, *short*
коротково́лновый, *short-wave* (*adj.*)
корпускуля́рный, *corpuscular*
корреля́ция, *correlation*
косми́ческий, *cosmic*
ко́стный, *osseous, bone* (*adj.*)
кость (*f.*), *bone*
кото́рый, *which, who*
коэффицие́нт, *coefficient*
ко́шка, *cat*
край, *edge*
кра́сный, *red*
кра́тер, *crater*
кре́мний, *silicon*
криво́й, *curved;* **крива́я,** *curve*
криста́лл, *crystal*
кристалли́ческий, *crystalline*
кровь (*f.*), *blood*
кро́лик, *rabbit*
кро́ме (+ gen.), *except*
круг, *circle*
кругосве́тный, *round the world*
кру́пный, *large*
кры́са, *rat*
кто, *who*
кто́-либо, *anybody, somebody*
кто́-нибудь, *anybody, somebody*
кто́-то, *somebody*
куб, *cube*
куби́ческий, *cubic*
куда́, *where, whither*
кузне́ц, *smith, blacksmith*
культура́льный, *cultural, culture* (*adj.*)
кусо́к (gen. **куска́**), *piece*

лаборато́рия, *laboratory*
лаборато́рный, *laboratory* (*adj.*)
ла́кмус, *litmus*
ла́мпа, *lamp, valve*
ле́вый, *left*
лёгкое, *lung*
лека́рство, *medicine, medicament*
ле́кция, *lecture*
лежа́ть, *to lie*
лес, *forest*
лесово́дство, *forestry*
лета́ть, *to fly*
лете́ть, *to be flying, to fly*
ле́то, *summer, year*
лече́бный, *therapeutic, medicinal*
лече́ние, *treatment*
ли́бо . . . ли́бо . . ., *either . . . or . . .*
лиза́т, *lysate*
лине́йный, *linear*
ли́ния, *line*
листово́й, *leaf* (*adj.*)

лить, *to pour*
лицо́, *face*
лиша́ть, лиши́ть, *to deprive*
лишь, *only*
лобово́й, *frontal*
ло́дка, *boat*
ло́коть (gen. **ло́ктя**), *elbow*
луна́, *moon*
лучево́й, *radial; radiation* (*adj.*)
лу́чший, *best, better*
лу́чше, *better*
любо́й, *any*
люминесце́нтный, *luminescent;* **л—ое свече́ние,** *chemi-luminescence*

ма́гний, *magnesium*
магни́т, *magnet*
магни́тный, *magnetic*
мазь (*f.*), *ointment*
ма́ксимум, *maximum*
ма́ленький, *small*
ма́ло, *few, little*
малоуглеро́дистый, *having a low carbon content, low-carbon*
манометри́ческий, *manometric, manometer* (*adj.*)
ма́сса, *mass*
масс-спектро́метр, *mass-spectrometer*
масс-спектрометри́ческий, *mass-spectrometer* (*adj.*)
матема́тик, *mathematician*
матема́тика, *mathematics*
математи́ческий, *mathematical*
материа́л, *material*
материалисти́ческий, *materialistic*
махро́вый, *double* (of flowers)
медици́на, *medicine*
медици́нский, *medical;* **медици́нская сестра́,** *nursing sister*
ме́дленный, *slow*
медь (*f.*), *copper*
ме́жду (+ inst.), *between;* **ме́жду тем,** *meanwhile*
межледнико́вый, *interglacial*
межплане́тный, *interplanetary*
мезо́н, *meson*
мембра́нный, *membrane* (*adj.*), *diaphragm* (*adj.*)
ме́ньше, *less, fewer, smaller*
ме́ньший, *smaller, less*
ме́стный, *local*
ме́сто, *place;* **име́ть ме́сто,** *to take place*
месторожде́ние, *deposit*
ме́сяц, *month*
метаболи́т, *metabolite*
мета́лл, *metal*
металли́ческий, *metallic*
металлу́рг, *metallurgist*
мета́н, *methane*
метеори́т, *meteorite*
ме́тод, *method*
механи́зм, *mechanism*
меха́ник, *mechanic; mechanician*
меха́ника, *mechanics*
механи́ческий, *mechanical, mechanistic*
микро́б, *microbe*
микробиоло́гия, *microbiology*
микро́бный, *microbe* (*adj.*), *of microbe(s)*
микрооргани́зм, *microorganism*
микроско́п, *microscope*
микроскопи́рование, *microscopy*
микроскопи́ческий, *microscopic*
микротро́н, *microtron*
микротро́нный, *microtron* (*adj.*)
микроци́д, *'microcide'*
миллиме́тр, *millimetre*
ми́ля, *mile*
минима́льный, *minimal*
мину́та, *minute*

мир, *world*
митоти́ческий, *mitotic*
мл. = миллили́тр, *millilitre*
млн. = миллио́н, *million*
мне́ние, *opinion*
мно́го, *much, many*
многокле́точный, *multicellular*
мо́жет быть, *perhaps, may be, possibly*
мо́жно, *one can, one may, it is possible*
мозг, *brain, marrow;* **головно́й мозг,** *brain, cerebrum*
мой, *my*
моле́кула, *molecule*
молекуля́рный, *molecular*
молодо́й, *young*
мо́лот, (*large*) *hammer*
моме́нт, *moment*
моне́та, *coin; coinage*
моне́тный двор, *mint*
мо́ре, *sea*
морска́я сви́нка, *guinea-pig*
морфологи́ческий, *morphological*
моча́, *urine*
мочь (**могу́, мо́жет, мо́гут** ; past **мог, могла́**), **смочь,** *to be able*
мы, *we*
мыть, *to wash*
мя́гкий, *soft*
мя́со, *meat, flesh*

на (+ acc. and prep.), *on, at*
наблюда́ть, *to observe*
наблюде́ние, *observation*
набро́сок (gen. **набро́ска**), *sketch, draft*
навига́ция, *navigation;* **меж-плане́тная н——,** *interplanetary flight*
нагля́дность (*f.*), *clarity*
нагре́в, *heating*
нагрева́ние, *heating*
нагрева́ть, нагре́ть, *to heat up*
над (+ inst.), *above, over*
на́до, *it is necessary*
наза́д, *ago, back*
называ́ть, назва́ть, *to call, to name;* **так называ́емый,** *so-called*
наибо́лее, *most*
наибо́льший, *greatest*
наиме́ньший, *least, smallest*
найти́, see **находи́ть**
наконе́ц, *at last, finally*
нали́чие, *presence*
наоборо́т, *on the other hand*
напомина́ть, напо́мнить, *to remind, to be reminiscent of*
направле́ние, *direction*
наприме́р, *for example*
напряжённость (*f.*), *intensity, tension*
нару́жный, *external, outer*
населённость (*f.*), *population* (literally '*populatedness*')
насле́дство, *inheritance, heritage*
насо́с, *pump*
настоя́щий, *present, real*
насыще́ние, *saturation*
нати́вный, *native*
на́трий, *sodium*
натурали́ст, *naturalist*
натура́льный, *natural*
нау́ка, *science*
нау́чный, *scientific*
нафто́л, *naphthol*
находи́ть, найти́, *to find, to come upon*
находи́ться, найти́сь, *to be found, to be*
нача́ло, *beginning: principal*
нача́льный, *initial:* **нача́льная то́чка,** *departure-point*
нача́ть, see **начина́ть**
начина́ть, нача́ть, *to begin*

наш, *our*
не, *not, is not, are not*
неакти́вный, *inactive*
небе́сный, *celestial*
не́бо, *sky*
небольшо́й, *small*
неви́димый, *invisible*
невозмо́жный, *impossible*
невооружённый, *unarmed;* **н—— глаз,** *naked eye*
недово́льный, *discontented, displeased, dissatisfied*
недоста́ток (gen. **недоста́тка**) *fault, flaw*
нейтро́н, *neutron*
не́кого, *there is nobody* (see Chapter 18)
не́которые, *some, several*
не́который, *a certain*
не́кто, *somebody*
нельзя́, *it is impossible,* (*one* etc.) *cannot*
неме́цкий, *German*
немно́го, *a few, a little*
ненасы́щенный, *unsaturated*
необрати́мый, *irreversible*
чеобходи́мый, *essential, necessary*
непосре́дственный, *immediate, direct*
непра́вильный, *incorrect, wrong*
непреме́нно, *definitely*
нерв, *nerve*
не́рвный, *nervous*
нерегуля́рный, *irregular*
несжима́емый, *uncompressed*
неспа́ренный, *unpaired*
нести́, *to be carrying, to be bearing, to be bringing*
несмотря́ на (+ acc.), *in spite of*
нет, *no, there is not, there are not*
не́чего, *there is nothing* (see Chapter 18)
не́что, *something*
неэлектромагни́тный, *non-electromagnetic*
ни, *nor, neither*
ни́же, *lower, below*
ни́зкий, *low*
никако́й, *no, not any*
ни́кель (*m.*), *nickel*
никогда́, *never*
никто́, *nobody*
нитра́т, *nitrate*
нить (*f.*), *thread*
ничто́, *nothing*
но, *but*
но́вый, *new*
ноль, нуль (*m.*), *zero*
но́мер, *number*
норма́льный, *normal*
ночь (*f.*), *night*
нукло́н, *nucleon*

о (об, обо), *about* (with prep.), *against* (with acc.)
о́ба (*m.* and *n.*), **о́бе** (*f.*), *both*
обеспе́чивать, обеспе́чить, *to secure, to ensure*
облада́ть (+ inst.), *to have, to possess*
о́бласть (*f.*), *province, region, sphere*
облуча́ть, облучи́ть, *to irradiate*
обнару́жение, *discovery*
обнару́живать, обнару́жить, *to discover, to reveal*
обнару́жить, see **обнару́живать**
оболо́чка, *envelope, shell*
обосно́вывать, обоснова́ть, *to found*
о́браз, *form, way, manner;* **гла́вным о́бразом,** *for the most part, principally;* **таки́м о́бразом,** *in this way, in that way, thus*

обра́зе́ц (gen. **образца́**), *sample, model*
образо́вывать, образова́ть, *to form, to shape*
обраще́ние, *revolution*
обсервато́рия, *observatory*
обсужда́ть, обсуди́ть, *to discuss*
о́бщество, *society*
о́бщий, *common, general, total*
объе́кт, *object, objective*
объём, *volume*
объясне́ние, *explanation*
объясня́ть, объясни́ть, *to explain*
о́вощи, *vegetables*
огро́мный, *huge*
оди́н (**одна́, одно́**), *one;* **одни́,** *some*
одина́ковый, *identical, same*
одна́ко, *however*
одновре́менный, *simultaneous*
одноро́дность (*f.*), *homogeneity*
одноро́дный, *homogeneous*
оказа́ть, see **ока́зывать**
оказа́ться, see **ока́зываться**
ока́зывать, оказа́ть, *to exert, to render*
ока́зываться, оказа́ться, *to turn out* (*to be*)
ока́нчивать, око́нчить, *to complete*
океа́н, *ocean*
окисле́ние, *oxid*(*is*)*ation*
окисля́ть, окисли́ть, *to oxidise*
о́коло (+ gen.), *about, around*
оконча́ние, *conclusion, completion*
око́нчить, see **ока́нчивать**
о́лово, *tin*
омыва́ть, омы́ть, *to wash*
он, *he, it;* **она́,** *she, it;* **оно́,** *it;* **они́,** *they*
онтогене́з, *ontogenesis*
опера́ция, *operation*
опи́сывать, описа́ть, *to describe*
определе́ние, *definition, determination*
определя́ть, определи́ть, *to determine, to define*
о́птика, *optics*
оптима́льный, *optimal, optimum* (*adj.*)
опти́ческий, *optical*
опублико́вывать, опубликова́ть, *to publish*
о́пухоль (*f.*), *tumour*
о́пыт, *experiment; experience*
орби́та, *orbit*
о́рган, *organ*
организа́ция, *organisation*
органи́зм, *organism*
органи́зовать, с-, *to organise*
органи́ческий, *organic*
ориентиро́вочный, *tentative, approximate*
оса́док (gen. **оса́дка**), *deposit*
осажде́ние, *precipitation, deposit*
освеще́ние, *illumination, lighting*
ослабле́ние, *weakening, attenuation*
осмо́тр, *inspection*
осно́ва, *basis, base*
основа́ние, *basis, grounds*
основно́й, *fundamental, basic, chief*
основополо́жник, *founder*
осо́бенность (*f.*), *peculiarity*
осо́бый, *special, particular*
остава́ться, оста́ться, *to remain*
остально́й, *remaining*
оста́ться, see **остава́ться**
осуша́ть, осуши́ть, *to dry*
осуши́тель (*m.*), *drying agent*
осуществле́ние, *realisation*
осуществля́ть, осуществи́ть, *to bring about, to realise*

ось (*f.*), *axis*
от (+ gen.), *from*
отбóр, *selection*
отвéт, *reply, answer*
отвéтственный, *responsible*
отворáчиваться, отвернýться, *to turn away*
отдéл, *section*
отделя́ть, отдели́ть, *to separate*
отклонéние, *deviation*
отклоня́ться, отклони́ться, *to deviate*
открывáть, откры́ть, *to discover, to open*
откры́тие, *discovery*
откры́тый, *open*
отличáть, отличи́ть, *to distinguish, to differentiate*
отмечáть, отмéтить, *to note*
относи́тельный, *relative*
относи́ться, отнести́сь (к), *to relate to, to concern, to refer to, to belong to*
отношéние, *attitude, relation;* **в отношéнии**, *as regards*
отправнóй, *departure* (*adj.*)
óтпуск, *leave-of-absence*
отрицáтельный, *negative*
отрывнóй, *escape* (*adj.*)
отсáсывать, отсосáть, *to suck off, to draw off*
отставáть, отстáть, *to lag behind*
оттесня́ть, оттесни́ть, *to force back*
отчёт, *report*
охлаждéние, *cooling, refrigeration*
оцéнивать, оцени́ть, *to evaluate*
óчень, *very*
очи́стка, *clean(s)ing*
очищáть, очи́стить, *to clean, to clean out*
ошибáться, ошиби́ться, *to make a mistake*
оши́бка, *mistake, error*
оши́бочность (*f.*), *erroneousness*

пáдать, пасть, *to fall*
пáлочка, *rod, bacillus*
пар, *steam, vapour*
парабиóнт, *parabiont*
парадóкс, *paradox*
параллéльный, *parallel*
парамагни́тный, *paramagnetic*
парáметр, *parameter*
партнёр, *partner*
пасть, see **пáдать**
патогéнный, *pathogenic*
патолóгия, *pathology*
пентадиéн, *pentadiene*
пéрвый, *first;* **пéрвое врéмя**, *at first*
перевáривать, перевари́ть, *to digest*
переводи́ть, перевести́, *to translate*
перегруппирóвка, *regrouping*
пéред (+ inst.), *in front of, before*
передавáть, передáть, *to transfer, to transmit*
перейти́, see **переходи́ть**
перемещéние, *transfer, shifting*
переноси́ть, пренести́, *to carry across, to undergo, to suffer*
перестрóйка, *rebuilding, reorganisation*
перехóд, *transition, transfer*
переходи́ть, перейти́, *to go/come across*
перечекáнка, *recoinage*
пери́од, *period*
периоди́ческий, *periodic*
перó (nom. pl. **пéрья**), *feather*
персонáл, *personnel, staff*
перхлорáт, *perchlorate*
печёночный, *hepatic, of the liver*

печь, *to bake, to roast*
печь, (*f.*), *stove, oven*
пигме́нтный, *pigment, pigmentary*
писа́ть, на-, *to write*
пить, вы́-, *to drink*
пи́ща, *food*
пищево́й, *alimentary, food* (*adj.*)
пла́мя (*n.*, gen. **пла́мени**), *flame*
план, *plan, scheme*
плане́та, *planet*
планета́рный, *planetary*
пласти́нка, *plate*
пластма́сса, *plastic* (*n.*)
пла́тина, *platinum*
пле́сень (*f.*), *mould*
плести́, *to weave, to plait*
плод, *fruit*
плуто́ний, *plutonium*
по (+ prep. and dat.), *after* (with prep.); *according to, through, by,* etc. (with dat.)
пове́рхность (*f.*), *surface*
по-ви́димому, *apparently, evidently*
повторя́ть, -и́ть, *to repeat*
повыша́ть, повы́сить, *to raise, to heighten*
пога́снуть, see **га́снуть**
поглоща́ть, поглоти́ть, *to absorb*
поглоще́ние, *absorption*
под (+ acc. and inst.), *under, beneath*
подава́ть, пода́ть, *to serve, to deliver*
подверга́ть, подве́ргнуть, *to submit, to subject*
подвижно́й, *mobile*
подлежа́ть (+ dat.), *to be subject to, to be open to*
поднима́ть, подня́ть, *to raise, to lift*
подтвержда́ть, подтверди́ть, *to confirm, to corroborate*
подро́бный, *detailed*
подъём, *rise, lifting*
подъёмный, *lifting;* **п——ая си́ла,** *lifting power*
позволя́ть, позво́лить, *to allow, to permit* (+ dat. of the person to whom permission is given)
позвоно́к (gen. **позвонка́**), *vertebra*
позвоно́чный, *vertebrate*
позитро́н, *positron*
пока́зывать, показа́ть, *to show*
покрыва́ть, покры́ть, *to cover*
по́ле, *field*
поле́зный, *useful*
полимериза́ция, *polymerisation*
полимеризова́ть, *to polymerise*
полиомиели́т, *poliomyelitis*
по́лный, *full, complete, total*
по́лностью, *completely, exhaustively*
положе́ние, *position, state; thesis*
положи́тельный, *positive*
полтора́ (gen. **полу́тора**), *one and a half*
получа́ть, -и́ть, *to receive, to obtain*
полуша́рие, *hemisphere*
по́льзоваться (+ inst.), *to make use of*
по́люс, *pole*
поля́рный, *polar*
помеща́ть, помести́ть, *to place*
помога́ть, помо́чь (+ dat.), *to help*
по́мощь (*f.*), *help, aid*
пониже́ние, *lowering, drop*
понима́ть, поня́ть, *to understand*
поня́тие, *idea*
поня́тный, *comprehensible*
поня́ть, see **понима́ть**
попада́ть, попа́сть, *to fall on, to strike, to reach*

поочерёдно, *in turn*
поря́док (gen. **поря́дка**), *order*
посвяща́ть, посвяти́ть, *to devote, to dedicate*
по́сле (+ gen.), *after*
после́дний, *last, latter*
после́довательно, *in succession, successively*
после́дующий, *following, subsequent*
послужи́ть, see **служи́ть**
постано́вка, *placing*
постепе́нный, *gradual*
постоя́нно, *constantly*
постоя́нство, *constancy*
построе́ние, *construction, building-up, synthesis*
пот, *sweat*
потенциа́л, *potential*
пото́к, *flow*
пото́м, *then*
потому́ что, *because*
похо́жий на (+ acc.), *like*
по́чва, *soil*
почему́, *why*
почти́, *almost, nearly*
поэ́тому, *therefore*
появле́ние, *appearance*
появля́ться, появи́ться, *to appear*
пра́вильный, *correct*
пра́вый, *right, right-hand*
пра́ктика, *practice;* **на п——е,** *in practice*
практи́чески, *practically, almost*
практи́ческий, *practical*
превраща́ть, преврати́ть, *to convert, to transform*
превраще́ние, *conversion*
предвари́тельный, *preliminary*
предви́деть, *to foresee*
преде́л, *limit;* **преде́л Пуанкаре́** *Poincaré's limit*
предлага́ть, предложи́ть, *to propose, to suggest, to offer*
предме́т, *object, subject*
пре́док (gen. **пре́дка**), *ancestor*
предполага́ть, предположи́ть, *to (pre)suppose, to conjecture*
предположе́ние, *supposition*
предположи́ть, see **предполага́ть**
представи́тель (*m.*), *representative*
представле́ние, *concept, idea*
представля́ть, предста́вить, *to present*
пре́жде, *before;* **пре́жде всего́,** *first of all, first and foremost*
прекраща́ть, прекрати́ть, *to curtail, to stop*
преоблада́ние, *preponderance*
препара́т, *preparation, compound*
при (+ prep.), *in, near, by, during*
прибавле́ние, *addition*
прибавля́ть, приба́вить, *to add*
приближе́ние, *approximation*
приблизи́тельный, *approximate*
прибо́р, *instrument, device*
приведе́ние, *bringing, adduction, adducing*
приводи́ть, привести́, *to bring*
придти́, see **приходи́ть**
признава́ть, призна́ть, *to recognise, to admit*
примене́ние, *application*
применя́ть, примени́ть, *to apply, to use*
приме́рно, *approximately*
примити́вный, *primitive*
принести́, see **приноси́ть**
принима́ть, приня́ть, *to take, to receive, to accept, to assume;* **п—— во внима́ние,** *to take into account*

приноси́ть, принести́, *to bring*
при́нцип, *principle*
при́нято, *it is accepted, it is usual*
приня́ть, see **принима́ть**
припи́сывать, приписа́ть, *to ascribe*
приро́да, *nature*
приспосо́бленность (*f.*), *adaptation*
приспособля́емость (*f.*), *adaptability, adjustability*
прису́тствовать, *to be present*
притти́, see **приходи́ть**
прихо́дится, *has to, have to;* (see also sentence 9, Exercise 27, Chapter 15)
приходи́ть, придти́/притти́/прийти́, *to come*
причи́на, *cause, reason*
проанализи́ровать, see **анализи́ровать**
пробле́ма, *problem*
про́бный, *test* (*adj.*)
проведе́ние, *conduct, conducting*
прове́рить, see **проверя́ть**
прове́рка, *checking, verification*
проверя́ть, прове́рить, *to verify*
проводи́ть, провести́, *to conduct, to draw in, to put in*
прогрева́ние, *heating, warming*
прогрева́ть, прогре́ть, *to warm up*
продолжа́ть, продо́лжить, *to continue*
проду́кт, *product*
прожо́рливый, *gluttonous*
производи́ть, произвести́, *to carry out, perform; to produce*
произво́дства, *production*
произойти́, see **происходи́ть**
произраста́ть, произрасти́, *to grow*
проиллюстри́ровать, see **иллюстри́ровать**
происходи́ть, произойти́, *to issue, to arise, to occur*
происхожде́ние, *origin*
проколлаге́н, *procollagene*
проника́ть, прони́кнуть, *to penetrate*
проникнове́ние, *penetration*
прони́кнуть, see **проника́ть**
проница́емость (*f.*), *penetrability*
просле́живать, проследи́ть, *to trace*
просто́й, *simple*
простра́нство, *space*
про́тив (+ gen.), *against*
прото́н, *proton*
профе́ссор, *professor*
про́филь (*m.*), *profile, section*
проходи́ть, пройти́, *to pass through*
прохожде́ние, *passage*
проце́нт, *per cent., percentage, percentile*
проце́сс, *process*
про́чный, *durable*
проявля́ть, прояви́ть, *to show, to manifest*
прямо́й, *straight, direct*
пуска́ть, пусти́ть, *to let, to allow;* **п—— в ход,** *to set in motion*
пусто́й, *empty*
пустота́, *vacuum*
путеше́ствие, *journey*
путь (*m.*), *path, way, road;* **путём,** *by means* (*of*)
пучо́к (gen. **пучка́**), *beam*
пыль (*f.*), *dust*
пыта́ться, по-, *to try*
пятна́дцать, *fifteen*
пятно́, *stain, patch, mark*
пять, *five*

рабо́та, *work*
рабо́тать, *to work*
рабо́чий, *working;* (*n.*) *worker*
равнове́сный, *balanced, equilibrium* (*adj.*)
ра́вный, *equal, like, congruent*
ра́дий, *radium*
радиоакти́вный, *radio-active*
радиолокацио́нный, *radio-locational, radar* (*adj.*)
радиопереда́тчик, *radio-transmitter*
радо́н, *radon*
раз, *once;* (' *time* ' as in **два ра́за,** *two times, twice*)
разбавля́ть, разба́вить *to dilute*
разбо́р, *analysis*
развива́ть, разви́ть, *to develop*
разви́тие, *development, growth, evolution*
разви́ть, see **развива́ть**
разли́чие, *difference*
разли́чный, *various, different*
разложе́ние, *resolution, decomposition*
разме́р, *dimension*
размножа́ться, размно́житься, *to multiply, to reproduce*
размноже́ние, *reproduction*
ра́зный, *different, various*
разраба́тывать, разрабо́тать, *to work out, to elaborate*
разре́з, *cut, section*
райо́н, *region, sphere, area*
рак, *cancer; crayfish*
раке́та, *rocket*
ра́на, *wound*
ра́нее, *earlier, previously*
раска́чивать, раскача́ть, *to sway, to swing*
распа́д, *decay, decomposition*
распада́ться, распа́сться, *to disintegrate*
располага́ть, расположи́ть, *to place, to arrange, to dispose*
расположе́ние, *disposition, distribution*
расположи́ть, see **располага́ть**
распределе́ние, *distribution*
распростране́ние, *spread, distribution*
рассма́тривать, рассмо́треть, *to examine*
расстоя́ние, *distance*
рассчи́тывать, рассчита́ть, *to calculate*
раство́р, *solution*
раствори́мость (*f.*), *solubility*
растворя́ть, -и́ть, *to dissolve*
расте́ние, *plant*
расти́ (past tense **рос, росла́, росло́,** *pl.* **росли́**), *to grow*
расщепи́ть, see **расщепля́ть**
расщепле́ние, *splitting*
расщепля́ть, расщепи́ть, *to split*
рацио́н, *ration*
реакти́вный, *reaction* (*adj.*); **р—— самолёт,** *jet aircraft*
реа́ктор, *reactor*
реа́кция, *reaction*
реализова́ть, *to realise, to bring about*
регенерацио́нный, *regenerative*
регенера́ция, *regeneration*
регули́ровать, *to regulate*
ре́дкий, *rare, rarefied*
режи́м, *régime, system, method*
резервуа́р, *reservoir, basin, tank*
рези́на, (*hard*) *rubber*
ре́зкий, *sharp, pronounced, marked*
резона́нс, *resonance*
результа́т, *result;* **в р——е,** *as a result, as the result*
реиспаря́ться, реиспа́риться, *to re-evaporate*

рентгеногра́мма, *X-ray plate*
рефле́кс, *reflex*
рециди́в, *relapse*
реша́ть, -и́ть, *to decide*
реше́ние, *decision, solution*
реши́ть, see **реша́ть**
рису́нок (gen. **рису́нка**), *sketch, diagram*
рог, *horn*
рогово́й, *horny*
роди́тель (*m.*), *parent*
рожь (*f.*), *rye*
рой, *swarm*
роль (*f.*), *part, role*
Росси́я, *Russia*
рост, *growth*
ртуть (*f.*), *mercury*
рубль (*m.*), *rouble*
рука́, *hand, arm*
ру́сский, *Russian*
ры́ба, *fish*
ряд, *row, series*

с (+ gen.), *from, off;* (+ inst.) *with;* **с тем, что́бы,** *in order that, in order to*
сад, *garden*
сади́ться, сесть, *to sit down*
сам (**сама́, само́,** *pl.* **са́ми**), *self;* **сам по себе́,** *of itself, by itself*
саме́ц (gen. **самца́**), *male, buck,* etc.
са́мка, *female, doe,* etc.
самолёт, *aircraft*
са́мый, *self;* with adj.=*most, very*
сантиме́тр, *centimetre*
са́хар, *sugar*
сбо́рка, *assemblage*
сва́рка, *welding*
свет, *light*
свет, *world*
светово́й, *light* (*adj.*)*;* **светово́й день,** *light-day*
свече́ние, *shimmer, luminosity;* **люминесце́нтное с——,** *chemi-luminescence*
свине́ц (gen. **свинца́**), *lead*
сви́нка, as in **морска́я с——,** *guinea-pig*
свинцо́вый, *leaden, of lead*
своба́дный, *free*
свой (**своя́, своё,** *pl.* **свои́**), *own* (see Chapter 18)
сво́йство, *property, attribute*
свя́зывать, связа́ть, *to connect*
связь (*f.*), *connection, link, bond*
сде́лать, see **де́лать**
себя́, reflexive pronoun (see Chapter 18)
се́верный, *northern*
се́веро-за́падный, *north-western*
седимента́ция, *sedimentation*
секре́ция, *secretion*
се́ктор, *sector, segment*
селезёнка, *spleen*
семе́йство, *family*
семикра́тный, *sevenfold*
семь, *seven*
се́мя (*n.* gen. sing. **се́мени,** gen. pl. **семя́н**), *seed*
се́ра, *sulphur*
середи́на, *middle*
се́рия, *series*
сероводоро́дный, *hydrogen sulphide, hydrosulphuric*
серьёзность (*f.*), *seriousness*
серьёзный, *serious*
сестра́, *sister*
сесть, see **сади́ться**
се́тка, *net, grid*
сече́ние, *section*
сжима́ть, сжать, *to compress*
сиде́ть, *to sit*
си́ла, *force, power*
си́льно, *strongly, considerably*
си́льный, *strong*

си́ний, *blue*
си́нтез, *synthesis*
синтети́ческий, *synthetic(al)*
синхроциклотро́н, *synchro-cyclotron*
систе́ма, *system*
системати́ческий, *systematic, pertaining to a system*
сия́ние, *aurora*
сказа́ть, see **говори́ть**
скла́дка, *fold*
ско́лько, *how much*
ско́рость (*f.*), *speed, velocity*
ско́рый, *quick, fast*
сла́бый, *weak*
слага́ть, сложи́ть, *to compose*
сле́довательно, *consequently*
сле́довать, по-, *to follow, to ensue* (see also Chapter 15)
сле́дует, *ought* (see Chapter 15)
сле́дующий, *following*
слепо́й, *blind*
сло́во, *word*
сло́жный, *complex, complicated*
слой, *layer*
служи́ть, по-, *to serve* (+ dat. of person served)
слу́чай, *case, occasion, incident, chance;* **в тако́м слу́чае,** *in that case*
слы́шать, у-, *to hear*
смесь (*f.*), *mixture*
смея́ться, *to laugh*
смотре́ть, *to look*
смочь, see **мочь**
снаря́д, *missile*
снег, *snow*
снижа́ть, сни́зить, *to lower*
сниже́ние, *decrease, lowering, diminution*
сни́зить, see **снижа́ть**
сни́мок (gen. **сни́мка**), *photograph*
собира́ть, собра́ть, *to gather*
со́бственный, *own*
соверша́ть, -и́ть, *to accomplish, to perform*
соверше́нный, *perfect*
сове́товать, по-, *to advise* (+ dat. of person advised)
сове́тский, *Soviet*
совме́стно, *in common, jointly*
совреме́нный, *contemporary*
согла́сно (+ dat.), *according (to), in accordance (with)*
согласова́ться, *to agree*
со́да, *common soda*
содержа́ние, *contents, content*
содержа́ть, *to contain*
соедине́ние, *compound*
соедини́тельный, *connective*
соединя́ть, -и́ть, *to connect, to combine, to unite*
созве́здие, *constellation*
создава́ть, созда́ть, *to create*
сок, *juice, sap*
сокраща́ть, сократи́ть, *to curtail*
со́лнечный, *solar*
со́лнце, *sun*
соль (*f.*), *salt*
сомнева́ться, *to doubt*
сомне́ние, *doubt*
сообще́ние, *communication*
соотве́тственный, *corresponding*
соотве́тствие, *accordance, correspondence*
соотве́тствовать (+ dat.), *to correspond (to)*
соотноше́ние, *relationship*
соприкаса́ться, соприкосну́ться, *to touch, to be adjacent*
сопротивле́ние, *resistance*
со́рок, *forty*
соста́в, *composition*
составля́ть, соста́вить, *to compose*

состоя́ние, *state*
состоя́ть (из), *to consist (of)*
сосу́д, *vessel*
сотру́дник, *collaborator;* **нау́чный с——,** *scientific worker, scientist*
сохраня́ть, -и́ть, *to preserve*
спать, *to sleep*
спектр, *spectrum*
специа́льный, *special*
специфи́ческий, *specific*
спин, *spin*
спира́ль (*f.*), *spiral*
спира́льный, *spiral* (*adj.*)
спирохе́та, *spirochete*
спирт, *spirit, alcohol*
сплав, *alloy*
сплавля́ть, спла́вить, *to fuse*
спосо́бность (*f.*), *ability, capacity*
спосо́бный, *capable*
спосо́бствовать (+ dat.), *to help, to promote*
спустя́, *later*
спу́тник, *satellite*
сравне́ние, *comparison;* **по с——ю,** *in comparison*
сравни́тельный, *comparative*
среда́, *milieu, medium*
среди́ (+ gen.), *among*
сре́дний, *central; average*
сре́дство, *means, instrument*
СССР, *U.S.S.R.*
стабилиза́ция, *stabilisation*
стаби́льный, *stable*
ста́дия, *stage*
сталь (*f.*), *steel*
стандáртный, *standard*
станови́ться, стать, *to become*
ста́нция, *station*
стать, see **станови́ться**
статья́, *article*
сте́пень (*f.*), *degree*
стира́ть, стере́ть, *to wipe off*
стиро́л, *styrene, styrol*
сто, *hundred*
стол, *table*
столе́тие, *century*
стоматоло́гия, *stomatology*
сторона́, *side*
стратосфе́ра, *stratosphere*
строе́ние, *construction, building structure*
стро́ить, по-, *to build*
строй, *order, structure*
структу́ра, *structure*
студени́стый, *jelly-like*
студе́нт, *student*
студе́нтка, *student (female)*
су́тки (gen. **су́ток**), *day, night and day, period of 24 hours*
сухо́й, *dry*
суще́ственный, *fundamental, essential, substantial*
существо́, *creature*
существова́ть, *to exist*
сфе́ра, *sphere*
сфери́ческий, *spherical*
сформули́ровать, see **формули́ровать**
схемати́чно, *schematically, in outline*
схемати́чный, *schematic, outline*
счита́ть, счесть, *to consider*
съесть, see **есть**
сын, *son*
сыро́й, *damp, raw*
сырьё, *raw material*

та, see **тот**
табли́ца, *table*
так, *so, thus;* **так же как,** *just as, in the same way as;* **так называ́емый,** *so-called;* **так что,** *so that*
та́кже, *also*

тако́й, *such;* **таки́м о́бразом,** *in that way, in this way, thus*
там, *there*
твёрдость (*f.*), *hardness*
твёрдый, *hard*
те, see **тот**
т.е. = **то есть,** *that is, i.e.*
телеско́п, *telescope;* **телеско́п-рефле́ктор,** *reflector telescope*
телефони́я, *telephony*
те́ло, *body*
тем, see **чем**
те́ма, *theme*
тёмный, *dark*
температу́ра, *temperature*
температу́рный, *temperature* (*adj.*)
тенде́нция, *tendency*
теоре́тик, *theoretician*
теорети́ческий, *theoretical*
тео́рия, *theory*
тере́ть, *to rub*
термодина́мика, *thermodynamics*
те́рмо-я́дерный, *thermo-nuclear*
террито́рия, *territory*
тётка, *auntie*
те́хника, *technics; technique*
тече́ние, *course, current, flow;* **в тече́ние** (+ gen.) *in the course of, during, for*
ти́хий, *quiet, pacific*
тип, *type*
тиф, *typhus;* **возвра́тный тиф,** *relapsing fever* (*typhoid*)
ткань (*f.*), *fabric, tissue*
то, see **тот**
тогда́, *then;* **тогда́ как,** *whereas*
ток, *current*
токси́н, *toxin*
то́лько, *only*
толщина́, *thickness*
то́нкий, *fine, thin*
том, *volume, tome*
то́нна, *ton* (metric ton = 1,000 kg, English ton = 1,105 kg.)
тонча́йший, *finest*
то́пливо, *fuel*
тормози́ть, за-, *to brake*
тот (*f.* **та,** *n.* **то,** *n. pl.* **те**), *that*
то́чка, *point*
то́чный, *precise, exact*
траекто́рия, *trajectory*
тре́бование, *demand, need*
тре́бовать, вос-, *to demand, require*
тре́тий (*f.* **тре́тья,** *n.* **тре́тье,** *pl.* **тре́тьи**), *third*
трёхфа́зный, *three-phase*
три, *three*
трио́дный, *triode* (*adj.*)
тройно́й, *triple, threefold*
тру́бка, *tube, pipe*
труд, *work*
тру́дный, *difficult*
туберкулёз, *tuberculosis*
тума́нность (*f.*), *nebula*
тут, *here*
тща́тельный, *thorough, careful*
ты́сяча, *thousand*
тяготе́ние, *gravitation*
тяжёлый, *heavy*
тя́жесть (*f.*), *gravity*

у (+ gen.), *at* (see also Ex. 6, note 1)
увели́чивать, увели́чить, *to increase*
угаса́ть, уга́снуть, *to go out, be extinguished*
углеводоро́д, *hydrocarbon*
углеки́слый газ, *carbon dioxide*
углеро́д, *carbon*
углеро́дистый, *carbonaceous, carbonic*
углово́й, *angular*

угнете́ние, *oppression, depression, suppression*
у́гол (gen. **угла́**), *corner, angle*
удава́ться, *to succeed;* see notes to Exercise 31, (8)
уда́рный, *shock* (*adj.*)
уде́льный, *specific*
удиви́тельный, *surprising*
удо́бный, *convenient, comfortable*
удовлетвори́тельный, *satisfactory*
удовлетворя́ть, удовлетвори́ть, *to satisfy*
у́же, *narrower*
уже́, *already*
у́зел (gen. **узла́**), *knot, node, ganglion*
у́зкий, *narrow*
узнава́ть, узна́ть, *to find out, get to know*
ука́зывать, указа́ть, *to indicate*
у́ксусная кислота́, *acetic acid*
ультрафи́льтр, *ultrafilter*
уменьша́ть, -и́ть, *to decrease, to diminish*
умира́ть, умере́ть, *to die*
умноже́ние, *multiplication*
унести́, see **уноси́ть**
университе́т, *university*
уноси́ть, унести́, *to carry off, to take away*
упада́ть, упа́сть, *to fall, to fall down*
уплотня́ть, -и́ть, *to thicken, to condense, to compress*
управле́ние, *guidance, guiding*
упру́гость (*f.*), *elasticity*
уравне́ние, *equation*
ура́н, *uranium*
у́ровень (*m.*), *level*
уси́ливать, уси́лить, *to strengthen*
ускори́тель (*m.*), *accelerator*
ускоря́ть, уско́рить, *to accelerate*
усло́вие, *condition, circumstance*
усло́вный, *conditional, conventional*
устана́вливать, установи́ть, *to establish*
устано́вка, *setting up; apparatus*
установле́ние, *establishment, determination, ascertaining*
устра́ивать, устро́ить, *to arrange, to organise*
уступа́ть, -и́ть, *to yield*
у́тка, *duck*
у́тро, *morning*
уча́сток (gen. **уча́стка**), *part, section, sector*
уче́ние, *teaching*
учёный, *learned;* as noun = *scholar, scientist*
уче́сть, see **учи́тывать**
учи́тель (*m.*), *teacher*
учи́тывать, уче́сть, *to take into account*
учи́ться, *to learn, to study*
ушиба́ть, ушиби́ть, *to knock, bruise*

фагоци́т, *phagocyte*
фагоцита́рный, *phagocyte* (*adj.*)
фа́за, *phase*
фа́зовый, *phase* (*adj.*), *phasal*
фазотро́н, *phasotron*
факт, *fact*
фа́ктор, *factor*
ферме́нт, *ferment*
ферромагни́тность (*f.*), *ferromagnetism*
фигу́ра, *figure*
фи́зик, *physicist*
фи́зика, *physics*
фи́зико-хими́ческий, *physicochemical*
физиологи́ческий, *physiological*
физиоло́гия, *physiology*

физи́ческий, *physical*
филосо́фия, *philosophy*
фильм, *film*
фитопланкто́н, *phytoplankton*
фо́рма, *form, shape*
формули́ровать, с-, *to formulate*
фосфа́тный, *phosphate (adj.)*
фосфори́т, *phosphorite*
фотографи́ческий, *photographic*
фотоси́нтез, *photosynthesis*
фотоэлектри́ческий, *photoelectric*
фракциони́рование, *fractionation*
фра́кция, *fraction, faction, group*
фу́нкция, *function*
фунт, *pound*

хао́с, *chaos*
хара́ктер, *character*
характеризова́ть, *to characterise*
хи́мик, *chemist*
хими́ческий, *chemical*
хи́мия, *chemistry*
хиру́рг, *surgeon*
хирурги́я, *surgery*
хлори́д, *chloride*
хлорофо́рм, *chloroform*
ход, *process, course*
ходи́ть, *to go*
холе́рный, *cholera (adj.)*
хоро́ший, *good*
хорошо́, *well*
хоте́ть, за-, *to want*
хотя́, *although,* **хотя́ бы,** *at least, if only*
хром, *chromium; chrome*
хромати́ческий, *chromatic*
хромосо́ма, *chromosome*
хру́пкий, *brittle*
хру́пкость (*f.*), *brittleness*

цвет, *colour*
цвето́к (gen. **цветка́**), *flower*
целесообра́зный, *expedient, convenient*
целлюло́за, *cellulose*
це́лостность (*f.*), *wholeness, entirety*
це́лый, *whole;* **в це́лом,** *as a whole*
цель (*f.*), *object, aim*
цеме́нт, *cement*
цена́, *price*
центр, *centre*
центра́льный, *central*
центрифуги́рование, *centrifuging*
цепо́чка, *chain*
цепь (*f.*), *chain*
це́рий, *cerium*
цикл, *cycle*
циклотро́н, *cyclotron*
цилиндри́ческий, *cylindrical*
цинк, *zinc*
циркули́ровать, *to circulate*
циркуля́ция, *circulation*
цитра́тный, *citrate (adj.)*
ци́фра, *figure, number*
цынга́, *scurvy*

чай, *tea*
час, *hour; o'clock*
части́ца, *particle*
части́чный, *partial*
ча́стность (*f.*), *particularity;* **в ча́стности,** *in particular*
ча́сто, *often*
частота́, *frequency*
ча́стый, *frequent*
часть (*f.*), *part;* **бо́льшей ча́стью,** *for the most/greater part*
чахо́тка, *consumption*
ча́ще всего́, *most often*
чей (*f.* **чья,** *n.* **чьё,** *pl.* **чьи**), *whose*

челове́к, *man*
чем, *than;* **чем** (+ comparative) **. . . тем** (+ comparative) = *the more . . . the more*
чередова́ться, *to alternate*
че́рез (+ acc.), *across, through, by way of*
чёрный, *black, dark*
четвёртый, *fourth*
четы́ре, *four*
число́, *number*
чи́стый, *clean, pure*
чита́тель (*m.*), *reader*
чита́ть, прочита́ть/проче́сть, *to read*
член, *member, limb*
что, *what, which; that;* **что за,** *what sort of*
что бы, *whatever*
что́бы, *in order to, in order that;* **для того́, что́бы** and **с тем, что́бы** = *in order to, in order that* **что́бы . . . не,** *lest*
что́-либо, *anything, something*
что́-нибудь, *anything, something*
что́-то, *something*
чу́вство, *feeling*
чугу́н, *cast-iron*

шаг, *step*
шар, *sphere*
шёл (*f.* **шла,** *n.* **шло,** *pl.* **шли**), past tense of **идти́** (*q.v.*)
шесть, *six*
широ́кий, *broad, widespread*
широ́тный, *latitudinal*
шок, *shock*
щека́, *cheek*
щелочно́й, *alkaline, basic*
щу́ка, *pike*

эбони́т, *ebonite*
эволюцио́нный, *evolutionary*
эволю́ция, *evolution*
эква́тор, *equator*
экрани́ровать, *to screen*
экспериме́нт, *experiment*
эксперимента́льно, *experimentally*
эксперимента́льный, *experimental*
экстра́кт, *extract*
электри́ческий, *electric(al)*
электро́д, *electrode*
электромагни́тный, *electromagnetic*
электро́н, *electron*
электропроводи́мость (*f.*), *electrical conductivity*
электроста́нция, *power-station*
электростати́ческий, *electrostatic*
электроте́хника, *electrotechnics, electrical engineering*
элеме́нт, *element*
элемента́рный, *elementary*
эмбриоло́гия, *embriology*
эмитти́ровать, *to emit*
энерге́тика, *energetics, power engineering*
эне́ргия, *energy*
энзи́м, *enzyme*
энтерото́мия, *enterotomy*
эти́ловый, *ethyl*
э́тот (*f.* **э́та,** *n.* **э́то,** *pl.* **э́ти**), *this, that;* (*pl.*) *these, those*
эфи́р, *ether*
эффе́кт, *effect*

юг, *south*
ю́жный, *south, southern*
Юпи́тер, *Jupiter*

я, *I*
яви́ться, see **явля́ться**
явле́ние, *phenomenon*

явля́ться, яви́ться (+ inst.), *to be, to appear*
ягнёнок (gen. **ягнёнка,** *n. pl.* **ягня́та**), *lamb*
я́дерный, *nuclear*
ядови́тый, *poisonous*
ядро́, *nucleus, kernel*
язы́к, *language*
я́ркий, *vivid, bright*
я́сный, *clear*

INDEX

See page 203 *for index of Russian words.*